# Thinking Theologically about Language Teaching

Christians are called to view all of life, including their vocations, through the lens of Scripture. This is all the more critical for language teachers, who are instructing students in a medium that is at the heart of God's identity as a Trinitarian, speaking God. Language teaching in itself is a theological endeavor. The essays in this volume bring out critical issues for Christian English language teachers to consider – from biblical foundations for language teaching, to creative interactions with language theory, to reflections on biblical methodology and pedagogy, to a theological ground for dialogue. They are not merely a welcome contribution to the field of Christian English language teaching; they are, in my opinion, required reading for Christian English teachers who want to approach their calling with biblical integrity. If you are a Christian involved in language teaching, let me put it tersely: please read this book.

**Pierce Taylor Hibbs**
Associate Director for Theological Curriculum and Instruction,
Westminster Theological Seminary, USA

What does language teaching have to do with theology? This book will convince you that for the Christian language teacher, the answer might well be . . . *everything*! With theological insights pertaining to language, teaching, second language acquisition, and the unique field of English language teaching, the chapters in this text explore how biblical theology might undergird and inform our vocation. A broad range of theological positions, educational perspectives, and teaching and learning contexts provides plenty of food for thought, and concrete applications in nearly every chapter address practical ways to live out our theology in the classroom. This volume will challenge Christian readers to grapple with how our faith commitment both reflects and is reflected in our language teaching, and should be required reading for anyone who is a committed Christian and is called to language teaching.

**Jan Edwards Dormer**
Author of *Teaching English in Missions*
Associate Professor of TESOL, Messiah College, USA

The contributors to this volume provide Christian teachers with ideas that are both theological and practical, informed by their rich experience around the world. This book will help readers in the field of language teaching discern their calling, choose methods, design materials, write lesson plans, manage their classrooms, and more – from a well-considered Christian perspective.

**Kitty Purgason**
Author of *Professional Guidelines for Christian English Teachers*
Professor of Applied Linguistics and TESOL,
Cook School of Intercultural Studies, Biola University, USA

# Thinking Theologically about Language Teaching

*Christian Perspectives on an Educational Calling*

Cheri Pierson and Will Bankston, Editors

GLOBAL LIBRARY

© 2017 by Cheri Pierson and Will Bankston

Published 2017 by Langham Global Library
*An imprint of Langham Publishing*
www.langhampublishing.org

Langham Publishing and its imprints are a ministry of Langham Partnership

Langham Partnership
PO Box 296, Carlisle, Cumbria CA3 9WZ, UK
www.langham.org

ISBNs:
978-1-78368-288-1 Print
978-1-78368-312-3 Mobi
978-1-78368-311-6 ePub
978-1-78368-313-0 PDF

Cheri Pierson and Will Bankston have asserted their right under the Copyright, Designs and Patents Act, 1988 to be identified as the Authors of this work.

All rights reserved. No part of this publication may be reproduced, stored in a retrieval system or transmitted, in any form or by any means, electronic, mechanical, photocopying, recording or otherwise, without the prior written permission of the publisher or the Copyright Licensing Agency.

Unless otherwise indicated, Scripture quotations are taken from the Holy Bible, New International Version®, NIV®. Copyright ©1973, 1978, 1984, 2011 by Biblica, Inc.™ Used by permission of Zondervan.

All the Scripture quotations in chapter 3 and chapter 9 are from The Holy Bible, English Standard Version® (ESV®), copyright © 2001 by Crossway, a publishing ministry of Good News Publishers. Used by permission. All rights reserved.

**British Library Cataloguing in Publication Data**
A catalogue record for this book is available from the British Library

ISBN: 978-1-78368-288-1

Cover & Book Design: projectluz.com

Langham Partnership actively supports theological dialogue and an author's right to publish but does not necessarily endorse the views and opinions set forth here or in works referenced within this publication, nor can we guarantee technical and grammatical correctness. Langham Partnership does not accept any responsibility or liability to persons or property as a consequence of the reading, use or interpretation of its published content.

**Dedication**

We dedicate this volume of essays to the glory of God and to the teachers and students who will use them in their vocational calling for the work of his kingdom.

# CONTENTS

Acknowledgements . . . . . . . . . . . . . . . . . . . . . . . . . . . . . . . . . . . . . . . xi

Introduction . . . . . . . . . . . . . . . . . . . . . . . . . . . . . . . . . . . . . . . . . . . . . 1

**Section I – Our Content: Theology and Language**

1.  Biblical Themes for Christians in Language Teaching . . . . . . . . . . . . 7
    *Michael Lessard-Clouston*

2.  Equipping Students to Read Theology with Discernment . . . . . . . . 29
    *Karin Spiecker Stetina*

3.  Using Words to Change the World:
    Wittgenstein and the Communication of Life . . . . . . . . . . . . . . . . . . 53
    *Will Bankston*

**Section II – Our Calling: Theology and the Teacher**

4.  Seeing Clearly:
    My Role as a Humble, Worshiping Educator . . . . . . . . . . . . . . . . . . . 83
    *Kaylene Powell*

5.  Imitating the Humility of Christ in Language Teaching. . . . . . . . . 107
    *Bradley Baurain*

6.  Transformational Teaching:
    Engaging in a Pneumatic Teaching Praxis . . . . . . . . . . . . . . . . . . . . 135
    *Robert L. Gallagher*

**Section III – Our Classroom: Theology and Practice**

7.  Exploring Method as Metaphor:
    A Historical Perspective for Second Language Educators . . . . . . . 165
    *Cheri Pierson*

8.  Managing Twenty-First-Century Classes Biblically . . . . . . . . . . . . 189
    *Marilyn Lewis*

9.  Dialogue, Divinity, and Deciphering the Self:
    Calling Out God's Image in the Language Classroom . . . . . . . . . . 209
    *Will Bankston*

10  Yahweh's Taxonomy of the Deeper Dimensions . . . . . . . . . . . . . . . 239
    *Melissa Smith*

Contributors. . . . . . . . . . . . . . . . . . . . . . . . . . . . . . . . . . . . . . . . . . . . . . 263

# Acknowledgements

We are indebted to many people who made this project possible. Special thanks to Audrey Welch, Hope Rozenboom and Mary Elizabeth Moore who served as our research assistants. They spent many hours researching, editing and formatting the text. They also spent time communicating with the contributing writers and the publisher. Audrey, Hope and Mary Elizabeth hold a Master of Arts in TESOL and Intercultural Studies from Wheaton College Graduate School. They have taught English as a foreign language in Europe, Asia and the United States. Their willingness to work with us has made this project a real joy. We also appreciate the assistance of Greg Morrison, Assistant Professor of Library Science, Wheaton College, for his advice throughout the project, and we would like to acknowledge the G. W. Aldeen Memorial Fund for providing funds to assist in the publication of this book.

We are grateful to the contributors who have spent time writing the insightful essays contained in this volume. Each author has caused us to think more deeply about our Christian faith as it relates to our profession of teaching and learning language. Each contributor has taken time from their busy schedules to write, submit, edit and resubmit the essays contained in this book.

We wish to thank Pieter Kwant and Langham Partnership for believing in the project and for preparing the manuscript for publication. Vivian Doub graciously answered many questions throughout the writing of this text.

We extend our personal thanks to our families and friends:

Cheri – I want to thank my husband, Dr Steven Pierson and my son David Pierson, for their ongoing support throughout the process of completing this project. I also want to thank my colleagues in the Intercultural Studies Department for their encouragement and support.

Will – I am especially grateful to my wife, Kristin, for our conversations through the years regarding what it means to live theologically, of which my essays in this book are only two of many such fruits. With that, I want to thank her and my sons, Ezra, Oren, and Maxwell, for their support, encouragement, and patience amid stretches of writing and editing. A huge debt of thankfulness is likewise due my parents for their continual encouragement and support. And of course, I owe much gratitude to the colleagues I have taught with and learned from during my time overseas, especially to Scott, Steven, and Jason.

*Cheri Pierson and Will Bankston*

# Introduction

We as Christians can often overlook the need to bring our daily vocations in accord with the reality that is created, sustained, and purposed through Christ (Col 1:16–18). Of course, this is another way of saying that we fail to work in a distinctly Christian way, which is certainly not less, but much more, than working with excellence. And so, a much more important question than "How can I be a good worker?" is "How can my work play its proper role in the cosmic narrative of creation, fall, redemption, and restoration?" For all Christians the answer to the second question is a complex one. And our particular answer as Christian language teachers is no exception. We find ourselves at an interdisciplinary crossroads where the paths of language, culture, and education merge. As such, we need a nuanced course of navigation that seeks to give God the specific glory that is uniquely generated by the language classroom.

Toward this end, we hold that the theological must justify the pedagogical and not vice versa. Certainly some essays in this volume will linger more in doctrine and others will spend more time in the resulting classroom practice, but all will flow from this conviction. The contributors themselves, as the reader will perceive, come from a range of evangelical traditions and denominations. Accordingly, we hope to foster a kind of vocational catholicity in which distinctions arise but divisions do not. There is, of course, much fertile theological ground here for a wide range of topical discussions as we engage the interdisciplinary elements that hold our field together. Language, for instance, has assumed an especially prominent place in many contemporary conversations. As Kevin Vanhoozer writes, "Indeed, it would be no exaggeration to say that language has become the preeminent problem of twentieth-century philosophy."[1] Likewise, culture has also been an issue of much recent excitement and exploration. We might even sum up the equal and opposite errors of modernism and postmodernism with the former awarding culture too little weight and the latter awarding it too much. In response, we must wisely navigate the tangled complexities of language and culture as

---

1. Kevin J. Vanhoozer, *Is There a Meaning in this Text? The Bible, the Reader, and the Morality of Literary Knowledge* (Grand Rapids, MI: Zondervan, 1998), 17.

we instruct students in the use of culturally situated languages often much different from their own local tongue. As the educational stewards of those who bear God's image and to whom God has accordingly bestowed the faculty of language, this is no small task. He is the God who reveals himself through the very medium in which we daily work: human language and culture. As J. Todd Billings assures us, in Scripture God did not "bypass the embodied, historical, culturally embedded life of human beings."[2] He is no gnostic, and, for that reason, our work is of great worth.

In fact, such importance does God grant our vocation, that any other significance offered by any other conception rooted in any other presupposition than the Triune God, pales in comparison. There is no greater purpose we can pursue than to join God's work of reconciling all things to himself through Christ. Even more, the very possibility of meaningful communication, which this purpose supposes, rests wholly on God himself. Therefore, the need to understand language education through a thoroughly theological lens presses itself onto all language teachers. Otherwise we run the risk of missing what God has done, is doing, and will do through the particulars of our profession. In so doing we will forfeit Christian distinction for a teaching philosophy and practice that looks no different than that of our non-Christian colleagues. At best, this approach will accord with the noble, yet often vague, ideals put forward by our respective cultures. For instance, such a teacher might rightly value classroom practices of mutual respect and appreciation for diversity, but not in a way that is specifically rooted in the person and work of Christ. At worst, such an approach will unknowingly proceed from the anti-Christian presuppositions sometimes present in the profession. For instance, stronger, non-moderated forms of reader-response theory ultimately entail that a "community cannot be corrected and reformed . . . from outside itself."[3] All that can we take from a text is that which we brought to it, namely ourselves. In effect, a foreign language no longer becomes an avenue through which students can learn from the other. And ultimately such presuppositions not only cut us off from the otherness of a foreign culture, but also from God's word, which originates from him alone, outside of any human community.

---

2. J. Todd Billings, *The Word of God for the People of God: An Entryway to the Theological Interpretation of Scripture* (Grand Rapids, MI: Eerdmans, 2010), 57.

3. Anthony C. Thiselton, *New Horizons in Hermeneutics: The Theory and Practice of Transforming Biblical Reading*, 20th ann. ed. (Grand Rapids, MI: Zondervan, 1992), 27.

These concerns, though they might seem merely theoretical and relegated only to the clouds above the classroom, play out in very practical ways. If we are always seeking to know why we are doing what we are doing, we will continually change, and hopefully improve, what we are doing. Of course improvement here refers to a pedagogical performance ever more fitting with Christ's comprehensive work of redeeming creation. With that said, each essay in this volume seeks to show both why theology must affect one's teaching method and what forms resulting methodological modifications can take. In fact, as we apply theological truths derived from Scripture to our vocational contexts, we will find that our understanding and embodiment of these truths has deepened. As John Frame points out, the more we apply Scripture to the various facets of our lives, the more fully we understand its meaning.[4] Frame is drawing from the philosophy of Ludwig Wittgenstein, who says of "a *large* class of cases . . . the meaning of a word is its use in the language."[5] Conversely, Wittgenstein also writes, "there are certain criteria in a man's behaviour for his not understanding a word: that it means nothing to him, that he can do nothing with it."[6] Just as a greater understanding of a word enables us to *use* it more effectively across a wider range of contexts, so does a greater understanding of Scripture enable us to apply, or *use*, its truth in ever more situations, vocational or otherwise. In discerning the particular scriptural application for which each situation calls, we must continually strive for a better understanding of the situations in which we find ourselves. Accordingly, Frame goes on to write, "The interesting result of that line of reasoning is that we need to know the world to understand the meaning of scripture."[7]

This is not pragmatism. Rather, it is applying the truth of reality to a specific part of reality, a process that brings a corresponding aspect of that truth into high relief. Toward that end, one specific kind of world knowledge that we have daily given ourselves to is that of the language classroom, and this particularity awards us unique interpretive insights in understanding Scripture's implications for this context. Having applied Scripture to our daily work, we will find our understanding of each has increased. It is this belief,

---

4. John Frame, *The Doctrine of the Knowledge of God: A Theology of Lordship* (Phillipsburg, NJ: P&R, 1987), 66–69.

5. Ludwig Wittgenstein, *Philosophical Investigations*, eds. P. M. S. Hacker and Joachim Schulte, trans. G. E. M. Anscombe, P. M. S. Hacker, and Joachim Schulte, 4th ed. (Chichester, West Sussex, UK; Malden, MA: Wiley-Blackwell, 2009), 43.

6. Ibid., 269.

7. Frame, *Doctrine of the Knowledge of God*, 67.

and the vocational imperatives that it presents, that have shaped the purpose of this book. And it is our hope that these essays will aid their audience in better understanding what it means to be a Christian language teacher. We work with words, a responsibility created, sustained, and purposed by the Word of God himself.

# Section I

# Our Content: Theology and Language

# 1

# Biblical Themes for Christians in Language Teaching[1]

*Michael Lessard-Clouston*

## Background

Despite some recent and helpful writings on faith and religion in language teaching and research, there has unfortunately been less focus on the Bible as it relates to second and/or foreign language (L2/FL) teaching.[2] As a result, this essay focuses on biblical themes that I believe are relevant for Christians in language teaching.

---

1. This chapter is based on plenary talks delivered at the Christians in English Language Teaching (CELT 2015 Toronto) conference in Toronto, Ontario, Canada, and the 15th Cornerstone University ESL Conference in April 2016, in Grand Rapids, MI, USA. It draws on, but also significantly expands upon, the framework introduced in Lessard-Clouston (2012). Although examples relate to English language teaching, my hope is that this chapter and the themes outlined will be useful to teachers of all languages.

2. K. Foye, "Religion in the ELT Classroom: Teachers' Perspectives," *The Language Teacher* 38, no. 2 (2014): 5–12; ibid.; Carolyn Kristjánsson, "(In)Visible Agents in the Academy: Locating the Discussion of Faiths and Practices," *JCFL Journal of Christianity and Foreign Languages: Journal of the North American Christian Foreign Language Association (NACFLA)* 14 (2013): 45–55; Earl Stevick and Carolyn Kristjánsson, "Faiths and Practices in Language Teaching," *Journal of Christianity and Foreign Languages* 14 (2013): 64–86; Mary Shepard Wong and A. Suresh Canagarajah, eds., *Christian and Critical English Language Educators in Dialogue: Pedagogical and Ethical Dilemmas* (New York: Routledge, 2009); Mary Shepard Wong, Carolyn Kristjánsson, and Zoltán Dörnyei, eds., *Christian Faith and English Language Teaching and Learning: Research on the Interrelationship of Religion and ELT* (New York: Routledge, 2013).

*Biblical themes* are simply concepts, ideas, or topics we find as we study the Bible.[3] Sometimes they are reflected in particular words, and they usually help us think about timeless theological truths. Those discussed here are ones that I believe can help us think about language teaching. In reference to *language*, Richards and Schmidt define it as "the system of human communication which consists of the structured arrangement of sounds (or their written representation) into larger units."[4] Although L2/FL *teaching* most often involves classrooms with students at various educational and proficiency levels, it is not limited to such contexts, although they are my main point of reference.

As Christians working in L2/FL education, the Bible is often central to our thinking, our worldview, and our identities. Identity is currently a major focus in applied linguistics, especially for teachers and English language teaching.[5] Writing on identity and language teaching, Norton states:

> If we agree that diverse identity positions offer learners a range of positions from which to speak, listen, read or write, the challenge for language educators is to explore which identity positions offer the greatest opportunity for social engagement and interaction. Conversely, if there are identity positions that silence students, then teachers need to investigate and address these marginalizing practices.[6]

Identity "positions" are key to how teachers and students relate to one another, and Norton indicates that they offer opportunities for language learning and use in our L2/FL classes, particularly through interaction and social engagement.[7] I believe that, for Christian language teachers, biblical themes can help us think theologically about our identities (i.e. who we are as individuals and as teachers) and our teaching (i.e. what we do in and out of class), as well as our relationships with both our students and our colleagues.

---

3. J. I. Packer, *God's Words: Studies of Key Bible Themes* (Downers Grove, IL: InterVarsity, 1981), 17.

4. Jack Richards and Richard W. Schmidt, *Longman Dictionary of Language Teaching and Applied Linguistics*, 4th ed. (Harlow, UK: Longman, 2010), 311.

5. Miri Tashma Baum, "'The Aspect of the Heart': English and Self-Identity in the Experience of Preservice Teachers," *Language and Intercultural Communication* 14, no. 4 (2014): 407–422; John Gray and Tom Morton, *Social Interaction and ELT Teacher Identity* (Edinburgh: Edinburgh University Press, 2014).

6. Bonny Norton, *Identity and Language Learning: Extending the Conversation*, 2nd ed. (Bristol: Multilingual Matters, 2013), 16.

7. Ibid.

In the discussion that follows, I draw upon four basic assumptions that help ground this consideration of biblical themes for Christians in language teaching. First, I believe that language finds its source in God and, as a result, language is central to an understanding of God, human beings, and God's creation.[8] Second, I believe the Bible is the inerrant written Word of God, and, following what it teaches about itself, it is authoritative, clear, necessary, and sufficient for knowing, trusting, and obeying God.[9] Third, a Christian perspective on language should therefore begin with the Bible and reflect what the whole Bible says about this topic, but unfortunately I cannot address everything the Bible might have to say about language in this essay.[10] Fourth, recognizing that God entrusts people with his common grace in all realms of life, I assume there are opportunities to learn from related writings, by people of various worldviews, and where helpful I will therefore mention key related references in elaborating on the biblical themes below.

My methodology for this ongoing study is principled yet somewhat eclectic. With an evangelical Christian perspective, I have read the Bible and reflected on any potentially relevant Scripture passages, and considered the themes and issues that appeared to emerge in relation to language. So while this is clearly a limited and personal study, I have nonetheless attempted to consider how seven resulting themes might guide our thinking about and work in language teaching. I recognize this is only *one* perspective, and that it has limitations. Yet I believe there are connections between Christian faith and theology and aspects of language teaching because language is significant to people's understanding of God, ourselves, and our world. This will hopefully become evident through the seven biblical themes which emerged from my reading and reflections.

---

8. William J. Vande Kopple, "Toward a Christian View of Language," in *Contemporary Literary Theory: A Christian Appraisal*, eds. Clarence Walhout and Leland Ryken (Grand Rapids, MI: Eerdmans, 1991), 200–201.

9. Wayne Grudem, "The Perspicuity of Scripture," *Themelios* from The Gospel Coalition 34, no. 3 (November 2009): 307–308.

10. IIndeed, the Bible has much to say about language. See, for instance, Vern S. Poythress, *In the Beginning Was the Word: Language – A God-Centered Approach* (Wheaton, IL: Crossway, 2009). Karen Ehman states, for example, that "the Bible reveals that God places great importance on the way we use our speech. In fact, the words *tongue, talk, speak, words, mouth*, and *silence* are used over 3,500 times in the Bible" (*Keep It Shut: What to Say, How to Say It, and When to Say Nothing at All* [Grand Rapids, MI: Zondervan, 2015], 15 [emphasis original]).

## Biblical Themes for Christians in Language Teaching

The biblical themes which emerged from my study concern creativity, understanding, communication, community, sin, diversity, and redemption. Each of these motifs is introduced in Table 1.1 on page 24 and is then discussed in the following sections, which note representative and relevant Scripture passages and the experiences of biblical characters.

### *Creativity*

The theme of language and creativity appears in the first chapters of the Bible with the Genesis creation narrative and continues through to Revelation, where we read about God creating a new heaven and a new earth, and we learn that God has communicated this reality to human beings in both oral and written form (Rev 21). Two striking features of Genesis 1 are that language appears to be central to God's nature, and it is connected to his creative work. God spoke audibly using language early in creation (on days 1 to 4) well *before* he created living creatures (on day 5) or human beings (on day 6) who might have heard his speech. Also, it is through spoken language that God carried out his creative activities. Psalm 148:5 summarizes the expected response of all creation to this creativity, encouraging everyone to praise God through language: "Let them praise the name of the Lord, for at his command they were created." As Silva noted, the fact that God did not create with a simple wave of his hand draws "attention not only to God's power but specifically the power that is attached to his *word*."[11]

A further observation is that God created human beings in his image (Gen 1:27) with the ability to understand and use language (Gen 1:28; 2:19–24). Language is meaningful, therefore, not only as a reflection of God's nature, but also to our identity as human beings and in our relationships. The fact that Adam was involved in naming God's creatures (Gen 2:19–20) also affirms that creativity in language is evident in humankind. Vande Kopple therefore views language as a creative gift God gave uniquely to human beings, observing that "even though all humans have a finite number of words to work with, they can produce an infinite number of well-formed sentences and cohesive sequences of sentences."[12]

---

11. Moisés Silva, *God, Language, and Scripture: Reading the Bible in the Light of General Linguistics* (Grand Rapids, MI: Zondervan, 1990), 21 (emphasis original).

12. Vande Kopple, "Toward a Christian View of Language," 202, 208.

I believe there are some potential applications of these truths for language teaching. First, creativity in, with, and through language is normal in any activities carried out through spoken and written language.[13] Second, people who appreciate idioms, jokes, and creative turns of phrase can praise God's goodness in language as a reflection of his common grace and rejoice when people reflect such creativity through language in creative writing (fiction, plays, poetry, etc.) and other art forms which involve language (e.g. film, music, etc.). Third, as Carter, Cook, Crystal, and Vande Kopple declare, in both language learning and language use, creative language play is not only the norm among both children and adults, it also appears to be helpful and should therefore be encouraged.[14] As a result, Christians involved in language teaching should remember, as McLain observed, that language is changing and dynamic, and we should thus be flexible and allow our teaching to reflect the creativity of God and others as much as possible.[15] Also, language teachers should look for new vocabulary and structures that result from such creativity, which we might then incorporate into our classes and teaching, and we should be aware of changing standards for language use in particular contexts.

As teachers who follow Jesus, the Master Teacher, we can look to how Jesus taught creatively in different contexts and with different groups, and recognize that he did not deal with every person or group in the same way.[16] Consider, for example, how differently Jesus dealt with Nicodemus in John 3 and the Samaritan woman at the well in John 4. In both cases Jesus teaches them who he is, and that he is the One who brings salvation. But in each case he does so very differently. Creative teachers may be encouraged by Jesus's creativity in teaching. But if one is not particularly creative, then we might be challenged to think of how to teach language more creatively to our students. There are many other biblical examples we could mention, where Jesus teaches crowds of people creatively. So we can look to Jesus and others as biblical models for creativity in our L2/FL teaching.

---

13. See, for example, Rodney H. Jones, ed. *The Routledge Handbook of Language and Creativity* (London; New York: Routledge, 2016), and especially the final section dealing with creativity in language teaching and learning.

14. Ronald Carter, *Language and Creativity: The Art of Common Talk* (London: Routledge, 2004); Guy Cook, *Language Play, Language Learning* (Oxford: Oxford University Press, 2000); David Crystal, *Language Play* (Chicago: University of Chicago Press, 2001); Vande Kopple, "Toward a Christian View of Language."

15. Charles MacLain, "Toward a Theology of Langauge," *Calvary Baptist Theological Journal* 12 (1996): 27–29.

16. Edward Kuhlman, *Master Teacher* (Old Tappan, NJ: Revell, 1987), 16.

## *Understanding*

Language and understanding is a second biblical theme that comes out of the Genesis account of creation and carries on throughout the Bible. Right through his creative activity God named things (e.g. day, night, sky, seas; Gen 1:5–10), and it is assumed in those early chapters that people understand language and the things, ideas, or concepts to which these words and this language refer. Similarly, when Adam named the creatures in Genesis 2:19 we read that "whatever the man called each living creature, that was its name." The understanding of what the creatures were (the concepts) and what they were called (the symbols) is taken for granted. In discussing the parable of the sower in Mark 4, Jesus reveals (quoting from Isa 6:9–10) that some will be hearing but not understanding. Jesus also indicates through this verbal teaching that when people do not understand, they usually need some explanation in order to comprehend (e.g. Mark 4:13–20). Finally, from 1 John 5:20 we know that Jesus, "the Son of God has come and has given us understanding, so that we may know him who is true."

In terms of possible applications of understanding to language teaching, names and signs or symbols for concepts and ideas may be random (e.g. Gen 2:19), as many linguists suggest, yet they work together in a comprehensive and comprehensible system.[17] As Vande Kopple noted, the language facility in human beings appears to be innate and involves a complex system of symbols and concepts that enable us to be creative with language and to understand the language and communication of God and others.[18] Some authors like Kramsch have tried to explain complicated connections between language, thought, and culture.[19] To a large extent Kramsch does so by removing the focus on language, thought, and culture and by shifting "toward more dynamic notions of speakers/writers, thinkers, and members of discourse communities."[20] While this may be helpful on some levels in addressing issues in L2/FL teaching, Silva makes a convincing and important point: "The question of whether thought is possible without language is theoretically interesting, but it has little practical relevance. As far as we can tell, all of the thinking that in fact goes on is inextricably tied to linguistic competence."[21] I believe we should recognize

---

17. Fredric W. Field, *Essays in the Design of Language* (Santa Ana, CA: Calvary Chapel, 2005).

18. Vande Kopple, "Toward a Christian View of Language," 209–213.

19. Claire Kramsch, "Language, Thought, and Culture," in *The Handbook of Applied Linguistics*, eds. Alan Davies and Catherine Elder (Oxford: Blackwell, 2006), 235–261.

20. Ibid., 255.

21. Silva, *God, Language, and Scripture*, 25.

language and understanding are inseparable, yet that we cannot explain all of the connections between them.

The Bible reflects our personal human experiences with difficulties in understanding when we read of "obscure speech and strange language" in passages like Ezekiel 3:5-6. Jesus makes clear in John 8:43-44, however, that misunderstanding may not just derive from a lack of clarity in language, but rather from sin or a lack of ability or desire to hear the truth. Some linguists, like Tannen, have done important and popular work in sociolinguistics to show how a lack of understanding may also relate to communication style, which is something that those of us in L2/FL education need to consider in our language teaching, too.[22]

In addition to Jesus, we can look to others in the Bible for examples of their approaches to teaching, and for the theme of understanding, Paul's experience in Athens in Acts 17 comes to mind. There he related what he wanted to teach to people's objects of worship. Paul said he had found an altar with the inscription "to an unknown god," and he then talked about God (Acts 17:23-31). Like Paul in that situation, L2/FL teachers can and should make connections for our students and with their prior experience and knowledge, in order to help them grow in learning both the target language and culture.

## *Communication*

The third theme, concerning communication, is perhaps the one most people imagine from the start. Indeed, the Bible is replete with examples of God and others using language to communicate. Genesis chapters 1-3 make evident that God created human beings to understand language and to communicate through it, just as God does. McLain states that communication involves a communicator, a message (through spoken or written language), and an audience, but he also made clear that communication cannot be said to have occurred unless the audience has understanding of the communicator's message.[23] Quoting 1 Corinthians 14:9, McLain notes that unless one's message is intelligible to their audience, then understanding and communication simply do not occur, and the communication is instead just "speaking into the air."[24]

---

22. Deborah Tannen, *You Just Don't Understand: Women and Men in Conversation* (New York: Quill, 2001).
23. MacLain, "Toward a Theology of Langauge," 21-22.
24. MacLain, "Toward a Theology of Langauge."

Psalm 19 indicates that communication can reflect the glory of God (v. 1), and that it can reveal both God's general (vv. 1–6) and special (vv. 7–11) revelation. In the Bible God communicates orally to people like Adam and Eve (Gen 3) and Moses (Exod 3), as well as through dreams (e.g. for Jacob, Gen 28:10–15) or visions (e.g. to Saul and Ananias, Acts 9:1–19), both of which also involve verbal communication, as well as in writing, such as with the Ten Commandments (Exod 31:18; 34:1). Whatever form of communication is used, the main issue here is that God communicates to people in ordinary, everyday human language.[25] In Exodus 33:11, for example, we learn that "The Lord would speak to Moses face to face, as one speaks to a friend." Throughout the Gospels we read of Jesus teaching and relating to people in ordinary language, sometimes even in their own vernacular (e.g. Mark 5:41). Accordingly, we also find that crowds were amazed at Jesus's teaching, because he "taught as one who had authority, and not as their teachers of the law" (Matt 7:28–29).

Perhaps the first implication of the communication theme for world language teaching is that ordinary, human languages have value. Beyond the many forms of communication they enable, God can and does reveal himself to people in and through any language, and no language is foreign to God and his glory (Ps 19:1–4).[26] While English is the current lingua franca, which might encourage English language teachers, the fact that God can and does communicate with people in every language should also motivate teachers to learn and use other languages, when doing so is helpful.[27] For L2/FL teachers, I believe this also means that we should teach everyday, regular language use.

A second application is that dialogue and interaction are human norms. In L2/FL education, then, this biblical theme should encourage us to consider and possibly value communicative approaches to language teaching, while in second-language acquisition theory we should perhaps be wary of simplistic behavioral, psycholinguistic or other approaches to language learning, and consider more dialogic ones, such as Johnson's philosophy of second-language acquisition (SLA).[28] In short, we are dealing with people in language teaching,

---

25. J. I. Packer, "The Adequacy of Human Language," in *Inerrancy*, ed. Norman Geisler (Grand Rapids, MI: Zondervan, 1980), 197.

26. Calvin Seerveld, "Babel, Pentecost, Glossalia and Philoxenia: No Language Is Foreign to God," *Journal of Christianity and Foreign Languages* 2 (2001): 14.

27. Donald B. Snow, "English Teachers, Language Learning, and the Issue of Power," in *Christian and Critical English Language Educators in Dialogue: Pedagogical and Ethical Dilemmas*, eds. Mary Shepard Wong and A. Suresh Canagarajah (New York: Routledge, 2009), 183.

28. Marysia Johnson, *A Philosophy of Second Language Acquisition* (New Haven: Yale University Press, 2004).

and should ideally focus on developing relationships and exchanging ideas through the target language and learning experiences. Thus while there may be different emphases in particular language classes, oral and written communication should usually be central, and go well beyond the simple memorization of grammar and vocabulary.[29] In SLA, I believe one's purpose should be to see students as whole people, and thus encourage learning that connects individuals and communities in and through language and communication.[30] Given that most of the world is at least bilingual, in SLA Cook's multicompetence perspective offers promise in understanding the complexity of individuals learning and using two or more languages.[31]

A third implication is to acknowledge that language can be used both positively (to bless, e.g. Gen 1:28) and negatively (to curse, Deut 11:26–28). Teachers should therefore be active and discerning in working to bring about good language practice and use that can bless others, both inside and outside of our classes. A final application here relates to the need and desirability, where helpful and possible, for communication with students in their own language in and out of class, both orally and in writing. In the Bible we see samples of this in Ezra (4:7) and Esther (1:22; 8:9), and in language teaching I believe this suggests we should question "target language only" policies where they are harmful, and instead be comfortable to use our students' first language(s) in our teaching when doing so is useful.

---

29. For recent treatments that go beyond simple presentation-practice-production (PPP) (e.g. Jeremy Harmer, *The Practice of English Language Teaching* [New York: Pearson Education, 2015]), see H. Douglas Brown and Heekyeong Lee, *Teaching by Principles: An Interactive Approach to Language Pedagogy*, 4th ed. (White Plains, NY: Pearson Education ESL, 2015), which may be used in various contextualized communicative teaching methods. I also often use the four strands approach of Paul Nation and Azusa Yamamoto, "Applying the Four Strands of Language to Learning." *International Journal of Innovation in English Language Teaching* 1, no 2 (2012): 167–181, with my teacher education students, within which equal emphasis is placed in the classroom on meaning-focused input, meaning-focused output, language-focused learning, and fluency development. I believe such views lend themselves quite easily to the incorporation of communication and relationship building.

30. Beyond the survey and ecology view of H. Douglas Brown, *Principles of Language Learning and Teaching: A Course in Second Language Acquisition*, 6th ed. (New York: Pearson Longman, 2014), see Lourdes Ortega, "Second Language Learning Explained? SLA across 10 Contemporary Theories." In *Theories in Second Language Acquisition: An Introduction*, edited by Bill VanPatten and Jessica Williams, 2nd ed. (New York: Routledge, 2015), 245–272. Ortega offers a good secular overview of contemporary SLA theories. See Dwight Atkinson, *Alternative Approaches to Second Language Acquisition* (London: Routledge, 2011), for alternative approaches to mainstream cognitive views. See critiques of some approaches to language learning in teaching in David I. Smith and Barbara Maria Carvill, *Learning from the Stranger: Christian Faith and Cultural Diversity* (Grand Rapids, MI: Eerdmans, 2000).

31. Cook, *Language Play, Language Learning*, 14.

One challenging example related to this is how Paul uses Greek, the lingua franca of the day, in Acts 21 as he is dealing with Roman commanders, but then in Acts 22 he uses Aramaic to share his testimony with the Jews gathered there that wanted to kill him. In English language teaching our focus is English, but there may be occasions when it is best to use our students' native language to help them understand and learn in our classes or other contexts.

## *Community*

Community is a fourth biblical theme for language teaching. In the creation narrative, for example, God clearly created human beings to be in community and fellowship with him, but he also commanded humanity to be fruitful and increase in number – a clear push for community (Gen 1:26–31; 2:15–18). In Genesis 2:18, God said it was in fact "not good for the man to be alone," and that is why he created a suitable helper in Eve for Adam. In Genesis 10, the table of nations, various communities existed, and verse 20 mentions language, referring to "the sons of Ham by their clans and languages, in their territories and nations."

After Babel in Genesis 11 it is evident there were different linguistic communities, and at Pentecost in Acts 2 people from numerous language communities are listed (vv. 7–12). The example at Pentecost also shows that through the Holy Spirit God can and does empower speech, communication, and understanding within and across language communities (vv. 4, 8, 11). In addition, community develops most often through language. In Revelation 3:20, for example, Jesus declares that he stands at the door and knocks. "If anyone hears [his] voice and opens the door," Jesus will go in and fellowship together with them. Also, community is clear when the elders fall down in Revelation 5 to worship the Lamb, and verse 9 declares that they will sing that he is worthy because with his blood he purchased "for God persons from every tribe and language and people and nation" – people from various types of communities.

Possible applications of the community theme to language teaching are evident first in relation to the importance of language for communication and understanding within and between communities. Communities usually cherish differences, and one may be an insider or outsider for different reasons, related to language, culture, race, nationality, and so on. Paul declared in 1 Corinthians 14:11, for example: "If then I do not grasp the meaning of what someone is saying, I am a foreigner to the speaker, and the speaker is a foreigner to me." To create communication and understanding both within and across communities, language and culture are central, as most L2/FL teachers are aware. Accordingly, Christian L2/FL teachers need to be sensitive to the guidance of the Holy Spirit in enabling communication and comprehension in our classes, as well as across language and cultural communities.

A second implication for community concerns its role in L2/FL education. In an insightful analysis of two approaches to community in language teaching, Smith and Carvill plainly reject community language learning and critical foreign language pedagogy approaches in favor of their views of hospitality and of the stranger (Paul's "foreigner") in L2/FL education.[32] Smith reiterated this take on community by insisting

> ... on a fully Christian understanding of hospitality as a welcoming of angels unawares, that is, of one who may well be greater than I and from whom I must learn, rather than as a virtuous retooling of the centered self ... Even such an interrogation of the idea of hospitality, however, carries with it the need for a further step, an admission that the self, and not merely the other, is a vulnerable stranger.[33]

This view of community may reflect something of the way Christ humbled himself for us, as John 1:14 declares: "The Word became flesh and made his dwelling among us."

One verse I wonder about in terms of community is 1 John 3:18, where we are challenged: "Let us not love with words or speech but with actions and in truth." How might we as L2/FL teachers love our students and class communities not only with words, but also with actions and in truth? One sacrificial example from the Bible that might inform how language teachers could potentially relate to our students and colleagues concerns how Paul loved both Philemon and his slave Onesimus, by sending Onesimus back to Philemon, although Onesimus was actually very useful to Paul while he was in prison (Phlm 13). It may well be that as language teachers we need to sacrifice in practical ways for our students and classes, too. In discussing transformed linguistic communities, Pasquale and Bierma provide case studies of churches that serve their communities sacrificially through ESL and other programs

---

32. David I. Smith and Barbara Maria Carvill, *Learning from the Stranger: Christian Faith and Cultural Diversity* (Grand Rapids, MI: Eerdmans, 2009), 173–190.

33. David I. Smith, "Editorial: The Gift of the Stranger Revisited," *Journal of Christianity and Foreign Languages* 7 (2006): 6.

because they value and aim to model God's plans for diversity, creativity, and linguistic hospitality.[34]

## *Sin*

The fifth biblical theme concerns sin, and finds its origins in Genesis 3:1–5, where the devil uses language to tempt Adam and Eve, largely through deception and the twisting of what God had said, and the same is true in Matthew 4:1–11 with the temptation of Jesus. One interesting observation is that there is no account of language or communication when Adam and Eve sinned by eating the fruit from the forbidden tree. However, in the passage that follows, it is clear that there are consequences to sin, in how Adam and Eve relate to God and in the way they each appear to blame others (vv. 8–13), as well as in God's response (vv. 14–24).

This theme is further developed in Genesis 11, the famous "Babel" passage. This Hebrew word means "gate of God" but sounds like "confused." In moving east and settling (vv. 2–3), the people rebelled with pride by building a tower and refusing to be scattered over the earth (v. 4). In response, the Lord came down, confused their language, scattered the people, and in doing so created a variety of different languages (vv. 5–9). A final point about language and sin is that we should remember Hebrews 4:12, which tells us that God's word is living and active: sharper than a double-edged sword it divides the soul and spirit and judges the thoughts and attitudes of the heart. So through God's word, language helps us to understand and be convicted of our sin, too.

Possible implications of this theme are straightforward. First, since the fall much of life has meant addressing various language-related human problems, and particularly in adulthood, learning a second or foreign language is often a challenge.[35] This situation is no doubt in large part due to our finitude, as well as to our existence as embodied creatures. Beyond childhood, it is often simply very difficult to learn how to produce particular sounds with our mouths, despite the fact that we are created in God's image to know and use language. Second, as McLain rightly observed, after Genesis 3 language

> . . . was affected by the Fall. As sin-affected people, we use a sin-affected language. We may not like the problems this creates and

---

34. Michael Pasquale and Nathan L. K. Bierma, *Every Tribe and Tongue: A Biblical Vision for Language in Society* (Eugene, OR: Pickwick, 2011).

35. H. Douglas Brown, *Principles of Language Learning and Teaching: A Course in Second Language Acquisition*, 6th ed. (New York: Pearson Longman, 2014), 53.

the implications that result, but we cannot deny this theological truth. Language is affected by the same decay and corruption that characterizes all creation since the Fall.[36]

It is not simply language, however. The infiltration of sin into our human faculties may be evident in every aspect of our humanity. The disobedience of Adam and Eve in Genesis 3 is reflected at Babel in Genesis 11, just as it is in our own lives and language use (Col 3:8–9). Third, as much as possible, Christians in L2/FL teaching should aim to be human "gates of God" who address various types of "confusion" in our classes and share our experience and knowledge of the target language, education, Christianity, and Scripture with those we work for and within various contexts, whether they are our students or our colleagues.

Research by Garcia, Garas, and Schweitzer with English, German, and Spanish indicated that, overall, positive words used on the Internet generally carry less information than negative words, perhaps because "the language used on the Internet is emotionally charged."[37] This fact may suggest why it is so important for us as Christians to avoid sinning through our use of language, and why as teachers we need to teach this.[38] Garcia et al.'s study considered written work online, where it is generally impossible, even with emoticons, to convey things nonverbally the same ways we might in face-to-face verbal interaction.[39] This reality, which is all too evident in how many people use social media, may be a result of the fall. From my perspective, this reality emphasizes how important it is for L2/FL teachers to address the power of both written and spoken communication, and the need to remember the people involved. In introducing a series of studies in a journal's special issue, Hodges, Steffensen, and Martin described "real-life empirical examples of caring-in-conversing," including within language learning.[40] In contrast to Garcia et al.,

---

36. MacLain, "Toward a Theology of Language," 27.

37. David Garcia, Antonios Garas, and Frank Schweitzer, "Positive Words Carry Less Information than Negative Words," *EPJ Data Sci. EPJ Data Science* 1, no. 1 (2012): 4, doi:10.1140/epjds3.

38. Although not specifically geared toward language teachers or teaching, for many insights and guidelines in this regard see Marilyn McEntyre, *Caring for Words in a Culture of Lies* (Grand Rapids, MI: Eerdmans, 2009), and Ehman, *Keep It Shut*.

39. Garcia, Garas, and Schweitzer, "Positive Words."

40. Bert H. Hodges, Sune V. Steffensen, and James E. Martin, "Caring, Conversing, and Realizing Values: New Directions in Language Studies," *Language Sciences*, Caring and Conversing: The Distributed Dynamics of Language 34, no. 5 (September 2012): 502, doi:10.1016/j.langsci.2012.03.006.

Hodge et al.'s work points to redemptive ways that caring is communicated in face-to-face oral interaction, reflecting how interlocutors can and do bless others, reversing sin's effects.[41]

One passage that comes to mind in regards to sin and language teaching is Matthew 12, where Jesus responds to the Pharisees, who had suggested Jesus did miracles through Beelzebub, the prince of demons (v. 24). Jesus sets them straight but goes on to teach the crowd that "every sin and slander will be forgiven" (v. 31), yet he also teaches that "the mouth speaks what the heart is full of" (v. 34). Language teachers tend to do a lot of talking, and we need to be connected to the vine, so that we speak out of a heart full of mercy and grace, and from a good relationship with Jesus Christ. Further, in Matthew 12:36 Jesus says that we will all "have to give account on the day of judgment for every empty word" we have spoken. May our words not cause us or our students to sin, but rather help both us and others to come to know God better.

## *Diversity*

Diversity is a sixth biblical theme for Christians in language teaching. In Genesis 10:20 and 31 we see references to "clans and languages," and the Genesis 11 passage already mentioned clearly reveals that one language and pride had led people to sin, so God confused their language and created instead a diversity of languages. The scattering of people mentioned in Genesis carried on with the Exodus, and by Nehemiah 13:24 it is evident that God's people and their children spoke a range of languages. In fact, parts of Ezra (4–6) were written in Aramaic rather than in Hebrew, and in Esther 8:9c Mordecai's "orders were written in the script of each province and the language of each people and also to the Jews in their own script and language."

The diversity of languages continues in the Bible with Daniel (1:4b), who in Babylon studied "the language and literature of the Babylonians" under the chief of the King's officials. In Daniel 3:7 "all the nations and peoples of every language fell down and worshiped the image of gold that King Nebuchadnezzar had set up," and the diversity of languages and their connections with varied peoples and nations is distinct. In the New Testament the diversity of languages is also evident in the interactions of Jesus (e.g. Mark 5:41) and Paul (e.g. Acts 21–22) with people in Aramaic and Greek, as well as in the variety of

---

41. Hodges, Steffensen, and Martin, "Caring, Conversing, and Realizing Values"; Garcia, Garas, and Schweitzer, "Positive Words."

languages used in Acts 2 at Pentecost. As Paul wrote in 1 Corinthians 14:10, "Undoubtedly there are all sorts of languages in the world, yet none of them is without meaning." The Pentecost experience and this perspective seem to point toward heaven, where John tells us in Revelation 7:9 that there is "a great multitude that no one could count, from every nation, tribe, people and language, standing before the throne and before the Lamb," praising God. From Babel to Pentecost to heaven, God has created ethnic, linguistic, and cultural diversity, as Smith and Carvill describe.

The applications of the diversity theme to language education are multiple. First, the Bible reflects our human experience of linguistic diversity in the world and reveals that varied languages and linguistic, cultural, and ethnic groups will continue to exist in heaven (e.g. Dan 7:13–14). We can rejoice that our multicultural experiences in this life prepare us for heaven. Second, while affirming linguistic diversity, the Bible also shows that there is a concept of native languages, as John 8:44 and Acts 2:6–11 attest. As the "native speaker" concept has been criticized in the applied linguistics literature in recent years, this fact gives Christians in language teaching pause and reason to reexamine our thinking on this issue.[42] The John 8:44 passage presents the idea of native languages in a negative light (comparing speech to lies), while Acts 2:6–11 views them positively, as something the people connected with at Pentecost (hearing the wonders of God in their own native tongues). Davies points out that most of the discussion about doing away with the native speaker concept is in relation to English, an international language, and comes from applied and educational linguists.[43] Davies also suggests that apart from learning a language early in life and over a very long time (key points for "native speakers" of languages), many proficient speakers of second and foreign languages can pass as native speakers when they develop the requisite competence in the language.[44] Third, the Bible makes clear that the diversity theme involves different types of and uses for language and communication, including plain versus figurative speech (e.g. John 16:25), confirming the value of recognizing different genres in spoken and written language currently central to L2/FL teaching. Finally, the fact that Jesus (Mark 5:41) and Paul (Acts 22:2) used different languages in diverse but

---

42. Alan Davies, *Native Speakers and Native Users: Loss and Gain* (Cambridge, UK: Cambridge University Press, 2013).

43. Ibid.

44. For more discussion on the issue of second language competence, see Liang, "Second Language Competence." For thoughtful reflections of a Christian non-native English-speaking teacher, see Liang, "The Courage to Teach as a Nonnative English Teacher."

specific settings reminds us as language teachers to help our students discern what type of language and what communication style is most helpful in order to communicate their messages most effectively to others.

## **Redemption**

The final biblical theme concerns redemption, a significant Christian concept. Again, this theme is evident from early in Genesis through to the end of Revelation. After the fall (Gen 3:15) we see God's intervention to deal with sin through judgment, and the promise he would "crush" the serpent. It is important that God communicated the consequences of Adam and Eve's sin to them verbally through language, as is the fact that God has revealed his plan of redemption both orally to people throughout the ages and in his trustworthy written Word.

In Genesis 11 we see God intervening again for good, coming down and limiting the people's sin by confusing their language and scattering them. This pattern of God's intervention in people's lives in and through language is the Bible narrative – God redeems people and saves them from their sins. In John 1 we read of Jesus Christ, the Word of God, becoming flesh and granting "to all who did receive him, to those who believed in his name . . . the right to become children of God" (v. 12). God's eternal purpose has been accomplished through Jesus Christ, and it is communicated to people through both spoken and written language.

The redemption theme is further evident in the "word of faith" that Paul proclaimed:

> If you declare with your mouth, "Jesus is Lord," and believe in your heart that God raised him from the dead, you will be saved. For it is with your heart that you believe and are justified, and it is with your mouth that you profess your faith and are saved. As Scripture says, "Anyone who believes in him will never be put to shame." (Rom 10:9–11)

In this passage the role of oral and written language in redemption is notable. People normally need speech to profess their faith and trust in Christ in order to be saved (cf. Acts 2:21). But Paul also refers specifically here to the written Scriptures (Isa 28:16), emphasizing their role in redemption, as in 2 Timothy 3:15–17. In Revelation 14:6 we similarly learn that an angel had "the eternal gospel to proclaim to those who live on the earth – to every nation, tribe, language and people."

There are several potential implications of this biblical theme of redemption for L2/FL education. First, the importance of both oral and written language in redemption reinforces the roles of orality and literacy, not only in faith and religion but also in education, including language teaching. In essence, language is used to communicate God's redemption, as well as many other truths. Second, because languages are important in communicating this redemption, those of us working in language teaching should carry on in our specific tasks personally and professionally, and on various levels (e.g. in theory, practice, and policy). Finally, clarity and thoughtfulness in our language teaching work are therefore part of our Christian and social responsibility, since language is connected to redemption, as Silva articulates.[45]

As I gain more life experience, I feel more convinced of the need to share the good news of redemption through Jesus Christ, but in my teaching I am also less convinced that I personally am necessarily the one who is going to lead people to Christ. It may be, like the formerly demon-possessed man in Mark 5, that our role as teachers is simply to tell people how much Christ has done for us, and how he has had mercy upon us (v. 19). Or like the Samaritan woman at the well in John 4, our role may be to share what we learn about Christ and to testify about him using redemptive words, so that others will come to know and follow Jesus (vv. 39–42). May all Christian language teachers be sensitive to the Holy Spirit and reflect humility in our teaching and relationships, imitating Christ's example in Philippians 2. There Paul and Timothy write in verse 13, "It is God who works in you to will and to act in order to fulfill his good purpose."

## Conclusion

This chapter has introduced biblical themes that I believe may be useful to Christians in language teaching. All seven themes, concerning creativity, understanding, communication, community, sin, diversity, and redemption, are connected with language, and as I have tried to indicate, there are therefore relevant possibilities for applications for Christians in language teaching. A study like this reminds me of God's goodness and faithfulness, and brings to mind the praises of the great multitude in heaven described in Revelation 7:9. May God grant each of us wisdom and guidance so we might apply these biblical themes to our work in L2/FL teaching.

---

45. Silva, *God, Language, and Scripture.*

Table 1.1 Biblical Themes for Christians in Language Teaching "At a Glance"

| Seven Biblical Themes | Relevant Bible Passages | Observations/Reflections/Realities |
|---|---|---|
| Creativity | Genesis 1<br>Genesis 2:19–24<br>Psalm 148:5<br>Numbers 22:21–41<br>Daniel 5<br>Revelation 21 | • God used language in creation (days 1–5), even before creating human beings (day 6).<br>• Adam was involved in naming creatures.<br>• God will create a new heaven and a new earth, and has communicated this to us in language, both oral (vv. 3–4) and written. |
| Understanding | Genesis 1:5, etc.<br>Genesis 2:19<br>Genesis 1:28–31<br>John 8:43–44<br>1 John 5:20 | • Throughout creation God named things ("day," "night," "sky," "land," "seas").<br>• It is assumed people understand language, and the things, ideas, and/or concepts to which language/names/symbols refer. |
| Communication | Genesis 1:28; 2:15–24; 3:19.<br>Psalm 19:1–4<br>Psalm 19:7–14<br>1 Corinthians 14:9 | • God created human beings to understand language and communicate through it.<br>• Communication reflects the glory of God.<br>• Communication can be used to reveal both God's general and special revelation. |
| Community | Genesis 1:26–31; 2:15–18, etc.<br>Acts 2 | • God created human beings to be in community and fellowship with him.<br>• Holy Spirit enables speech/understanding. |
| Sin | Genesis 3<br>Matthew 4:1–11<br>Genesis 11 | • The devil uses language to tempt people, and language is tainted by sin/the Fall.<br>• There are consequences to sin. |
| Diversity | Genesis 11:1–9<br>Revelation 7:9<br>1 Corinthians 14:10 | • One language led humans to sin, and as a result God created a diversity of languages.<br>• There are many languages, with meaning. |
| Redemption | Genesis 11:5, 8–9<br>Ephesians 3:10–12<br>Romans 10:9–11<br>Revelation 14:6–7 | • In his mercy, God intervenes for us.<br>• God's manifold wisdom involves faith in Christ and thus freedom and confidence.<br>• Speech/Scripture are key for salvation. |

| Potential Applications for Language Teaching (and authors or passages to consider) |
|---|
| ☐ Language is creative, and creativity should be the norm in activities with language, including teaching.<br>☐ In language learning and use, creative language play is usual and should be encouraged, if possible (e.g. Carter, Cook, Crystal, Jones, Vande Kopple).<br>☐ Be flexible and look for changes in language use. |
| ☐ Language is a comprehensive system; do our lessons reflect this? Teach connections if possible.<br>☐ Language, thought, and culture are interconnected (Kramsch, Silva,); reveal this to students.<br>☐ Note and teach different communication styles. |
| ☐ Ordinary languages have value and should be taught.<br>☐ Dialogue/interaction is a human norm (Johnson).<br>☐ Language can be used positively (to bless, Gen 1:28) or negatively (to curse, Deut 11:26–28).<br>☐ Use students' L1 where useful in language teaching. |
| ☐ Language is key to community/communication.<br>☐ Language and culture are interconnected.<br>☐ Recognize the role of community (Smith/Carvill). |
| ☐ Language is affected by sin, decay (McLain).<br>☐ Train people to use language in positive ways.<br>☐ Learners/teachers can be human "gates of God." |
| ☐ We need to teach not only varied languages and groups, but also different ways of speaking, etc.<br>☐ Teach different types of genres in language. |
| ☐ Orality and literacy are key in learning/teaching.<br>☐ Language communicates God's redemption.<br>☐ Learn and teach with humility, imitating Christ's example (Phil 2:1–18). Mark 5:19, John 4:39–42. |

## Bibliography

Atkinson, Dwight. *Alternative Approaches to Second Language Acquisition*. London: Routledge, 2011.

Brown, H. Douglas. *Principles of Language Learning and Teaching: A Course in Second Language Acquisition*. 6th ed. New York: Pearson Longman, 2014.

Brown, H. Douglas, and Heekyeong Lee. *Teaching by Principles: An Interactive Approach to Language Pedagogy*. 4th ed. White Plains, NY: Pearson Education ESL, 2015.

Carter, Ronald. *Language and Creativity: The Art of Common Talk*. London: Routledge, 2004.

Cook, Guy. *Language Play, Language Learning*. Oxford: Oxford University Press, 2000.

Crystal, David. *Language Play*. Chicago: University of Chicago Press, 2001.

Davies, Alan. *Native Speakers and Native Users: Loss and Gain*. Cambridge, UK: Cambridge University Press, 2013.

Ehman, Karen. *Keep It Shut: What to Say, How to Say It, and When to Say Nothing at All*. Grand Rapids, MI: Zondervan, 2015.

Field, Fredric W. *Essays in the Design of Language*. Santa Ana, CA: Calvary Chapel, 2005.

Foye, K. "Religion in the ELT Classroom: Teachers' Perspectives." *The Language Teacher* 38, no. 2 (2014): 5–12.

Garcia, David, Antonios Garas, and Frank Schweitzer. "Positive Words Carry Less Information than Negative Words." *EPJ Data Science* 1, no. 1 (2012). doi:10.1140/epjds3.

Gray, John, and Tom Morton. *Social Interaction and ELT Teacher Identity*. Edinburgh: Edinburgh University Press, 2014.

Grudem, Wayne. "The Perspicuity of Scripture." *Themelios* from The Gospel Coalition 34, no. 3 (November 2009): 288–308.

Harmer, Jeremy. *The Practice of English Language Teaching*. New York: Pearson Education, 2015.

Hodges, Bert H., Sune V. Steffensen, and James E. Martin. "Caring, Conversing, and Realizing Values: New Directions in Language Studies." *Language Sciences, Caring and Conversing: The Distributed Dynamics of Language* 34, no. 5 (September 2012): 499–506. doi:10.1016/j.langsci.2012.03.006.

Johnson, Marysia. *A Philosophy of Second Language Acquisition*. New Haven, CT: Yale University Press, 2004.

Jones, Rodney H., ed. *The Routledge Handbook of Language and Creativity*. London; New York: Routledge, 2016.

Kramsch, Claire. "Language, Thought, and Culture." In *The Handbook of Applied Linguistics*, edited by Alan Davies and Catherine Elder, 235–261. Oxford: Blackwell, 2006.

Kristjánsson, Carolyn. "(In)Visible Agents in the Academy: Locating the Discussion of Faiths and Practices." *JCFL Journal of Christianity and Foreign Languages: Journal*

*of the North American Christian Foreign Language Association (NACFLA)* 14 (2013): 45–55.
Kuhlman, Edward. *Master Teacher*. Old Tappan, NJ: Revell, 1987.
Lessard-Clouston, Michael. "Seven Biblical Themes for Language Learning." *Evangelical Missions Quarterly* 48 (2012): 172–179.
Liang, John. "The Courage to Teach as a Nonnative English Teacher: The Confession of a Christian Teacher." In *Christian and Critical English Language Educators in Dialogue: Pedagogical and Ethical Dilemmas*, edited by Mary Shepard Wong and A. Suresh Canagarajah, 163–172. New York: Routledge, 2009.
———. "Second Language Competence: Native Speaker Competence or User Competence?" In *The NNEST Newsletter* 7, no. 2 (2005).
MacLain, Charles. "Toward a Theology of Language." *Calvary Baptist Theological Journal* 12 (1996): 17–41.
McEntyre, Marilyn. *Caring for Words in a Culture of Lies*. Grand Rapids, MI: Eerdmans, 2009.
Nation, Paul, and Azusa Yamamoto. "Applying the Four Strands of Language to Learning." *International Journal of Innovation in English Language Teaching* 1, no 2 (2012): 167–181.
Norton, Bonny. *Identity and Language Learning: Extending the Conversation*. 2nd ed. Bristol: Multilingual Matters, 2013.
Ortega, Lourdes. "Second Language Learning Explained? SLA across 10 Contemporary Theories." In *Theories in Second Language Acquisition: An Introduction*, edited by Bill VanPatten and Jessica Williams, 2nd ed., 245–72. New York: Routledge, 2015.
Packer, J. I. *God's Words: Studies of Key Bible Themes*. Downers Grove, IL: InterVarsity, 1981.
———. "The Adequacy of Human Language." In *Inerrancy*, edited by Norman Geisler, 197–226. Grand Rapids, MI: Zondervan, 1980.
Pasquale, Michael, and Nathan L. K. Bierma. *Every Tribe and Tongue: A Biblical Vision for Language in Society*. Eugene, OR: Pickwick, 2011.
Poythress, Vern S. *In the Beginning Was the Word: Language: A God-Centered Approach*. Wheaton, IL: Crossway, 2009.
Richards, Jack, and Richard W. Schmidt. *Longman Dictionary of Language Teaching and Applied Linguistics*. 4th ed. Harlow, UK: Longman, 2010.
Seerveld, Calvin. "Babel, Pentecost, Glossalia and Philoxenia: No Language Is Foreign to God." *Journal of Christianity and Foreign Languages* 2 (2001): 5–30.
Silva, Moisés. *God, Language, and Scripture: Reading the Bible in the Light of General Linguistics*. Grand Rapids, MI: Zondervan, 1990.
Smith, David I. "Editorial: The Gift of the Stranger Revisited." *Journal of Christianity and Foreign Languages* 7 (2006): 3–9.
———. *The Gift of the Stranger: Faith, Hospitality, and Foreign Language Learning*. Grand Rapids, MI: Eerdmans, 2000.

Smith, David I., and Barbara Maria Carvill. *Learning from the Stranger: Christian Faith and Cultural Diversity*. Grand Rapids, MI: Eerdmans, 2009.

Snow, Donald B. "English Teachers, Language Learning, and the Issue of Power." In *Christian and Critical English Language Educators in Dialogue: Pedagogical and Ethical Dilemmas*, edited by Mary Shepard Wong and A. Suresh Canagarajah. New York: Routledge, 2009.

Stevick, Earl, and Carolyn Kristjánsson. "Faiths and Practices in Language Teaching." *Journal of Christianity and Foreign Languages* 14 (2013): 64–86.

Tannen, Deborah. *You Just Don't Understand: Women and Men in Conversation*. New York: Quill, 2001.

Tashma Baum, Miri. "'The Aspect of the Heart': English and Self-Identity in the Experience of Preservice Teachers." *Language and Intercultural Communication* 14, no. 4 (2014): 407–422. doi:10.1080/14708477.2014.934379.

Vande Kopple, William J. "Toward a Christian View of Language." In *Contemporary Literary Theory: A Christian Appraisal*, edited by Clarence Walhout and Leland Ryken. Grand Rapids, MI: Eerdmans, 1991.

Wong, Mary Shepard, and A. Suresh Canagarajah, eds. *Christian and Critical English Language Educators in Dialogue: Pedagogical and Ethical Dilemmas*. New York: Routledge, 2009.

Wong, Mary Shepard, Carolyn Kristjánsson, and Zoltán Dörnyei, eds. *Christian Faith and English Language Teaching and Learning: Research on the Interrelationship of Religion and ELT*. New York: Routledge, 2013.

# 2

# Equipping Students to Read Theology with Discernment

*Karin Spiecker Stetina*

*But you must always keep in mind that an article of faith is not something that the faithful assume. Faith, for those who have it, is the most certain form of knowledge, not a tentative opinion.*

Mortimer J. Adler[1]

In one of his sermons, Charles Spurgeon recalls an old American military tale. He writes of a man passing by a group of soldiers hard at work lifting a heavy piece of timber. The corporal of the regiment calls out to his men, "Heave there, heave ahoy!" giving them lots of directions. A passerby dismounts his horse and asks the corporal, "What is the good of your calling out to those men, why don't you help them yourself and do part of the work?" The corporal responds indignantly, "Perhaps you are not aware to whom you are speaking, sir; I am a corporal." "I beg your pardon," replies the onlooker. "You are a corporal are you; I am sorry I should not have insulted you." The traveler removes his coat and begins to help the soldiers build the fortification. When he finishes he says, "Mr Corporal, I am sorry I insulted you, but when you have any more fortifications to get up, and your men won't help you, send for

---

1. Mortimer Adler and Charles Lincoln Van Doren, *How to Read a Book: The Classic Guide to Intelligent Reading* (New York: Simon & Schuster, 2014), 286.

George Washington, the commander-in-chief, and I will come and help them." Feeling ashamed of himself, the corporal despondently walked away.[2]

Similarly, Christ, our commander-in-chief, gives us an example of how to lead those entrusted to us. Christ did not lead his disciples by standing apart from them and shouting out commands. Rather, the Gospels reveal Jesus walking alongside them, assisting them, and modeling godly living. Jesus Christ did not just convey head knowledge, but equipped his disciples with the tools to live a godly life. Christ trained them to know God and recognize their utter dependence upon God (John 15:15). Christ invited them to listen to God, seek God's ways, and put off the ways of this world (Matt 6:33). Christ called his followers to abandon worldly knowledge and seek godly wisdom (John 17:17).

In a similar vein, we too need to humbly walk beside our students and help them fulfill their Christian call to love the Lord God with all their heart and love their neighbor as themselves (Matt 22:37). How is this pursued in the higher learning context? The role of a Christian educator, as Helmut Thielke points out in his classic text, *A Little Exercise for Young Theologians*, is to see our "students not only as students but also as souls entrusted" to us.[3] He warns that "Theology is a very human business, a craft, and sometimes an art. In the last analysis it is always ambivalent. It can be sacred theology or diabolical theology. That depends on the hands and hearts which further it."[4] How do we help students, especially students learning in a language different from their native tongue, discern the sacred from the diabolical?

Higher learning in general requires that one go beyond merely understanding the words printed on the page in the pursuit of knowledge. Christian higher learning is unique in that the end goal is not just knowledge, but godly wisdom. In *The Discipline of Spiritual Discernment*, Tim Challies acknowledges that for the Christian, knowledge is never the end in and of itself. Rather the goal is "to better know, understand, and serve God," and this begins with understanding "the character of God."[5]

J. I. Packer gives a helpful definition of wisdom as "the power to see, and the inclination to choose, the best and highest goal, together with the surest means of attaining it. Wisdom is, in fact, the practical side of moral

---

2. Spurgeon, *A Home Mission Sermon*, No. 259–5:273, delivered 26 June 1859 (Green Forest, AR: Attic Books, 2012).

3. Helmut Thielke, *A Little Exercise for Young Theologians* (Grand Rapids, MI: Eerdmans, 1962), 1.

4. Ibid., 37.

5. Tim Challies, *The Discipline of Spiritual Discernment* (Wheaton, IL: Crossway, 2007), 55.

goodness." It is only fully found in God, as "He alone is naturally and entirely and invariably wise."[6] Christ, being fully God and fully man, not only teaches what true wisdom is, but incarnationally reveals true wisdom and calls us to imitate him (John 14:6).

How can Christian educators promote the godly wisdom which Christ exemplifies and calls us to emulate? In particular, how can Christian educators equip language learners to recognize, understand, and respond to God's truth? While this is most certainly a challenge that can and should be applied to all of life, the scope of this essay will focus on the specific task of equipping language learners how to read theological texts with discernment.

## The Word as Our Source of Truth

As Christians we are called to live a life informed by the Word, which includes both Christ and the Holy Scriptures. Psalm 119 declares the beauty and value of God's Word. The psalmist opens with the words "Blessed are those whose ways are blameless, who walk according to the law of the Lord." In verses 33–34 the psalmist cries out, "Teach me, Lord, the way of your decrees, that I may follow it to the end. Give me understanding, so that I may keep your laws and obey it with all my heart." He continues in verse 105, "Your word is a lamp for my feet, a light on my path." A few verses later, the psalmist cries out, "[God] give me discernment that I may understand your statutes." The author of this psalm recognizes the vital importance of God's Word and turns to it for understanding and direction (vv. 130–133). While the source of light and wisdom is clear, the understanding and application are not always as evident.

How do we interpret God's Word? Often we turn to theologians, pastors, friends, and the even the Internet as a guide. One of the challenges we face in a world inundated with resources that are just a few keystrokes away is deciding whom we listen to. Charlotte Mason rightly recognizes the importance of this question, writing,

> None of us can be proof against the influences that proceed from the persons he associates with. Wherefore, in books and men, let us look out for the best society, that which yields a bracing and wholesome influence. We all know the person for whose

---

6. J. I. Packer, *Knowing God* (Downers Grove, IL: InterVarsity, 1973), 80.

company we are the better, though the talk is only about fishing or embroidery.[7]

Before we can even ask the question of *whom* we listen to, or "for whose company we are the better," we need to examine *how* we are to listen. Being a good listener or what I will call here "a discerning reader" has become virtually a lost art. Part of our calling as believers is to be wise, and as educators our duty is to train others up to be discerning. When applying this idea to the higher learning context, one needs to go beyond merely understanding the words on the page to reading with a more learned discernment.

## Biblical Call to Discernment

In the book of Philippians, Paul implores the church to think about whatever is true, honorable, just, pure, commendable, excellent, and praiseworthy (Phil 4:8). He is calling Christians to godly thinking. As Proverbs 23:7 points out, what a person thinks, a person is. Scripture teaches that the things we choose to dwell on impact who we are. Jonathan Edwards makes a similar point in *Freedom of the Will*, saying "the ideas and images in men's minds are the invisible powers that constantly govern them."[8]

In the book of Ephesians, Paul begins to unpack what kinds of things we are to dwell on, urging his readers to avoid being deceived by false teachings. Christians are to seek unity in the body of Christ by being one in faith and practice. But what does Paul mean by unity? Often this concept is misunderstood as ecumenical or interfaith unity. Paul, however, is calling us to something radically different. He is calling believers to Christian maturity, so that they are no longer like children who are "tossed to and fro by the waves and carried about by every wind of doctrine, by human cunning, by craftiness in deceitful schemes" (Eph 4:1–16). Paul makes a similar point to the Corinthian church in 2 Corinthians 11, warning believers not to be led astray from their pure devotion to Christ by "false apostles, deceitful workmen, disguising themselves as apostles of Christ" (2 Cor 11:1–15). He recognizes the vital importance of godly teachers in this process. Christ, Paul proclaims, gave the church apostles, prophets, evangelists, shepherds and *teachers*, to "equip

---

7. Charlotte Mason, *Home School Series*, vol. 4, p. 15, accessed November 2015, https://www.amblesideonline.org/CM/vol4complete.html.

8. Jonathan Edwards, "Christian Classics Ethereal Library," *Freedom of the Will*, online: http://www.ccel.org/ccel/edwards/will.iii.ix.html?highlight=the,ideas,and,images,in,men%20s,minds,are,invisible,powers,that,constantly,govern,them#highlight, accessed November 2015.

the saints for the work of ministry" and the building of the body of Christ (Eph 4:12). How can we practically equip our students to be discerning? When they leave our classroom and our sphere of influence, what tools will they need in order to know *whom* to listen to and *how* to listen?

## Recognizing Our Ignorance and Shortcomings

As Christian educators, it is clear that we are to guide our students toward truth that ultimately produces a greater love for God and for neighbor (Matt 22:36–40). Fourteenth-century English theologian Richard Rolle insists that true love of Christ is proved "in three areas of your life – in your thinking, in your talking, and in your manner of working."[9] Before we can begin as educators training students in godly thinking, or in being discerning readers, however, it is important to acknowledge one important difference between us and Christ – we are fallen. While Christ is perfect, we are fallen. Our fallenness impacts our whole being.

Steven Turner points out how our sinful nature can impact artists, writing, "Artists, even those who are Christian, are fallen people observing a fallen world." Part of the task of an artist is "to take notice of its brokenness and acknowledge it in our work. Being that we ourselves are fallen we have to monitor our perceptions, because we know that they can be distorted by sin." Therefore, "we should hesitate before calling anything we do Christian art because we don't know how much of our own pride, selfishness or ignorance has polluted our vision."[10] This same thing can be said of an educator or a student. We struggle in our fallen condition to have true discernment. Our thinking is often "futile" and hearts often "darkened" (Rom 1:18–23). We need to constantly recognize our fallenness and the noetic effects of sin and humbly seek God's help to correct our vision; or even better, as Proverbs 3:5–6[11] and the well-known eighth-century Irish hymn convey, to lean not our own understanding, but cry out to God to "Be Thou My Vision."

---

9. Quoted in Alan Jacobs, *A Theology of Reading: The Hermeneutics of Love* (Boulder, CO: Westview Press, 2001), 10.

10. Steve Turner, *Imagine: A Vision for Christians in the Arts* (Downers Grove, IL: InterVarsity, 2001), 68.

11. "Trust in the Lord with all your heart, and do not lean on your own understanding. In all your ways acknowledge him, and he will make your paths straight."

## Offering the Tools of Careful Inspection

Having recognized the Christian call to discernment and the negative impact of our fallen nature on our understanding, we now have the task of determining how to best train our students to be discerning readers of theology. One practical way to help them is to offer our students the tools of careful inspection. While the skill of discernment can be applied to almost any field, for the Christian, the task of knowing *who* to read and *how* to read theological works is vital to learning *how* to interpret the Word of God as part of the body of Christ.[12]

As the editors of a volume on theological methods point out, "everyone interprets the Bible in their own way."[13] Whenever we come away from a Bible study or a sermon, we are well aware of the truth of this statement. Each reader has a lens by which he or she interprets Scripture and the world. It is extremely helpful, therefore, when approaching theological texts to be able to read between the lines, discerning the different perspectives, so that one is able to understand and evaluate the theology being taught. Equipped with the tools of careful inspection, the reader is more able to glean the truths contained in the work, and avoid the "deceitful schemes." This is of particular importance for foreign language learners, who not only have to overcome language barriers, but also the cultural nuances of a text. We can train these students to be discerning by teaching them *how* to listen to a text, like listening to a conversation partner.[14]

As educators, we can provide a type of scaffolding to guide our students in *how* to listen to theological texts. Russian cultural-historical psychologist Lev Vygotsky suggests that teachers can aid students in the learning process by providing scaffolding, or assistance, until the learner can accomplish the task

---

12. Both Dorothy Sayers in *The Lost Tools of Learning* and Mortimer Adler in *How to Read a Book* recognize the vital importance of equipping students with the tools of learning. Neither, however, seeks to specifically train students for godly discernment, nor focus primarily on training students how to read theology.

13. Steven L. McKenzie and Stephen R. Haynes, eds., *To Each Its Own Meaning: An Introduction to Biblical Criticisms and Their Application* (Louisville, MO: Westminster John Knox, 1999), 1.

14. Richard Langer of Biola University advocates for a conversational model for the integration of faith and learning. See for example online: http://open.biola.edu/resources/the-conversational-model-of-integration-topics, accessed on December 2015. His conversational model has implications not just for how we can approach other academic disciplines, but how we can approach texts that locate themselves within the Christian tradition. Similarly, Alan Jacobs endorses a conversational approach challenging his readers to approach texts by the "law of love," reading them "lovingly," just as we are called to love God and love neighbor. See his, *A Theology of Reading: The Hermeneutics of Love* (Boulder, CO: Westview, 2001).

alone.¹⁵ It is not enough to give them the information they need to understand and respond to theological texts. Instead, we are to be like George Washington and come alongside our students and assist them in developing the ability of *how* to approach theological texts. A practical way to equip them in becoming a discerning reader is to help to them be good conversation partners with theological works by training them to ask the right kinds of questions and assisting them in how to find the answers. These questions can be broken down into the following categories: discerning the context, the theological genre, and the author's view. Once they have the tools of careful inspection, they will be equipped to dialogue with texts on their own and will be better able to discern the theological truths communicated in them.

## *Discerning the Context*

When one enters into a conversation with a text, rather than merely reading a text like an instruction manual, one's posture toward the text completely changes. To be a good conversation partner, one needs to be able to not only listen to the speaker, but to accurately perceive what is truly being communicated by the speaker. It is much the same with a theological text. In *Is There a Meaning in the Text?*, Kevin Vanhoozer insightfully refers to theological texts as "communicative action" and suggests that the authors be seen as "communicative agents" speaking out of a particular historical situation.¹⁶ Building off of N. T. Wright, Vanhoozer suggests that if one is to understand a theological text, one must understand the "intentionality" of the author.¹⁷ That idea can be applied to both the author and the reader of a

---

15. M. Elizabeth Lewis Hall suggests that scaffolding can serve as a helpful approach to Christian scholarship in her chapter "Structuring the Scholarly Imagination: Strategies for Christian Engagement with the Disciplines" in Thomas M. Crisp, Steven L. Porter, and Gregg Ten Elshof, *Christian Scholarship in the Twenty-First Century: Prospects and Perils* (Grand Rapids, MI: Eerdmans, 2014), 97–124.

16. Kevin J. Vanhoozer, *Is There a Meaning in This Text?: The Bible, the Reader, and the Morality of Literary Knowledge* (Grand Rapids, MI: Zondervan, 1998), 232. He writes, "Understanding the text involves determining what an author has done, for a text is a communicative action fixed by writing." I am grateful for my colleague Uche Anizor's insights on the importance of understanding "a theology's backstory" or the context that it emerges out of. He practically fleshes out some of Vanhoozer's insights about the significance of context in the book he is writing, *Engaging Doctrine*.

17. Ibid., 233. On page 95 in *The New Testament and the People of God* (Minneapolis, MN: Fortress, 1992), N. T. Wright writes, "At its basic level, the 'meaning' of history may be held to lie in the intentionalities of the characters concerned (whether or not they realize their ambitions and achieve their aims)."

theological work. The discerning reader will recognize that there is a person behind the text that is attempting to communicate something that needs to be accurately heard.

Neither the author nor the reader, however, exists in a vacuum. Both are shaped by a variety of factors that influence their perspectives and their manner of communicating. In order to understand the text, therefore, one must not only comprehend the intentions of the author, but also something of the world or *context* they inhabit: the socio-political situation, the ecclesiastical setting, and their personal background and context.

The same can be said of the reader. Each reader approaches a text from a particular context. As Vanhoozer points out, this can often lead readers to treat books like a "mirror," only seeing themselves, rather than the author.[18] This can be especially true for foreign language learners, who have the extra interpretative work of attending to the linguistic elements of the text before they can even begin to unpack the contextual elements that may be at work. One needs only to think about simple idiomatic phrases to see the challenges that foreign language students may face. I remember receiving strange looks in college when I used the common Midwest idiom, "You are walking on thin ice." Though we were all native English speakers, many of my classmates in California had never even experienced ice, much less thin ice. They were utterly confused by the saying. After a few months, I learned to say, "You are walking on eggshells" to communicate that there was a delicate situation where one needed to proceed with caution. To understand an idiom one must understand more than the words used. Context plays a key role in the meaning.

So it is with theological works. The phrase *sola Scriptura*, for example, has a slightly different connotation for Martin Luther than Ulrich Zwingli. Though it can be translated "Scripture alone" in both instances, each theologian has a different application of this phrase. For Luther, beliefs should not be held if they contradict Scripture. Zwingli, on the other hand, took a bolder stand on the unique authority of Scripture, suggesting that beliefs should not be held unless they were derived from Scripture. Though they use the same phrase, both had a different view of how Christians were to apply this idea. It is vital to understand the context and the presuppositions that each Reformer held about Scripture and tradition, if one wants to truly understand the meaning of

---

18. Quoting Søren Kierkegaard, Vanhoozer writes of the dangers of interpreting a text in light of oneself, "'A book is a mirror. If an ass peers into it, you can't expect an apostle to look out.' ... Do we see only ourselves and our own concerns and those of our interpretive community, in the mirror?" (*Is There a Meaning*, 164).

*sola Scriptura*. How can teachers help equip students to understand the *context* that authors speak from? Some practical ways an educator can train students to discover the contextual information is to teach them to examine textual features and publication information and know how to discover background information about the author and the text.

**Examining Textual Features and Publication Information**
Much can be discovered about a theological text just by looking at the footnotes/endnotes, the bibliography, the foreword, the introduction, the original publication date, and the publisher. All of these elements can help a reader identify the context and authorial intent. The footnotes/endnotes and the bibliography point out the sources that the author directly acknowledges that he or she has relied upon or is dialoguing with in the text. When examining the footnotes/endnotes and bibliography as well as the text itself, one can begin to answer some important questions, such as:

- What types of sources does the author rely on? Reason, science, philosophy, Scripture, personal experience, or something else?
- What parts of Scripture does the author cite? The gospels, the epistles, narrative texts, prophetic texts, wisdom literature, poetic texts?
- Who has influenced the author? Specific theologians, philosophers, schools of thought, etc.
- Who is the author dialoguing with?

For example, if someone is studying 1 Peter and is confused by what is meant in verses 1–2 by "elect" and the "foreknowledge of God" it might be helpful to turn to a resource such as *Divine Foreknowledge: Four Views*.[19] How should one approach this text with discernment? In particular, what can be gleaned from Greg Boyd's open-theism view on divine foreknowledge? Quite a bit can be understood about his perspective before one even begins to read his chapter.[20] In his footnotes, Boyd references scientific and philosophical sources, including the chaos theory, as well as theologians such as John Sanders and Dietrich Bonhoeffer in support of his view. He also identifies some of his opponents, including United Methodist theologian Thomas Oden and Orthodox Presbyterian minister Robert Strimple. The footnotes also reveal that

---

19. James K. Beilby, Paul R. Eddy, and Gregory A. Boyd, *Divine Foreknowledge: Four Views* (Downers Grove, IL: InterVarsity, 2001).

20. Greg Boyd, "The Open-Theism View," in *Divine Foreknowledge: Four Views,* eds. James K. Beilby, Paul R. Eddy, and Gregory A. Boyd (Downers Grove, IL: InterVarsity, 2001), 13–64.

Boyd favors narrative and prophetic texts, especially from the Old Testament, over the Law and the epistles. This is in sharp contrast to the chapters in the same book by Paul Helm and David Hunt.

Publication information can also help shed light on context of the work. Examining publication information can help answer some of the following questions:

- Who published the work?
- When was the work originally published?
- Who was the intended audience?
- What was the purpose of its publication?

Returning to the example of Greg Boyd's chapter on open theism, it is significant to note that it was published by InterVarsity Press, an extension of InterVarsity Christian Fellowship, an evangelical organization that seeks to serve those in "the university, the church, and the world by publishing resources that equip people to follow Jesus as Savior and Lord of all life."[21] This book was first published in 2001. The introduction to the work identifies that it was published amid heated debates going on in evangelical circles over divine foreknowledge, particularly over the orthodoxy of open theism.[22]

The introduction also enlightens us to the target audience: "educated laypeople and college students who have had a first course in philosophy or theology."[23] All of this information is helpful in discerning not only *what* Boyd is communicating, but also *why* he is communicating it in the manner that he does. InterVarsity Press, an evangelical publishing company, has a very different mission than for instance, Covenant Communications, a publishing company that seeks to "reflect the values espoused by the church of Jesus Christ of the Latter-Day Saints."[24] The copyright and introduction alert the reader that this work was written in the beginning of the twenty-first century. The climate in North America was very different in 2001 than it was in 1971, prior to the publication of *The Chicago Statement on Biblical Inerrancy*, which was written to defend biblical inerrancy from more liberal conceptions of Scripture. As the introduction of *Divine Foreknowledge* indicates, many, particularly in

---

21. "About InterVarsity Press," InterVarsity Press, accessed December 2015, http://www.ivpress.com/about/.

22. Beilby et al., *Divine Foreknowledge*, 9.

23. Ibid., 11.

24. "Submission Guidelines," Covenant Communications, Inc., accessed December 2015, http://www.covenant-lds.com/submissions.

North America, saw open theism as one of the next great threats to evangelical orthodoxy.[25]

The example above illustrates the value of publication information and introductions. Both offer insights into the author's context and purpose. Through them we can discover that Boyd is primarily targeting an educated evangelical audience who has some basic philosophical and theological knowledge and is interested in the ongoing debate about divine foreknowledge. When we train our students to begin the reading process by examining the textual features and publication information first, they will have a head start on identifying important contextual information.

### Getting Acquainted with the Author and the Background of the Work

A second step in discovering important contextual information is to become acquainted with the author and the background of the work. This step includes identifying the specific socio-political situation, the ecclesiastical setting, and the background of the author. Some of the questions that need to be addressed are the following:

- What is the specific context of the work? This includes examining the socio-political and ecclesiastical context that the theological work emerges out of.
- Why did the author write the work? In other words, what are the explicit and implicit motives and goals of the author?
- What is the author's background? This includes the author's religious/denominational background, educational training, ethnic background, socio-political background, etc.
- What is the author's frame of reference? An author can speak as a feminist, liberation theologian, Arminian, Calvinist, biblical theologian, systematic theologian, American, etc. An author can speak from the position of narrator, pastor, scientist, philosopher, teacher, historian, etc. An author's presuppositions include his or her views about where we came from, who God is, who we are, what's wrong, what's the remedy, what is authoritative, etc.

In general, this process begins, like the previous step, before one even starts reading the theological work. Often reliable biographical and background information can be found in the book itself. For example, much can be learned about Greg Boyd's work, as we have already seen, in the introduction and

---

25. Beilby et al., *Divine Foreknowledge*, 9.

footnotes of the book. The introduction identifies Boyd as a North American evangelical and a proponent of open theism, historically a relatively rare view. One can also discover that Boyd has exegetically and philosophically defended open theism in a number of other books, including one that aims to address the problem of evil.[26] This information gives us a clue about some of his presuppositions and possible motives for arguing for open theism. Open theism, for Boyd, is not merely an abstract theological discussion, but one that helps answer the pastoral question how God can be both sovereign and not the author of evil. A question that has been a stumbling block for many people.

At other times, however, one needs to go beyond the theological text to find reliable information about the author and the context of the work. Further information about an author can often be discovered on publishers' websites and other reputable academic websites, such as the websites for the university, church, or the ministry that the author works for. InterVarsity's website, for example, reveals that Boyd received his PhD from Princeton Theological Seminary, is a pastor at Woodland Hills Church in St Paul, Minnesota, and was formerly a professor at Bethel University, a Christian university that is sponsored in part by the churches of Converge (formerly known as the Baptist General Conference). The website also states that he has published books responding to Revisionism, Skepticism, and theodicy. To gain further insights about Boyd, one can also look at the Woodland Hills website,[27] his personal websites,[28] and sites that give reliable information about Boyd's departure from Bethel University.[29] From his websites we learn that Boyd claims to boldly defend "a Christian faith that embraces science, rejects religion, transcends politics and nationalism, and that calls for a radical, socially engaged form of discipleship defined by the self-sacrificial love of the Cross."[30] We also discover that Boyd was a "former atheist who surrendered his life to Christ in 1974" and studied philosophy and theology, including process theology, at the University of Minnesota and Yale Divinity School prior to attending Princeton.[31] From his

---

26. Beilby et al., *Divine Foreknowledge*, 10; Gregory A. Boyd, *Satan and the Problem of Evil: Constructing a Trinitarian Warfare Theodicy* (Downers Grove, IL: InterVarsity, 2001).

27. Online: http://whchurch.org/about, accessed December 2015.

28. Online: http://reknew.org/ and http://gregboyd.blogspot.com/, accessed December 2015.

29. Online: http://www.desiringgod.org/articles/we-took-a-good-stand-and-made-a-bad-mistake, accessed December 2015.

30. "Greg Boyd," ReKnew, accessed December 2015, http://reknew.org/about/greg-boyd/.

31. "Greg Boyd's Profile," Blogger, accessed December 2015, https://www.blogger.com/profile/02240222413585189390.

church website we learn that the former Bethel professor no longer identifies himself with the Baptist General Conference, but is the head pastor of a nondenominational mega church which is exploring the possibility of affiliating itself with the Anabaptist/Mennonite Church USA.[32] In order to unpack the meaning of this information, it is helpful look to resources such as Walter Elwell's *Evangelical Dictionary of Theology* and H. Wayne House's *Charts of Christian Theology and Doctrine*.[33] Both of these sources will help readers of theology begin to understand the background information that they discover, such as what is theodicy, process theology, and atheism.

The more one knows about the author and the context, the more one is equipped to be a good dialogue partner. Just as one has a deeper understanding of what is being communicated by a friend than by a stranger, so is it with a theological text that one has taken time to get to know. If, for example, you overhear a stranger say that she loves a movie, you are much less likely to give her opinion the same weight that you would a trusted friend. When the theologian you are reading stays a stranger, it is difficult to know whether you should value his or her perspective, much less have confidence that you even understand what he or she is trying to say.

### *Discerning Theological Genres: Identifying Types and Methods*

While knowledge about the context and the author are vital, the discerning reader should also be able to identify the type of work and the method the author is using to express his or her theological views. Both of these pieces of information help unpack the meaning of the text. This step, however, can be one of the most challenging tasks of reading theology with discernment, in part because most readers are not very familiar with the different types of theological works, much less the various methodological approaches. There is also the added problem that many authors do not necessarily consciously work out of one approach. In ascertaining the type of work and method, the reader should seek to discover the following:

---

32. "About Us," Woodland Hills Church, accessed December 2015, http://whchurch.org/about.

33. Walter A. Elwell, *Evangelical Dictionary of Theology* (Grand Rapids, MI: Baker Book House, 1984); H. Wayne House, *Charts of Christian Theology and Doctrine* (Grand Rapids, MI: Zondervan, 1992).

- What type of theological work is it? Is it a sermon, theological treatise, polemic, response, commentary, systematic work, story/novel, poem, autobiography, etc.?
- What theological method(s) does the author utilize? Some of the possible methods are:[34]
  - *Dialectic* – pursuit of truth through questions/dialogue.
  - *Experimental/rational* – pursuit of truth by experience or rational observation.
  - *Feminist* – pursuit of truth through women's experience.
  - *Historical-critical*[35] – pursuit of truth by understanding the world behind the text.
  - *Literal exegetical (historical-grammatical)* – pursuit of truth by uncovering the author's intended meaning of the text.
  - *Narrative/story* – pursuit of truth in story rather than in propositional statements.
  - *Postmodern* – pursuit of truth through deconstructing texts, etc.
  - *Reader-response* – pursuit of truth through the reader's construction of it in response to the text.
  - *Revisionist* – pursuit of truth by discovering correlation between the Christian tradition and contemporary understanding of human existence.
- What types of sources does the author rely on? Primarily Scripture, reason, science, philosophy, personal experience, etc.?

One only needs to think about the impact of literary techniques such as sarcasm on meaning to begin to grasp the significance of the type of theological work and method employed. What if one reads literally, for example, Exodus

---

34. Understanding methods of biblical interpretation can be overwhelming, even for theologians. This list is by no means intended to be exhaustive or sufficient in explaining all the interpretative approaches. Further descriptions and examples of the various methodological approaches can be found in William W. Klein, Craig Blomberg, Robert L. Hubbard, and Kermit Allen Ecklebarger, *Introduction to Biblical Interpretation* (Dallas, TX: Word Pub, 1993); Stephen R. Haynes and Steven L. McKenzie, *To Each Its Own Meaning: An Introduction to Biblical Criticisms and Their Application* (Louisville, KY: Westminster John Knox, 1999); and Stanley E. Porter, Beth M. Stovell, and Craig Blomberg, *Biblical Hermeneutics: Five Views* (Downers Grove, IL: IVP Academic, 2012).

35. The historical criticism can be further broken down into various methodologies such as: canonical criticism, form criticism, redaction criticism, source criticism, tradition criticism, etc. See Richard N. Soulen, *Handbook of Biblical Criticism* (Atlanta, GA: Westminster John Knox, 1981), 79. For the purpose of introducing students to methodologies, however, I would advocate using a simplified list that helps them begin to recognize the use of different methodologies and how they help us understand the author's perspective.

14:11, "Is it because there are no graves in Egypt that you have taken us away to die in the wilderness? What have you done to us in bringing us out of Egypt?"[36] Are the Israelites actually wondering if Moses brought them out of Egypt because there was no place to bury them or are they murmuring against Moses? Theological genres, like literary techniques, greatly impact the communication of theological knowledge.

One can have a very different impression of the theology of eighteenth-century American theologian Jonathan Edwards, for example, if one reads *Freedom of the Will, Sinners in the Hands of an Angry God,* or his *Personal Narrative*. While each of these works has similar themes of human depravity and God's sovereign grace, Edwards employs different theological genres to critique libertarianism, to promote revival, and to share his personal experience of grace. One is a theological treatise/polemic, one a sermon, and one an autobiographical work. One text primarily employs an experimental/rational approach, one an exegetical approach, and one a more narrative approach. Each of Edwards's texts serves the same aim of communicating human depravity and God's grace, but each is tailored to a different audience and context. If his use of different theological genres is ignored, one could misread Edwards as strictly a deterministic philosopher, a hellfire preacher, or a religious mystic. Discerning theological genres is essential, especially for the language learner, in order to grasp the meaning of the text. The work of reading a theological piece does not end with being able to read the words. One must also be able to understand *how* the words are being used. Identifying the type of work and the theological method employed are vital to unpacking the meaning of the text.

Returning to Greg Boyd's chapter, for example, it is helpful to recognize that his work is a theological defense of open theism. From the introduction and the opening paragraphs of his chapter, one is informed that Boyd intends to use a literal exegetical approach to Scripture.[37] It is significant to note, that while he shares this approach with the three other authors of the book, he employs it on different types of biblical texts than his opponents do. Boyd primarily focuses on narrative and prophetic texts, whereas the other authors tend to focus on the epistles and historical texts. While the open theist argues that he holds the most biblically based position in the book, he also heavily

---

36. More examples of sarcasm are given at http://literaryterms.net/sarcasm/, accessed December 2015.

37. "Since exegesis should always drive our philosophy, instead of the other way around, and since this essay must be restricted in terms of its length, my defense of the openness view shall be almost exclusively along exegetical lines," (Boyd, "The Open-Theism View," 14).

utilizes science, philosophy, and human experience to defend his position.[38] If the reader truly wants to understand Boyd, he or she must be able to appreciate this author's theological approach.

The ability to identify theological genres increases as one becomes more conscious of *how* the author presents his or her ideas. Awareness begins before one even begins reading, by looking at information given by the publisher, author, or even outside sources. It often continues by reading the text and the footnotes/endnotes. Sometimes authors will explicitly state their theological approach, other times they will be much more covert. Identifying the theological genres will help the reader gain a deeper knowledge of a theologian's true convictions.

### *Identifying the Author's View: Thesis, Main Arguments, and Key Terms*

The heart of dialoguing with anyone is being able to actively listen and grasp what is really important to that person. Good communication, namely communication that involves being open to considering another person's perspective, is a basic element of true friendship and understanding. The same can be said of reading theology. In order to be a good conversation partner with a theological text, like any academic text, one must be able to consider the author's viewpoint. This dialogue becomes possible once the reader is able to do the following:

- Identify the thesis and key points.
- Restate the thesis and key arguments in one's own words.
- Define unknown words in the text.
- Identify and define the words that are important to the author's arguments, even if the reader knows what the word means.

Mortimer Adler points out that the "person who says he knows what he thinks but cannot express it usually does not know what he thinks."[39] This same statement can be applied to an undiscerning reader. If a reader cannot

---

38. Boyd utilizes chaos theory and dialogues with "process thought" in this work. Boyd writes "Chaos theory is deterministic but nevertheless supports the coherence of the openness view of the future insofar as it demonstrates that predictability and unpredictability are complementary, not antagonistic, principles" (18). Boyd holds that humans are free agents, like process thought, he however, sets his view apart by arguing that "God chose to create this world and give agents power to resist him" (43). He uses the analogy of the horrific human experience of children being kidnapped to argue that suffering isn't ordained by God (45–47).

39. Adler, *How to Read a Book,* 49.

clearly and concisely restate a theologian's thesis, key arguments, and key terms, then he or she probably does not really understand what the author is saying. If one can accurately restate the author's ideas in his or her own words, then one has opened the door to true communication and ultimately to theological discernment.

In teaching students how to identify theological arguments, it is helpful to encourage them to look beyond the topic headings, the questions asked by the author, and key phrases. While these are helpful devices in following the author's ideas, instead the reader should be able to identify the main point that the theologian is trying to communicate, which is usually found at the beginning of the work. The key arguments, then, are the points that serve to support the theologian's thesis.

When one is reading Boyd, for example, one should avoid seeing the section dividers such as *The Biblical Foundation of the Classical Position*, as the core of Boyd's argument. This approach would mislead one into thinking that Boyd is actually supporting the classical position on divine foreknowledge. Instead, the reader should be able to identify Boyd's thesis as

> . . . the reality that God perfectly knows, not only excludes some possibilities as what might have been but also includes other possibilities as what might be. Reality, in other words, is composed of both settled and open aspects. The sovereign Creator settles whatever he wants to settle . . . he leaves open what he wants to leave open.[40]

To put it concisely, in my own words, Boyd argues that God knows what God has settled in the future and knows all the possible outcomes of every possible choice made by free human agents. The open theist defends this view by arguing that the Bible does not warrant that the future is exhaustively settled by God, pointing out that science demonstrates that the future is partly open, and shows biblically that God is able to predict human behaviors but does not determine them, that God operates with creative flexibility in responding to creation, and that God can change his mind, be surprised, and experience frustration and regret. Understanding Boyd's thesis and arguments in support of open theism, prepares the reader to be able to evaluate his view.

Identifying and defining key terms is also essential to listening with discernment. It is important to define the terms by the author's usage. One should avoid, whenever possible, going to a dictionary, even a theological

---

40. Boyd, "The Open-Theism View," 14.

dictionary, to define the key terms because the author may not be using the term according to a dictionary's definition. This practice can be an especially dangerous pitfall for language learners. One only needs to order "chips" in both an American restaurant and an English pub to recognize how a common word can mean two very different things depending on the context. So it is often the case with theological texts. Each author of *Divine Foreknowledge: Four Views*, for example, has a different understanding of divine foreknowledge. All of them, in fact, suggest that they have the most biblical understanding of the term. If one were to read each as using Webster's definition of foreknowledge, to have "previous knowledge of; to know beforehand especially by paranormal means or by revelation," one would not be able to discern the differences between in *Divine Foreknowledge: Four Views* between open theism, simple-foreknowledge, middle-knowledge, and the Augustinian-Calvinist view.[41] As illustrated, relying on dictionaries may only serve to further confuse the reader. While outside resources may be helpful to understand some of the general terms, it is as essential to know how an author uses key terms.[42] These terms help unpack the arguments being presented.

## Going beyond Socrates: Evaluating and Applying the Text

As Rene Descartes aptly states, "the reading of all good books is like a conversation with the most honorable people of the past ages." He continues, "theology teaches one how to reach heaven."[43] The theological conversation between the author and reader ultimately becomes valuable when the reader moves beyond merely reading the words on the page, or even understanding the meaning of the author, and is brought closer to God. As Descartes points out, this step is only possible if one is able to know the "true worth" of the

---

41. "Foreknowledge," *Merriam-Webster Dictionary*, accessed December 2015, http://www.merriam-webster.com/dictionary/foreknow.

42. For general terms, where it not essential to know how the author is using the word, one can consult resources such as Justo L. González, *Essential Theological Terms* (Louisville, KY: Westminster John Knox, 2005); William A. Dyrness, Veli-Matti Kärkkäinen, Juan Francisco Martínez, and Simon Chan, *Global Dictionary of Theology: A Resource for the Worldwide Church* (Downers Grove, IL: IVP Academic, 2008); Donald K. McKim, *Westminster Dictionary of Theological Terms* (Louisville, KY: Westminster John Knox, 1996); and Stanley J. Grenz, David Guretzki, and Cherith Fee Nordling, *Pocket Dictionary of Theological Terms* (Downers Grove, IL: InterVarsity, 1999).

43. Rene Descartes, *Philosophical Essays and Correspondence* (Cambridge: Hackett, 2000), 48.

author's words so as "to guard against being deceived by" false teaching.[44] Once one has been trained in how to listen to the author, discerning the context, the theological genre, and the author's view, one can move from merely asking questions of the text to giving an informed response. This process includes being able to evaluate the text and seeing its possible application in one's own life.

### *Evaluating the value of the work*

Before one can wisely agree or disagree with someone, one must understand what has been said. As Mortimer Adler put it, "To agree without understanding is inane. To disagree without understanding is impudent."[45] Once the hard work of careful inspection is done, the reader is in the position to critically evaluate the value of the work. Assessing a work prior to reading it using the tools of discernment, is like judging a competition without being qualified to do so or giving an opinion on a food without having tasted it. One becomes a qualified judge or food critic when one becomes an expert in the field or has a developed palate. Yet often educators train students to ask "what do you think?" prior to "what does the author think?" This approach can lead students to give uninformed opinions or even reject the value of a work prior to having truly understood it. Furthermore, the reader can come away seeing the text as merely a mirror of their own thoughts, rather than a window into other perspectives on a topic. If we coach our students, however, to listen to the text like they would listen to a dear friend, they will be more open to appreciating the merit of the work, even if they find themselves in disagreement with it. The value of a theological work does not merely rest in how readable it is or how closely it aligns with our own beliefs, but in how it moves us toward loving God and loving others. Sometimes this happens when the work points us toward truth, sometimes when it helps point out flaws in our own thinking, or sometimes its value is in making us aware of the dangers of holding a "diabolical theology."

One only needs to enter into a conversation with Nietzsche, one of the most infamous critics of Christianity, to recognize that one can value a work even when one does not agree with it. One can reject Nietzsche's views on Christianity and truth and still see the importance of the questions that he raises on free will, morality, and the value of religion. Mortimer Adler argues

---

44. Ibid.
45. Adler, *How to Read a Book,* 141.

that "a good book can teach you about the world and about yourself." By engaging with good books, particularly good theological books, you do not just become more knowledgeable, but you become wiser by growing "more deeply aware of the great and enduring truths of human life."[46] Sometimes this happens simply by dialoguing with an author with whom you find yourself in disagreement.

Our evaluative process should begin, as Solomon did, with recognizing our fallenness and asking God to give us an "understanding mind" so that we "may discern between good and evil" (1 Kgs 3:9). Then, as Tim Challies suggests, making a "deliberate effort" to distinguish "between what is true and what is false."[47] We can help our students do this by teaching them to do the following:

- Test and evaluate the text against Scripture. How biblical are the author's ideas?
- Discover the implications of the text. What does it teach about God, about ourselves, and about the world? What are the implications of this work for Christianity and society?

Just as bank tellers learn how to recognize counterfeit bills by studying real money, readers of theology should learn to recognize heresy by studying the Word of God. Students should be steeped in prayer and Scripture so that when they read theology, or any academic text, they are able to discern where God's truth is being proclaimed. As Hebrews 4:12 declares, "the Word of God is living and active, sharper than any two-edged sword, piercing to the division of soul and of spirit, of joints and of marrow, and discerning the thoughts and intentions of the heart." This principle can work in two directions, helping readers discern their own heart as well as the heart of authors. Often we approach a theological work or even Scripture with preconceived notions that inhibit us from seeing anything but what we expect to see. When one is steeped in prayer and Scripture, one opens the door to the conviction of the Holy Spirit and to recognizing God's voice (Eph 1:17–18; 1 Cor 2:14–16).

If the purpose of reading theology is not worldly knowledge, but wisdom, or as Calvin puts it, true knowledge of God and ourselves, then it is not enough to read theology for understanding or even for evaluative purposes.[48] One should also read it with an eye towards its implications. If Calvin is correct,

---

46. Ibid., 340.

47. Challies, *The Discipline of Spiritual Discernment*, 67.

48. John Calvin, *Institutes of the Christian Religion* 1.1.1, ed. J. T. McNeill, trans. F. L. Battles (Philadelphia, PA: Westminster, 1960), 35.

we should seek to discover the practical implications the text has on our view of God, ourselves, and the world that we inhabit. Discovering the practical implications of ideas is foundational to significant learning experiences. One can see the importance of the implications of a work when reading scholastic theology or liberation theology. Many contemporary readers struggle to see the value of medieval scholastic theology due to its more abstract, theoretical nature that tends to offer fewer implications for faith and daily life. One only needs to examine Thomas Aquinas's lengthy discussion of angels in the *Summa Theologica* to see why scholastic theology has been criticized as impractical.[49] On the other hand, liberation theology primarily focuses on the praxis of theology, seeking to promote social change. The practical focus of liberation theology, however, has often overshadowed a focus on orthodoxy.[50] In both cases, it is important for the reader to consider both the orthodoxy and the practical implications of the theological ideas being asserted.

After one has carefully read Boyd's chapter on open theism and understands the context, the theological genre, and his view, one is prepared to begin the task of evaluating it. This process includes testing his views against Scripture as well as examining the implications of open theism. In looking at Boyd's understanding of foreknowledge as limited based on God being bound by time, for example, one may look at what Scripture has to say about time and God's relation to it. Does Scripture uphold God as existing within time or outside of time? Boyd points to passages such as Jeremiah 3:19–20, which speaks about God expecting Israel to respond to him, but Israel does not, to show how God's knowledge is bound by time. He writes, "If God wasn't certain how Israel would behave, this must mean that this information didn't yet exist; for if it did exist, God would certainly have known it."[51] Genesis 1:1, which says "in the beginning God created the heavens and the earth," however, can be seen as a challenge Boyd's view. This passage, which points to God creating time, and Isaiah 48:3, which says that God has declared the former things from the beginning, poses a challenge the notion that God cannot know the future until

---

49. Thomas Aquinas, *Summa Theologica* vol. 9 (London: Burns, Oates, & Washburne, 1920–1942) (Ia. 50–64). Aquinas has even been falsely accredited with asking the question, "How many angels could dance on the head of a pin?" The practical implications of such discussions seem less relevant today.

50. Gutiérrez, for example, emphasizes that to know God is to do justice, especially in liberating the poor. Gustavo Gutiérrez, *A Theology of Liberation: History, Politics, and Salvation* (Maryknoll, NY: Orbis Books, 1973).

51. Boyd, "The Open-Theism View," 25.

it happens. These passages and many others seem to indicate that God exists both within and outside of time.[52]

In evaluating Boyd's view, the reader should also recognize that Boyd self-consciously seeks to address how we are to understand God's knowledge in connection with human freedom. He argues that his relational view of divine foreknowledge helps address the problem of evil, promotes the power of prayer, and gives us a more biblical picture of God. Some of the conscious implications are that humans, not God, are responsible for evil; that there is power in prayer, since God can change his mind; and that when we suffer, God is empathetic and loving. These implications have a great appeal, particularly in the current North American culture, which has witnessed great evil and suffering and wants to understand where God is amid it. There are also a number of unconscious implications, such as the idea that God is not sovereign over all, since God leaves the future partially open and that God cannot answer prayers that infringe on human free will. The value of reading Boyd is not only found in understanding his view of divine foreknowledge, but also in being able to converse with him about God's nature, our nature, and what that means for how we live our lives. Once we have read a theologian, such as Boyd, with discernment we are more prepared to not only identify his beliefs, but also our own on a particular topic. The process of reading theology, or for that matter any academic text, with Christian discernment, opens the door to being sharpened through the engagement with others, as Proverbs 27:17 suggests.[53]

## Conclusion

Scripture calls us to "guard the good deposit entrusted to us" by the power of the Holy Spirit (2 Tim 1:14). In his exhortation, Paul is concerned both with the *truth*, or the good deposit God has entrusted us with, as well as the preservation of it in *faith* and *love*. As *The Expositor's Bible Commentary* points out, believers cannot accomplish this on their own, but rather by the power of the Holy Spirit who "is the great Conservator of orthodoxy."[54] As Christian educators, a primary task is to help our students guard the "good deposit." We are, like George Washington, to come alongside our students and assist them in

---

52. Some of the passages that seem to indicate that God is not bound by space or time and that God created time are Isa 46:9–11, John 4:24, Eph 1:4, and 2 Tim 1:9.

53. "Iron sharpens iron, and one man sharpens another."

54. Frank E. Gaebelein, ed., *The Expositor's Bible Commentary: Vol 11: Ephesians – Philemon* (Grand Rapids, MI: Zondervan, 1978), 397.

identifying and upholding God's truth. One way to do this is to equip them *how* to read theology and likewise any academic text with discernment. With the proper tools, language learners can approach theological texts with confidence and intentionality, learning to find worthy dialogue partners who can assist them in knowing God and knowing themselves better and hopefully how to live a life worthy of their calling in Christ. The very same principles used to read theology with discernment can be applied to almost any academic text, if one wants to be prepared to recognize, understand, and respond to God's truth.

## Bibliography

Adler, Mortimer and Charles Lincoln Van Doren. *How to Read a Book: The Classic Guide to Intelligent Reading*. New York: Simon & Schuster, 2014.

Aquinas, Thomas. *Summa Theologica* vol. 9. London: Burns, Oates, & Washburne, 1920–1942.

Beilby, James K., Paul R. Eddy, and Gregory A. Boyd. *Divine Foreknowledge: Four Views*. Downers Grove, IL: InterVarsity, 2001.

Boyd, Gregory A. "The Open-Theism View." In *Divine Foreknowledge: Four Views*, edited by James K. Beilby, Paul R. Eddy, and Gregory A. Boyd, 13–64. Downers Grove, IL: InterVarsity, 2001.

———. *Satan and the Problem of Evil: Constructing a Trinitarian Warfare Theodicy*. Downers Grove, IL: InterVarsity, 2001.

Calvin, John. *Institutes of the Christian Religion*. Edited by John T. McNeill. Translated by Ford Lewis Battles. 2 vols. Philadelphia: Westminster Press, 1960.

Charlotte Mason, *Home School Series*, vol. 4, p. 15. Accessed November 2015, https://www.amblesideonline.org/CM/vol4complete.html.

Challies, Tim. *The Discipline of Spiritual Discernment*. Wheaton, IL: Crossway, 2007.

Crisp, Thomas M., Steven L. Porter, and Gregg Ten Elshof. "Structuring the Scholarly Imagination: Strategies for Christian Engagement with the Disciplines." In *Christian Scholarship in the Twenty-First Century: Prospects and Perils*. Grand Rapids, MI: Eerdmans, 2014.

Descartes, Rene. *Philosophical Essays and Correspondence*. Cambridge: Hackett, 2000.

Dyrness, William A., Veli-Matti Kärkkäinen, Juan Francisco Martínez, and Simon Chan. *Global Dictionary of Theology: A Resource for the Worldwide Church*. Downers Grove, IL: IVP Academic, 2008.

Gaebelein, Frank E., ed. *The Expositor's Bible Commentary: Vol 11: Ephesians – Philemon*. Grand Rapids, MI: Zondervan, 1978.

González, Justo L. *Essential Theological Terms*. Louisville, KY: Westminster John Knox, 2005.

Grenz, Stanley J., David Guretzki, and Cherith Fee Nordling. *Pocket Dictionary of Theological Terms*. Downers Grove, IL: InterVarsity, 1999.

Gutiérrez, Gustavo. *A Theology of Liberation: History, Politics, and Salvation*. Maryknoll, NY: Orbis, 1973.

Jacobs, Alan. *A Theology of Reading: The Hermeneutics of Love*. Boulder, CO: Westview, 2001.

Klein, William W., Craig Blomberg, Robert L. Hubbard, and Kermit Allen Ecklebarger. *Introduction to Biblical Interpretation*. Dallas, TX: Word, 1993.

McKenzie, Steven L. and Stephen R. Haynes, eds. *To Each Its Own Meaning: An Introduction to Biblical Criticisms and Their Application*. Louisville: Westminster John Knox, 1999.

McKim, Donald K. *Westminster Dictionary of Theological Terms*. Louisville, KY: Westminster John Knox, 1996.

Packer, J. I. *Knowing God*. Downers Grove, IL: InterVarsity, 1973.

Porter, Stanley, E., Beth M. Stovell, and Craig Blomberg. *Biblical Hermeneutics: Five Views*. Downers Grove, IL: IVP Academic, 2012.

Soulen, Richard N. *Handbook of Biblical Criticism*. Atlanta, GA: Westminster John Knox, 1981.

Spurgeon, Charles. *A Home Mission Sermon*. No. 259–5:273. Delivered 26 June 1859. Green Forest, AR: Attic Books, 2012.

Thielke, Helmut. *A Little Exercise for Young Theologians*. Grand Rapids, MI: Eerdmans, 1962.

Turner, Steve. *Imagine: A Vision for Christians in the Arts*. Downers Grove, IL: InterVarsity, 2001.

Vanhoozer, Kevin J. *Is There a Meaning in This Text?: The Bible, the Reader, and the Morality of Literary Knowledge*. Grand Rapids, MI: Zondervan, 1998.

Wright, N. T. *The New Testament and the People of God*. Minneapolis, MN: Fortress, 1992.

# 3

# Using Words to Change the World: Wittgenstein and the Communication of Life

## Will Bankston

"The confusions which occupy us arise when language is, as it were, idling, not when it is doing work," says Ludwig Wittgenstein.[1] That is, when we think about language as an abstract system removed from the natural context of everyday life, we miss how it actually works and, thereby, much of what it actually is. The trouble lies in our tendency to envision language as a mere sign-system, mistaking the richly diverse facets of this complex human activity for an exercise in semiotics. We reduce successful use of language to correct labeling. If I say a word and you mentally fasten on the corresponding object, then, so it seems, communication has been achieved.

But surely, speaking is more than this picture would suggest. If our words continually fail to refer to the objects that they signify, then communication will certainly break down. However, things get complicated quickly. For instance, in which situations should I refer to that four-legged family pet as a dog? Or when would canine, doggy, or the suspicious superlative "man's best friend" constitute the more appropriate moniker? Whether I am addressing

---

1. Ludwig Wittgenstein, *Philosophical Investigations*, ed. P. M. S. Hacker and Joachim Schulte, trans. G. E. M. Anscombe, P. M. S. Hacker, and Joachim Schulte, 4th ed. (Chichester, West Sussex, UK; Malden, MA: Wiley-Blackwell, 2009), 132.

a zoological conference or looking at a picture book with my son makes all the difference in the world.[2] So then, we are left not just with denotation, signifying our intended object, but also with issues of connation, using the appropriate label for a particular context. Even more puzzling, what happens when we move beyond mere nouns and noun phrases? That is, what object am I ultimately referring to when I say "hello" or utter the words "I apologize?" Mere labeling, it seems, is not enough. Something much more intricate, nuanced, and involved is being carried out through the words we speak.

This realization takes us back to Wittgenstein's emphasis on how language actually works, which constitutes a major focus in his later writings. Given the complexity of language, it is a wonder that it does, in fact, work. However, too often this complexity has been abstracted from the successful communicative encounters of the day to day. Down that path lurks the postmodern practice of Deconstruction.[3] And, of course, language does work, at least well enough for the purposes to which we put it. It is from this easily observable premise that linguistic investigations are best begun. To be sure, the last century saw no shortage of philosophical forays into language. As Nicholas Wolterstorff comments, "Central in the philosophical thought of our century has been the topic of language."[4] Kevin Vanhoozer echoes this assessment, writing, "Indeed, it would be no exaggeration to say that language has become the preeminent problem of twentieth-century philosophy."[5] However, the philosophy of language can quickly hurl us over an esoteric edge, making us so referentially minded that we are no earthly good. However, Wittgenstein shows us another way, trading speculation for observation and pretension for practice. We would expect nothing less from a thinker who took his philosophical cue from our ordinary use of language.

As we will see, a main thrust of his later work is the notion that speaking is much more than referring. Speaking as mere referring would be like reducing a musical performance to a matter of simply matching one's produced pitches to black dots on a page. Even the most inept ear can tell that a well-played

---

2. This example is based on a similar one used by Michael D. C. Drout in his lecture series *The Modern Scholar: Way with Words: Writing Rhetoric and the Art of Persuasion* (Prince Frederick, MD: Recorded Books, 2006).

3. See Anthony C. Thiselton, *New Horizons in Hermeneutics*, 20th ann. ed. (Grand Rapids, MI: Zondervan, 1992), ch. 3.

4. Nicholas Wolterstorff, *Divine Discourse: Philosophical Reflections on the Claim That God Speaks* (Cambridge: Cambridge University Press, 1995), ix.

5. Kevin, J. Vanhoozer, *Is There a Meaning in This Text?: The Bible, the Reader, and the Morality of Literary Knowledge* (Grand Rapids, MI: Zondervan, 1998), 17.

piece constitutes much more than that. And so, too, is speaking much more than matching. Speaking is acting. We use words to do things, to navigate the many contexts that collectively comprise our life, be it ordinary or otherwise. Among other actions, we assert, command, apologize, forgive, and promise. That is to say, we use words for particular purposes in specific situations. Our speaking is acting.

Of course, we are not the only ones who use words for such ends. God likewise acts through words. As Vanhoozer writes, "The core concept in action is not bodily movement but bringing about a change in the world – directly or indirectly – by an act of will, decision, or intention. The Bible depicts God as performing some speech-acts directly (e.g. authoring the Ten Commandments) and others indirectly (e.g. speaking through the prophets)."[6] Again, words certainly do refer, but an exclusive focus on reference not only obscures our understanding of human words, but also our understanding of God's words. It fails to account for the communicative complexity of the image of God that we bear, which constitutes much more (and certainly not less) than exchanging information. Rather, words must be understood as mediators of the fullness of life in all its many manifestations. Michael Horton makes a similar point in critiquing theologies that rely on expressly non-Christian conceptions of knowing. He writes of God's self-communication, "Instead of reducing divine revelation to a Platonizing (and Cartesian) model of communicating one idea from one mind to another, we must recover the biblical (i.e. covenantal) epistemology that calls not only for observation, reflection and description, but for trust and obedience to a Thou."[7] That is, God communicates to bring us into a binding relationship with himself, not that we would simply know something new, but that we would actually become something new. God's words do not merely inform us; they transform us. He turns hostile enemies into humble servants.

Accordingly, Wittgenstein's insights help bridge the gap between theology and language pedagogy, providing us a much richer understanding of speaking, an action common to both us and our Creator. It helps us understand language in a way that not only casts light on everyday exchanges, but also on the divine intrusions of our great and gracious God into the lives of his communicating creatures. There will certainly be points of departure from Wittgenstien's

---

6. Kevin J. Vanhoozer, *Remythologizing Theology: Divine Action, Passion, and Authorship*, Cambridge Studies in Christine Doctrine (Cambridge: Cambridge University Press, 2012), 210.

7. Michael Horton, *Covenant and Eschatology: The Divine Drama* (Louisville, KY: Westminster John Knox, 2002), 143.

ideas, as Christian commitments ultimately come to contrasting conceptions of reality, but even then, such differences will stir us to dig deeper into the wonder of God's own self-communication. And so, as we explore Wittgenstein's later works, treading a path intermixed with both agreement and estrangement, our hope is that by better understanding that aspect of creation we know as human language, we will thereby be better enabled to use it and to teach it in accordance with the will of its Creator.

## No Meaning without Life

What is likely Wittgenstein's most quoted passage reads as follows: "For a *large* class of cases of the employment of the word 'meaning' – though not for *all* – this word can be explained in this way: the meaning of a word is its use in the language."[8] Eschewing the abstraction of language from everyday life, he is calling us to look at the "use" of our words in their authentic and assorted communicative contexts. In promoting this view, he is not insisting that words do not refer, that they do not signify objects. His very next line reads, "And the *meaning* of a name is sometimes explained by pointing to its *bearer*."[9] That is, sometimes identifying the object that a word signifies does demonstrate the word's meaning. Arguably the best way to explain the meaning of "dog" is to show someone the animal in question. But certainly many words such as conjunctions, articles, and interjections, to name only a few broad categories, function in a way that precludes this kind of identification. Even more, as Anthony Kenny points out, even if a word does have a corresponding object, this object and the word's meaning are not necessarily equivalent.[10] As Kenny warns, "We must beware of confusing the bearer of a name with a meaning of the name."[11] For instance, as mentioned above, Wittgenstein tells us that the meaning of a word can be "explained" at times by identifying its bearer. This action functions as a kind of visual definition of the word, what Wittgenstein calls an ostensive definition. Suppose though that every dog went extinct. In that case, despite the fact that "dog" would lack any corresponding referents, the word would be far from meaningless. We could still use it and be easily understood. That is, its meaning would remain alive and well. And certainly,

---

8. Wittgenstein, *Philosophical Investigations*, 43 (emphasis original).
9. Ibid., 43 (emphasis original).
10. Anthony Kenny, *Wittgenstein*, rev. ed. (Malden, MA: Wiley-Blackwell, 2006), 124–125.
11. Ibid., 125.

as mentioned above, while "canine" and "doggy" refer to the same object, they are *used* quite differently.

Elaborating on this notion, Wittgenstein writes, "Think of the tools in a toolbox: there is a hammer, pliers, a saw, a screwdriver, a ruler, a glue-pot, glue, nails and screws. – The functions of words are as diverse as the functions of these objects."[12] Tools are things we use to enact our intentions on the world around us. Just as we use a saw to cut a piece of wood, so we use words to make a new acquaintance. Bare hands in the former case and silence in the latter will likely leave the wood uncut and the person unmet. Accordingly, before carpenters embark upon any project, they must consider what tools will be needed for the task. In a similar fashion, as we approach the language classroom, we must never fail to consider what "projects," communicatively speaking, our students will be undertaking, and what "tools," that is, words, do such tasks require. In a sense, we are imparting linguistic craftsmanship.

This focus on use also shows us that naming does not exist in separation from the other actions that compose our life. For instance, Fergus Kerr points out, "it is impossible to isolate naming, or any of its surrogates, from a cluster of activities"[13] because "what matters is being acquainted with the innumerable different situations in which the word is *used.*"[14] We must have a reason for using this name, which entails a familiarity with the circumstances in which it would be employed. As Wittgenstein writes, "One has already to know (or be able to do) something before one can ask what something is called."[15] He goes on to say, "it only makes sense for someone to ask what something is called if he already knows how to make use of the name."[16] That is, we must already have a "post" at which "the new word is stationed."[17] And so we see that naming assumes that we have something in mind that we would like to do with that name, some action we hope it will enable us to carry out. We acquire names to use them for intentional ends. For instance, consider the following example from Wittgenstein in which he shows the ambiguity of naming that lacks a particular purpose:

---

12. Wittgenstein, *Philosophical Investigations*, 11.
13. Fergus Kerr, *Theology after Wittgenstein*, 2nd ed. (London: SPCK, 1997), 70.
14. Ibid., 71 (emphasis original).
15. Wittgenstein, *Philosophical Investigations*, 30.
16. Ibid., 31.
17. Ibid., 257.

Now, one can ostensively define a person's name, the name of a colour, the name of a material, a number-word, the name of a point of the compass, and so on. The definition of the number two, "that is called 'two'" – pointing to two nuts – perfectly exact. – But how can the number two be defined like that? The person one gives the definition to doesn't know *what* it is that one wants to call "two"; he will suppose that "two" is the name given to *this* group of nuts! – He *may* suppose this; but perhaps he does not.[18]

In a successful case, the pointing would be situated among the observer's recognized need, and corresponding ability, to use the name "two." He would know that numbers are the "posts" that need to be filled in his lexicon. This supposes that there is some activity involving counting that he would like to perform. Similarly, suppose the pointer intended to show the color brown by pointing to the nuts. The same rule would apply. As Wittgenstein writes, "A child must learn the use of colour words before it can ask for the name of a colour."[19] The intended use of the name removes the categorical ambiguity present in the example. It makes the ostensive definition intelligible, or we might say, *useful*.

In turn, not only do some words function in a way that prevents naming, having no extra-linguistic referent, but naming itself finds its necessity amid the greater purpose of *use* in the varied exchanges of one's life. We grow into the activity of naming as we are socialized into the life of a linguistic community, which is itself set within the real world of things like materials, colors, and numbers. "Naturally," Wittgenstein says, "the child who is just learning to speak has not yet got the concept *is called* at all."[20] Use, in this sense, is like the product of two reactants: the human community and the world it inhabits. As Kerr notes, "the locus of meanings is not the epistemological solitude of the individual consciousness but the practical exchanges that constitute the public world which we inhabit together."[21]

This is not unnoticed in studies of theology. For instance, drawing on the philosophy of Wittgenstein, John Frame writes, "The meaning of Scripture is

---

18. Ibid., 28 (emphasis original).
19. Wittgenstein, "On Certainty," in *Major Works: Selected Philosophical Writings* (New York, NY: Harper Perennial Modern Classics, 2009), 548.
20. Ibid., 536 (emphasis original).
21. Fergus Kerr, *Theology after Wittgenstein*, 58.

its application."[22] He gives the example of two scholars debating whether or not the commandant "Thou shalt not steal" applies to the act of embezzlement. It is clear that the scholar who understands the eighth commandment as a condemnation against this crime has better grasped its meaning. This has two important implications. First, because there is now such an activity as embezzlement, the eighth commandment, which Frame refers to as a "sentence," is able to be applied to a situation unknown to its Israelite forbearers. This application to a new situation supplies the church a richer understanding of the commandment's meaning, as it has increased its range of use. Frame puts this well, stating, "Knowing the meaning of a sentence is not merely being able to replace it with an equivalent sentence . . . Knowing the meaning is being able to use the sentence, to understand its implications, its powers, its applications."[23] Conversely, "When one lacks knowledge of how to 'apply' a text, his claim to know the 'meaning' becomes an empty-meaningless-claim."[24]

Second, this has the surprising consequence of connecting our understanding of Scripture to that of the world. That is, to plunge ever deeper into the meaning of Scripture, we must strive to apply this text with increasing wisdom to more and more of the situations that comprise our lives as humans. In Frame's words, "The interesting result of that line of reasoning is that we need to know the world to understand the meaning of Scripture."[25] Thus dispassionate observation, as much as such an orientation is possible, does not procure knowledge but prohibits it. Likewise, Andrew Walls makes a similar point from a missiological perspective. Showing the inseparable interplay between life and theology, he writes, "In mission studies we see theology 'en route' and realize its '*occasional*' nature, its character as response to the need to make Christian decisions. The conditions of Africa, for instance, are taking Christian theology into new areas of life, where Western theology has no answers, because it has no questions."[26] That is, many aspects of the lives of Africans, on a cultural level, look different than that of the Western world. Differing cultural actions have enabled Scripture to be used in situations unknown to Western theologians, thereby supplying the global church a wider application of the text and, thereby,

---

22. John M. Frame, *The Doctrine of the Knowledge of God: A Theology of Lordship* (Phillipsburg, NJ: P&R, 1987), Ch. 2, Section D.1.b.
23. Ibid.
24. Ibid.
25. Ibid.
26. Andrew Walls, *The Missionary Movement in Christian History: Studies in the Transmission of Faith* (Maryknoll, NY; Edinburgh: Orbis, 1996), 146 (emphasis original).

a fuller understanding of its meaning. We can understand then why Vanhoozer has called the church a "living commentary" of the Word of God.[27]

However, in looking at these examples, we are, so to speak, beginning our investigation mid-stream. We are examining the way in which words are used inside a language, but can we similarly examine the way that language, in its entirety, is used? From Wittgenstein's perspective, the answer is no. This would require someone to stand outside the activities that give human language its meaning. But outside such activities language would have no meaning for us since it would have no use. Accordingly, Wittgenstein notes, "Words have meaning only in the stream of life."[28] The only proper place for such an investigation would be outside of all human language systems, which, of course, is somewhere we can never stand because it is a place outside of the human life. As Wittgenstein writes of this place beyond our life and language, "We have got on to slippery ice where there is no friction, and so, in a certain sense, the conditions are ideal; but also, just because of that, we are unable to walk. We want to walk: so we need *friction*. Back to the rough ground!"[29] D. A. Carson expresses a similar sentiment, writing, "Finite human beings have no culture-free access to truth, nor can they express it in culture-free ways."[30] And so we would never be in a position to assert that language, as a comprehensive system, had a use, let alone identify the nature of this use. In resignation to the constraints of human finitude, Kenny thereby declares that "language as a whole is not an instrument for a particular purpose specifiable outside language."[31] Of course, we know that there is one who stands outside of all human activities and languages. Even more, we know that he has chosen to enter into them. We must therefore go back to the source of all things, language included, and see how God uses "language as a whole."

---

27. Vanhoozer, *Is There a Meaning in This Text?*, 441.

28. *Remarks on the Philosophy of Psychology*, vol. 1., ed. G. E. M. Anscombe and G. H. von Wright, trans. G. E. M. Anscombe (Oxford: Blackwell, 1980), 687, quoted in Kerr, *Theology after Wittgenstein*, 134.

29. Wittgenstein, *Philosophical Investigations*, 107 (emphasis original).

30. D. A. Carson, "Recent Developments in the Doctrine of Scripture," in *Collected Writings on Scripture*, ed. Andrew David Naselli (Wheaton, IL: Crossway, 2010), 102.

31. Kenny, *Wittgenstein*, 140.

## Use: A Surprisingly Christian Concept

As a first step, we do well to reflect theologically on the notion of *use*, which may, up to this point, have struck certain readers as distasteful. Perhaps it seems most at home amid modern-day mantras of "whatever works best for you" and accompanying idols such as efficiency. But use, as we will use it, is something quite different, something quite Christian, in fact. Far from pragmatism, this entails living in accordance with the way things actually are. Such a goal is both possible and profitable. That is, God has both revealed reality to us and, through the person and work of Christ, enabled us to live in right relation to it. Nothing, in fact, could be more *useful* than living in harmony with reality. Vanhoozer helps pull these strands together reminding us, "Reality is divine rhetoric, the universe a poetic work of triune artistry."[32] We ourselves are "divine rhetoric," created through the Word of God. And just like our rhetoric, so too does God's rhetoric have a use.

John Webster equates God's use of his creatures with the way in which they are "elected, shaped, and preserved."[33] He tells us, "creaturely realities are sanctified by divine use."[34] Through being used by God we are purposed "to undertake a role in the economy of salvation."[35] Our use, therefore, remains inseparable from our purpose. That is, we are *used* for God's purpose, the goal toward which all of his outward actions culminate. As B. B. Warfield writes, "That God acts upon a plan in all his activities, is already given in Theism . . . For person means purpose."[36] Describing the fulfillment of this purpose, he goes on to elaborate, "And as, when Christ comes, we shall each of us be like him, when we shall see him as he is, so also, when Christ comes, it will be to a fully saved world, and there shall be a new heaven and a new earth, in which dwells righteousness."[37] This accords well with Paul's pronouncement that God in Christ means "to reconcile to himself all things, whether on earth or in heaven, making peace by the blood of his cross" (Col 1:20).[38] We are *used* by God as instruments to bring about the redemption and restoration

---

32. Vanhoozer, *Remythologizing Theology*, 469.
33. John Webster, *Holy Scripture: A Dogmatic Sketch*, Current Issues in Theology (Cambridge: Cambridge University Press, 2003), 21.
34. Ibid.
35. Ibid.
36. B. B. Warfield, *The Plan of Salvation: Five Lectures Delivered at Princeton School of Theology: June, 1914* (Philadelphia, PA: Presbyterian Board of Publication, 1915), 12.
37. Ibid., 130.
38. All Scripture passages in this essay have been quoted from the ESV.

of all things, a purpose made possible by Christ and powerful by the Spirit. Accordingly, if this is our ultimate and encompassing use, then surely the human faculty of language finds its *usefulness* as an "instrument" (to use Kenny's terminology) aimed towards this end. Our life-embedded language and our language-embedded life have the privilege of being tools in the hands of the master craftsman. But how is this so? How is our language used as an instrument of redemption?

To answer this question, we must investigate how we ourselves came to be tools in God's plan of cosmic reconciliation. That is, we were not always so. We were once opposed to this purpose and, in relation to this proper end, we were, so to speak, *useless*. However, we were reconciled to God through Christ and thereby made *useful* as tools of his ongoing reconciliation by the use of another tool. That is to say, we ourselves have been expertly crafted. As Paul declares, "For we are his workmanship, created in Christ Jesus for good works, which God prepared beforehand, that we should walk in them" (Eph 2:10). So then, we must ask, if we are his workmanship, by what tool have we been created? Quite simply, God made us, the church, through the words of Scripture. Webster orients us to God's use of his word, writing, "Holy Scripture serves the spiritually visible, apostolic church as the *instrument* through which the Spirit breaks and reforms the community."[39] In this relationship, Scripture is the tool, the Holy Spirit the craftsman, and the church the finely fashioned product. We might summarize such insights by saying that Scripture is the tool that the Holy Spirit uses to create the church. And with that, as Webster points out, comes the sanctifying processes of being broken and reformed. How does the Spirit carry out this act of creation? Or, more astutely asked, how does he recreate us?

The Spirit uses Scripture to give the church an object of faith, by which we are justified, and an object of adoration, by which we are sanctified. This object, on both counts, is Christ. As Vanhoozer writes, framing the issue in terms of purpose, "Scripture is 'holy' not because the Bible possesses magical properties but because of its ultimate communicative agent and its ultimate communicative aim: to bring us to Jesus Christ and to sanctify us in the truth."[40] Elaborating on this "communicative agent," Vanhoozer goes on to explain, "The Spirit ministers the word that communicates Christ, the words

---

39. Webster, *Holy Scripture*, 47 (emphasis mine).

40. Kevin J. Vanhoozer, *The Drama of Doctrine: A Canonical Linguistic Approach to Christian Doctrine* (Louisville, KY: Westminster John Knox, 2005), 71.

that relates us to Christ, the word that enables communion with Christ."[41] We might paraphrase these thoughts by saying that Scripture is holy because of its *user* and its *use*. That is, Scripture testifies to Christ, our Savior and Lord, a testimony that the Spirit makes efficacious through his divine use, saving us through Christ's person and work and submitting us to his cosmic kingship.

Similarly, concerning sanctification, the Spirit makes Christ, as revealed in Scripture, an object of adoration, which is much more than an object of mere observance. That is, what we adore most is what we worship and worship constitutes the reorientation of our whole life and all its activities around that object. This is transformative, conforming us to our object of worship, of which Christ is the only proper candidate. Accordingly, as the Spirit gives us greater adoration for Christ, he makes us ever more like Christ. Paul expounds this transformational truth, writing, "And we all, with unveiled face, beholding the glory of the Lord, are being transformed into the same image from one degree of glory to another. For this comes from the Lord who is the Spirit" (2 Cor 3:18). And so we see that the words of Scripture do not merely serve as transmitters of information but as tools of transformation. Such is how God uses words, communicating not just principles but the very person of Christ.

Herman Bavinck makes a similar point, quoting Scripture's own evaluation of its purpose, that is, "to make us wise unto salvation (2 Tim 3:15)."[42] He then goes on to elaborate on this biblically mediated salvation, explaining, "Salvation is in the one who considered nothing human as alien and through his Holy Spirit joins us to himself through a word that is also fully human and wholly true."[43] The eternal Son took on humanity in all its finite fullness and deemed human language to be an effective medium for revealing himself. And these words that reveal him, when joined with the Spirit, connect us to him and communicate salvation itself. Let us therefore never cease to wonder at what human words, so used by the Spirit, can do. Accordingly, Scripture serves as the proper paradigm for the use of human language. For what the inspired words of Scripture accomplish decisively, language in general can accomplish in degrees. To be sure, despite the latter's lack of being "wholly true," both have the prescribed purpose of communicating Christ. Speaking

---

41. Ibid., 208.

42. Herman Bavinck, *Reformed Dogmatics, Vol. 1: Prolegomena*, ed. John Bolt, trans. John Vriend (Grand Rapids, MI: Baker Academic, 2003), 389.

43. Ibid.

of the church, Vanhoozer writes, "Its core practice is listening, responding, to, and performing biblical testimony."[44]

So then, as the church, we are called to communicate Christ by faithfully applying Scripture to all of the situations that comprise the human life across its many cultural forms. In so doing we bring all of human life under the submission of Scripture. With that said, we cannot forget that our use of language requires a linguistic craftsmanship that realizes different situations call for different tools. We certainly find ourselves in very different cultural and societal settings than those who have come before us and, as Vanhoozer points out, "To repeat the same words in a new situation is in fact to say something different."[45] Our aim then, as the church, is to use our words to communicate Christ amid what Wittgenstein calls "the whole hurly-burly of human actions, the background against which we see any action."[46] This is certainly no simple task. But, thankfully, we are not alone. That is, "The Spirit thus equips the church with a new communicative capacity: to witness to the word of life and, in so doing, communicate life itself."[47] And by this use of our capacities through the Spirit, we are being made holy. Thereby, may God's pronouncement of Saul also be true of us, that is, "he is a chosen *instrument* of mine to carry my name before the Gentiles and kings and the children of Israel" (Acts 9:15).

*Use*, then, is not a matter of pragmatics, but one of purpose. God *uses* words towards his own intentional ends. Our language finds its proper place only within his purposes of redemption and restoration. And so, Wittgenstein does not find himself alienated from Christian categories with his focus on use. Certainly there can be illegitimate uses of anything, words included. Even more, as sinful creatures we have rebelled against God's use for all aspects of his creation, subjecting it to "futility" (Rom 8:20). Again, language is not outside this subjugation. However, use demands intention, reminding us that God, like all speakers of human language, has purposes that he intends to enact upon the world. In fact, if we misunderstand his intentions, we misunderstand his use of words, which is as much to say, the meaning of those words. As Wolterstorff writes, "What, then, emboldens us to undertake interpreting God's discourse? The conviction, apparently, that we can and do know something of God and

---

44. Vanhoozer, *The Drama of Doctrine*, 201.

45. Ibid., 125.

46. *Zettel*, ed. G .E .M. Anscombe and G. H. von Wright, trans. G. E. M. Anscombe (Oxford: Blackwell, 1967), 567, quoted in Anthony C. Thiselton, *The Two Horizons: New Testament Hermeneutics and Philosophical Description* (Grand Rapids, MI: Eerdmans, 1980), 376.

47. Vanhoozer, *Remythologizing Theology*, 267–268.

of God's intentions."⁴⁸ Therefore we must dive into particulars, looking at how specific instances of language use become meaningful. In so doing, we will find regularities capable of connecting intention and interpretation. And these regularities apply not only to our use of words, but also to God's use.

## Much More than Checkers and Chatter

Weaving together the strands of use, meaning, and intention, Barry Stroud writes,

> The "use" of an expression as it is relevant to meaning is the distinctive role the expression plays in the activities in which human beings utter it: and respond to it as they do. Those actions and responses can help identify that meaning only if they are seen and understood as intentional; to ascribe them to those agents is to ascribe attitudes with intentional contents.⁴⁹

Each phrase then plays a "distinctive role" in a particular activity and when a phrase is used in accordance with that recognized role, a speaker's intention is intelligible. We know what the speaker is doing with the words. This most everyday of human phenomena is best captured by Wittgenstein's notion of *language-games*, a concept by which he likens communicating to playing a game. In employing this comparison he is not attempting to trivialize communication, making it something meant for mere amusement. Instead, he aims to show the similarities between the ways in which the two are conducted.

Towards this end, he notes, "For naming and describing do not stand on the *same* level: naming is preparation for describing. Naming is not yet a move in a language-game – any more than putting a piece in its place on the board is a move in chess."⁵⁰ In chess, we find a number of different pieces that are each employed by a player in its own unique manner. Without the game of chess, there would be no naming of these pieces, but because chess is a game, the naming, as is always the case, is not an end in itself. We name in order to play, that is, to use. For instance, suppose that despite our ability to successfully identify each piece on the board, the only piece we show competence in using

---

48. Wolterstorff, *Divine Discourse*, 224.

49. Barry Stroud, "Mind, Meaning, and Practice," in *The Cambridge Companion to Wittgenstein,* eds. Hans D. Sluga and David G. Stern (Cambridge; New York: Cambridge University Press, 1996), 310.

50. Wittgenstein, *Philosophical Investigations*, 49 (emphasis original).

is the pawn. We may know the names of the wooden figurines tucked away in the back row, but we do not really *know* them. If we *knew* them then we could *use* them towards the intentional end of checkmating our opponent. In fact, it might be argued that our pawn-confined play amounts to something more akin to checkers than chess. In effect, two different games are being played on the same board, which constitutes a breakdown in what properly counts as a game.

Similarly, let us imagine a student in the language classroom who has memorized thousands of vocabulary terms. He is in no shortage of names. But can he *use* those names? Can he properly put that vocabulary to use? And what exactly does it mean to use a word rightly? Returning to the analogy of the chess game supplies us a much-needed orientation for answering these queries. Like a befuddled chess player incapable of moving any pieces but pawns, this language student might have a much lower functional vocabulary than first appears. In Wittgenstein's assessment, "there are certain criteria in a man's behaviour for his not understanding a word: that it means nothing to him, that he can do nothing with it."[51] In these terms, if you cannot *use* a word, then you do not *understand* it. It remains functionally meaningless to you. Of course, technically speaking, knowing a word is not a dichotomous "know or not know" phenomenon. There are words that we can recall and produce and others that we can only recognize in the course of some contextually relevant discourse. But let us not lose Wittgenstein's forest for the psycholinguistic trees. And so just as a certain turn at a specific point in a chess game with a certain arrangement of pieces on the board calls for the particular use of a particular piece, so the contextually situated events of our lives call for the particular use of particular words. Returning to an earlier example, the use of "canine" over "doggy" could mark the difference between tenure and censure. And just as using a piece in the wrong way causes a breakdown in the game of chess, so, too, does the incorrect application of a word similarly affect communication.

Even more, just as every conversation is different, so is every game of chess. If each instance of play followed the same sequence of moves from both players, then something other than a game would be unfolding. This would be too robotic, a trait that good games never show. Games are governed, but not enslaved, by rules, which allows for the phenomenon of structured free-play. In further cementing a connection between communication and games, Wittgenstein says of a word, "It is not everywhere bounded by rules; but no more are there any rules for how high one may throw the ball in tennis,

---

51. Ibid., 269.

or how hard, yet tennis is a game for all that, and has rules too."[52] Moving from chess to tennis, he points out that there are only certain things a tennis ball is permitted to do in a match, but within these limitations, there exist numerous possibilities of free-play. Our words show a similar, yet much greater, freedom within their prescribed boundaries, a truth best exemplified in looking specifically at particular language-games identified by Wittgenstein.

He offers such examples as "giving orders," "requesting, thanking, cursing, greeting," and "reporting an event."[53] Each of these constitutes a complicated interchange with a level of rule-governed complexity that far surpasses that of tennis or chess. Even more, many of the words we use in the course of such language-games are not employed as a means of referencing some extra-linguistic object. Instead, they are used to convey things as numerous and diverse as politeness, concern, humor, respect, and agreement by acting in accordance with a staggering roster of rule-governed conventions. The field of pragmatics has demonstrated both the complexity of these interactions and the essentially limitless ways in which they can be conducted. For instance, in expressing sympathy, it is not uncommon for Vietnamese students of English to earnestly utter, "What a pity," which amounts to a rather direct translation of the Vietnamese "tiec qua." Let us call this language-game consoling. However, to the ears of modern, native English speakers, the phrase "what a pity" carries more sarcasm than sincerity. It is the stuff of jokes, at best, and insults, at worst. According to such linguistic-cultural conventions, "what a pity" has not been *used* correctly, and the stakes of this mistaken application will likely prove much higher than an unexpected checkmate. However, only a speaker's creativity marks the boundary of what words and phrases could be employed appropriately. Anything from the simple "I'm sorry" to the contextually conditioned "I'm sure the next exam will go better" could be properly used to console.

In effect, we see that just as words find their meaning in the context of particular language-games, so too do language-games find their meaning within a larger context. This context seems to be something culturally specific in part, but also something universally human. This backdrop is what Wittgenstein deemed a *form of life*. Michael Kober sheds light on this concept commenting, "Forms of life . . . require a community sharing practices,

---

52. Ibid., 68.
53. Ibid., 23.

customs, uses, institutions."⁵⁴ Without this "sharing," communication becomes not only impossible, but also purposeless, or, perhaps as Wittgenstein might say, *useless*. Wittgenstein tells us, "If a lion could talk, we wouldn't be able to understand it."⁵⁵ That is, even despite this feline's linguistic enlightenment, we would still experience an utterly different form of life from it, thereby precluding verbal communication with the beast. Reflecting on the ways our form of life frames the acquisition of our first language, Stroud writes, "We get into language at all, not by following instructions or explanations of how to do it, but only because we share enough natural responses, interests, and inclinations with those who already speak."⁵⁶

The notion of a form of life appears five times in Wittgenstein's *Philosophical Investigations* and, by subjecting his terminology to his own espoused method of enquiry, we see that it appears to be used in three slightly different ways. This issue deserves more treatment than can be given here, but a cursory survey will enable us to use the term more appropriately for our own purposes and show how he employs his own terms with the elastic, yet restrained, meaning of ordinary speech. Nicholas Lash, in building on the work of Kerr, identifies forms of life as "micro-practices" of which language-games constitute the language used in the particular activity.⁵⁷ That is, he understands language-games as "the linguistic component of a type of behavior, or 'form of life.'"⁵⁸ This seems to accord with one instance of Wittgenstein's use of the term, which treats forms of life as activities within a larger, shared culture.⁵⁹ Both Kenny and Kober, however, treat form of life as something akin to culture at large. As Kenny writes, "the comparison of language to a game . . . was meant to bring out the connection between the speaking of a language and non-linguistic activities."⁶⁰ Not only is speaking a form of acting, but language-games connect our language to our life, including all of the non-linguistic behaviors therein. In that sense, language-games, contra Lash, include more than just the words we speak. Kenny goes on, "Indeed the speaking of language is part of a communal

---

54. Michael Kober, "Certainties of a World-Picture: The Epistemological Investigations of *On Certainty*," in *The Cambridge Companion to Wittgenstein*, eds. Hans D. Sluga and David G. Stern (Cambridge; New York: Cambridge University Press, 1996), 418.
55. Wittgenstein, *Philosophical Investigations*, xi: 327.
56. Stroud, "Mind, Meaning, and Practice," 318.
57. Nicholas Lash, "How Large Is a 'Language Game'?" *Theology* 87, no. 715 (1984): 19–28.
58. Ibid., 23; for a similar analysis by Kerr see *Theology after Wittgenstein*, 28–31.
59. Wittgenstein, *Philosophical Investigations*, 23.
60. Kenny, *Wittgenstein*, 130.

activity, a way of living in society which Wittgenstein calls a 'form of life' (PI, 1, 23)."[61] Similarly, Kober says that a form of life "describes, or labels, the setting in which (e.g. discursive) language-games are practiced. That is to say: the concept of a practice or a language-game has to be linked with the concept of a community."[62] Wittgenstein appears to use language-games in this way in three of the five instances in his *Investigations*.[63] Lastly, Gordon Graham argues that the most accurate paradigm for forms of life is one that denotes a distinction in kinds of creatures.[64] In so doing he alludes to the quotation about the speaking lion above and cites an instance in the *Investigations* in which dogs and humans are said to have different forms of life.[65] In looking at these three uses, and as much as a definition is possible, we might do well to understand forms of life more generally as a shared background of life, at varying levels, which makes language-games possible.

## The God Who Communicates Christ

The question then arises, how could God and man ever participate together in a language-game? God and humanity exist at a much greater ontological distance from each other, infinite in fact, than do the finite life forms of humans and lions. However, and let us never cease to wonder at this, he has made himself a player in our language-games. Accordingly, we can know God's intentions, which is to say, how he uses his words. That is, we can know what actions his words are carrying out and, thus, what his words mean. Towards that end, the work of John Searle, who draws heavily on Wittgenstein in his development of speech-act theory, will be of help here. It will aid us in understanding two important dynamics that make God's communication of salvation in Christ possible: (1) he has entered into our form of life, thereby embracing not only human language but also the cultural conventions that give it life, and (2) we bear his image.

Alluding to Wittgenstein's imagery of a chess game, Searle writes, "If we ask ourselves under what conditions a player could be said to move a knight correctly, we would find preparatory conditions such as that it must be his

---

61. Ibid.
62. Kober, "Certainties of a World-Picture," 418.
63. Wittgenstein, *Philosophical Investigations*, 19, 241, xi: 345.
64. Gordon Graham, *Wittgenstein and Natural Religion* (Oxford: Oxford University Press, 2014), 43–45.
65. Wittgenstein, *Philosophical Investigations*, i, 1.

turn to move, as well as the essential condition stating the actual positions the knight can move to. There are even sincerity conditions for competitive games, such as that one does not cheat or attempt to 'throw' the game."[66] Although Searle would not exactly equate it as such, for our more general purposes, we can conceptualize the following of social conventions as playing chess in accordance with its rules. Similarly, if it is to truly be a game, both players must play sincerely, which, in chess, means competitively.

To see how the elements of conventions and intentions orchestrate actual actions, let us consider some examples. It should be noted that Searle specifically uses the term illocution to denote the following actions, which he equates with a speech-act, but these directly overlap with many of Wittgenstein's language-games. In turn, we would not be mistaken to regard them as such. To begin with, giving an order requires, conventionally speaking, that the speaker occupy a place of authority in regards to the hearer.[67] Intentionally speaking, the speaker should want the hearer to actually carry out the requested action. In the case of asserting, the conventions "include the fact that the hearer must have some basis for supposing the asserted proposition is true . . ." and, in terms of intention, the speaker must wish to inform the hearer and believe the fact to be true.[68] In the case of a greeting, "The preparatory condition is that the speaker must have just encountered the hearer, and the essential rule is that the utterance counts as a courteous indication of recognition of the hearer."[69] In these cases, the intentions can be assumed. In fact, in normal cases we never stop to question whether the conditions of "sincerity" have been met. As Wittgenstein retorts to the qualm of misusing the words in our language-games, "But ask yourself: how did the child learn the expression?"[70] That is, the fact that there exists such a language-game means that it functions with enough regularity (and therefore sincerity) to be acquired in the first place.

However, for Searle, the paradigmatic speech-act is the promise, and it is this example that will bridge us to God's entrance into human language-games. The conventions surrounding a promise, as identified by Searle, but in a form much simplified from his analytic rigor, involve the commitment of the speaker (S) to do some action (A) for the hearer (H), an action for which

---

66. John Searle, *Speech Acts: An Essay in the Philosophy of Language*, reprint ed. (Cambridge: Cambridge University Press, 1970), 63.
67. Ibid., 64.
68. Ibid.
69. Ibid., 64–65.
70. Wittgenstein, "On Certainty," 581.

"S believes H would prefer his doing A to his not doing A."[71] Even more, regarding this action, "It is not obvious to both S and H that S will do A in the normal course of events."[72] And, of course, S must believe that speaking certain words in this context will commit him to performing A. Lastly, and this is crucial, S must actually intend to perform A. In summary, if I promise to do something for you, then conventionally speaking, I believe that the action is both good for you and something that you could very well imagine me not doing. Intentionally speaking, I must see the words composing my promise as binding, and I must intend to carry out the action to which my words bind me. If these conventional and intentional guidelines have been met, then I have performed the speech-act of promising. In a similar way, if I have moved my knight two spaces forward and one space over with the competitive intention of checkmating my opponent, then I have successfully made a move in the game of chess.

However, it turns out that it is not only Searle who places special attention on the promise. God likewise awards this language-game a unique emphasis. In fact, it becomes the framework of our very salvation. Michael Horton, in appealing to Searle's analysis of what makes for a successful promise, demonstrates this redemptive reality with an astute eye to covenantal conventions. Examining God's covenant with Abraham in Genesis 15, Horton shows that all of the conventions of promise making are met in this encounter.[73] For instance, surveying the basic conditions, we see that God pledges himself to perform for Abraham actions that will be in Abraham's best interest. God tells him that his "reward shall be very great," assuring him that his offspring will be as the number of the stars and that he will be given "this land to possess" (vv. 1, 5, 8). Similarly, Abraham could easily imagine God not bestowing these blessings. Certainly God does not owe Abraham any such thing. And so, we can understand why in verse 8 Abraham asks of the land, "O Lord God, how am I to know that I shall possess it?" However, God, in his great graciousness, clearly communicates his intention to bind himself to his words of promise through the cultural conventions of the covenant. This commitment is all of grace. It is pure gift. As Horton explains, "Yahweh is utterly free to enter or not enter into a covenant with creatures. But upon choosing to do so, God *creates* and *accepts* an obligation for the future."[74] Therefore, in response to

---

71. Ibid., 58.
72. Ibid., 59.
73. Horton, *Covenant and Eschatology*, 127–131.
74. Ibid., 130 (emphasis original).

Abraham's question, he right away tells him to bring him a heifer, a goat, a turtledove, and a young pigeon. This might seem strange to us, or at least beside the promissory point, but not to Abraham. Excluding the birds, he cuts the animals in half. That is, according to covenantal conventions, the two participating parties would walk between the severed animals as an "oath of self-malediction."[75] That is, if they did not keep the conditions to which they had committed themselves, then they were to meet the same fate as the butchered beasts. In fact, we see this ceremony play out according to these very conditions in Jeremiah 34 between slaves and masters as the former are granted freedom.[76] Thus, when the masters went back on their promise and took back their slaves, God declares that he will "make them like the calf that they cut in two and passed between its parts" (Jer 34:18).

However, as Wittgenstein tells us, a game "is not everywhere bounded by rules."[77] And so within framework of a game, we can imagine variations that, though irregular, would still communicate their intended meaning. In fact, certain deviations, in their manipulation of prescribed procedures, might even do so stronger than their customary counterparts. We might consider, for instance, "Casey at the Bat," Ernest Thayer's iconic poem about baseball. Casey ignores two pitches, receiving two strikes, before the crowd realizes his intentions and quiets their calls for the life of the umpire. The crowd comes to recognize that, by veering from the prescribed batting procedure, Casey intends to shame the pitcher and highlight his own athletic prowess. He has placed himself into a "do or die" situation to amplify both his success and the pitcher's failure. Of course, he fails to connect with the ball on his next swing and, to the surprise of all, he strikes out. The rules of baseball are certainly not meant to reveal a player's character, but the lawful modification of regular play can express much more than a player's skill. Accordingly, through Casey's deviation from procedure, something of his character is brought into the light. His pride becomes evident to all.

Language-games allow for a similar departure from the normalized. Such is what we see in God's covenant with Abraham, albeit as an expression not of pride but of the utmost humility. That is, only God passes through the carcasses. Like the crowd that came to recognize Casey's less than admirably intentions, we too must understand the meaning of this covenantal modification. To

---

75. O. Palmer Robertson, *The Christ of the Covenants* (Phillipsburg, NJ: P&R, 1981), 130.
76. Ibid., 132–133.
77. Wittgenstein, *Philosophical Investigations*, 68.

Abraham, however, God's intentions are quite clear. Abraham has been freed from any threat of retribution for failing to live according to God's standard of obedience, which is, of course, perfection. As Horton writes elsewhere, "Instead, God alone takes that walk, assuming all of the responsibility for carrying the promise through to the end and bearing all of the curses for its breach."[78] The meaning, and thus intention, of this action is nothing less than salvation. God will take upon himself the punishment of all our sin, of all the ways we have not honored God as God. And, of course, this is exactly what he did in Christ's death, and utter God-forsakenness, on the cross. As the church, we have been saved by grace through faith in Christ and grafted into this covenant of grace. For ultimately, the children of Abraham are the multitudes worldwide who name Christ as their savior. Likewise, the land is much more than Canaan. It is the new heaven and the new earth of the age to come in which we will dwell fully with God.[79]

Furthermore, God's actions within the language-game of making a covenant change the world. J. L. Austin points out the ability of such speech-acts to alter reality in the example of the utterance of "I do" amid the proper context and conventions of the marriage ceremony.[80] These words, so to speak, change things. They are actions with actual effects. To say nothing of the great spiritual implications of becoming one flesh, the bride and the groom are now one entity in the eyes of the state. These words have altered everything regarding their legal status. Austin goes on to cite other speech-acts and, at the end of his investigation, he loosely groups them into five different categories. One such grouping is that of "commissives" which "commit the speaker to a certain course of action."[81] In this category he places both "promise" and, perhaps a bit unexpectedly to the eyes of modern readers, "covenant."[82] The point is that these speech-acts, these language-games, do something much more than convey information. And because of God's covenant with Abraham, which is fulfilled in Christ, we know that God changed, is changing, and will change his fallen world. More specifically, we know that his intention is to redeem

---

78. Michael Horton, *Introducing Covenant Theology* (Grand Rapids, MI: Baker, 2009), 33.

79. For a very helpful and clear summary of how God's covenant with Abraham fits into God's greater scheme of salvation see Michael G. Brown and Zach Keele, *Sacred Bond: Covenant Theology Explored* (Grandville, MI: Reformed Fellowship, 2012), 85–100.

80. J. L. Austin, *How to Do Things with Words*, eds. J. O. Urmson and Marina Sbisà, 2nd ed. (Cambridge, MA: Harvard University Press, 1975), 5.

81. Ibid., 157.

82. Ibid.

and restore all of creation, reconciling all things to himself in Christ. This is his intention in all that he does to his creation. And because of that, we can be certain of the purpose for which he uses words. Quite simply, God speaks to save us. Like the minister who unites the couple with the pronouncement that they have become man and wife, so God pronounces that we have been united to Christ, attributing Christ's perfect fulfillment of the covenant to us. For human marriage itself finds its referent in the union of "Christ and the church" (Eph 5:33).

Even more, there is a dignity here bestowed on humanity, his image bearers, that we must not miss. To be sure, the particular language-game of covenanting described here is one that takes a particularly human form. Likewise, God condescends to enter into it through his communicative graciousness. However, as Louis Berkhof points out, "the archetype of all covenant life is found in the Trinitarian being of God, and what is seen among men is but a faint copy."[83] For what is called the covenant of redemption constitutes an agreement between the persons of the Trinity prior to time and all of creation. In this covenant, the Triune God commits to bring about salvation for his people. As Horton writes of this pact, "The Father elects a people in the Son as their mediator to be brought to saving faith through the Spirit."[84] And so this covenant, which underlies all of God's covenants with his people, lays onto Christ a great burden that he humbly undertakes, a burden that entails his perfect life in the flesh and his total hell on the cross. Elaborating on this purpose founded in eternity past, Jesus says, "For the works that the Father has given me to accomplish, the very works that I am doing, bear witness about me that the Father has sent me" (John 5:36). The Father has assigned necessary works for the salvation of his people. Jesus has accomplished all of these. And now, the Spirit applies this completion to the church in the form of salvation. For our present purposes though, our point is not to delve deeply into this basis of redemption. Rather it is to show that just as God condescends to us, so does he also pull us up into his own Trinitarian language-games (if they can be so called). We bear his image and, ultimately, the reason we can participate in any and all language-games, the reason we can use words at all, is because we bear the image of the communicating God. Through all of eternity, in loving communion, he has spoken. And to us, his image bearers, he has gifted the privilege of speech. By this faculty, when used by him, we are not merely informed, but wholly

---

83. *Systematic Theology* (Grand Rapids, MI: Eerdmans, 1996), 263, quoted in Brown and Keele, *Sacred Bond*, 16.

84. Horton, *Introducing Covenant Theology*, 70.

transformed. And with that we enter what might be called a new human form of life, which is, to be sure, the only proper one. As Webster writes, "Through the Spirit, Jesus Christ the exalted one generates a new mode of common human life, the life of the Church."[85]

## Concluding Classroom Considerations

In many ways, Wittgenstein's insights on language accord well with recent trends in language education. For instance, looking to how a word is actually used in everyday speech resonates with the advent of corpus linguistics, in which actual samples of authentic language are analyzed. For instance, a recent corpus examined the verb "cause," finding that 90 percent of its instances of use were negative. And so, rather than speaking of "causing" beneficial effects, samples such as "to cause embarrassment, to cause havoc, to cause chaos, to cause distress," and "to cause pain to" are much more common.[86] Accordingly, students with their eyes on authentic use would know that "cause" is much better suited for the language-game of criticizing than commending. As Wittgenstein writes, "And the fact that a word means such-and-such, is used in such-and-such a way, is in turn an empirical fact, like the fact that what you see over there is a book."[87] And so corpus linguistics generates a great abundance of such "empirical" evidence.

Likewise, the concept of language-games largely overlaps with that of language functions, which might also be understood as the things we do with language. For instance, regarding syllabus design, the popular notional-functional syllabus "is organized around the communicative purposes, called functions, for which people *use* language (e.g. to obtain information or to apologize) and the notions that are being communicated (e.g. time and space)."[88] In this approach, teachers must take into account what students wish to do with the language in accordance with an utterance's context and content. Additionally, remembering the inseparable link between language and culture, we should have an eye to the language-games that particular cultures

---

85. John Webster, *Holiness* (Grand Rapids, MI: Eerdmans, 2003), 1–2.
86. John Morgan and Mario Rinvolucri, *Vocabulary*, 2nd ed. (Oxford: Oxford University Press, 2004), 10.
87. Wittgenstein, "On Certainty," 519.
88. Kathleen Graves, "Syllabus and Curriculum Design for Second Language Teaching," in *Teaching English as a Second or Foreign Language*, eds. Marianne Celce-Murcia, Donna M. Brinton, and Marguerite Ann Snow, 4th ed. (Boston, MA: Heinle ELT, 2013), 50 (emphasis mine).

expect to be played in the classroom itself. For instance, in contrast to other countries, scholastic proficiency in America, as Beatrice Mikulecky points out, "requires a person to be able to *use* language to: talk about an ongoing sequence of events, compare one phenomenon or text with another, explain causes and effects, render near-verbatim retellings, tell topic-centered stories, realize that printed materials are a source of new information," and "examine ideas from multiple points of view."[89] Again, as the quote makes clear, these are purposes for which we "use language" amid the form of life constituted by the American classroom, a context in which such actions have been deemed *useful*. We should therefore be prepared to offer extra help to students not yet acquainted with these particular language-games and their prescribed play.

However, we cannot stop here at these observations of mere practice. We must push further into the greater significance of teaching "Christianly." Towards that end, we must remember that we are teaching our students how to enter the *form of life* of another culture, one that is profoundly foreign yet inescapably human. This means that we need to train them in the use of their words against an unfamiliar backdrop. For instance, they need to know when "what a pity" is appropriate and when it is not, when it is the right tool for the job and when it should be set aside, when it is the right move in the game and when it violates the rules. In this case, they need to understand the cultural variations of the familiar language-game of consolation. As such, we must show them that a much better question than "How do I say 'tiec qua' in English?" is "What do I say to console someone?" or "What do I say to someone who is grieving?" Language-games are a framework that we should train our students to think within. Just as we only understand pawns and rooks in the bigger context of chess, so we cannot really understand our words outside of the socio-cultural contexts in which we put them to use.

This brings us back to Vanhoozer's observation. That is, "To repeat the same words in a new situation is in fact to say something different."[90] As Christians to whom the Spirit has given the "new communicative capacity" of communicating Christ, we must strive to understand the variations in language-games across cultures.[91] For instance, if we do not understand that the covenant ceremonies found throughout Scripture constitute a kind of

---

89. Beatrice Mikulecky, *A Short Course in Teaching Reading: Practical Techniques for Building Reading Power*, 2nd ed. (White Plains, NY: Pearson Education ESL, 2011), 15 (emphasis mine).

90. Vanhoozer, *The Drama of Doctrine*, 125.

91. Vanhoozer, *Remythologizing Theology*, 267.

promise making, then we will have missed everything. The fulfillment of a promise presupposes a promise having been made. Therefore, if we fail to identify this language-game, we will likewise miss Christ's fulfillment of it. We will have performed the communicative equivalent of moving all the pieces on a chessboard as if they were mere checkers. In both cases, we will lack the categories for which to make sense of the death of the king.

Accordingly, in the classroom, we must strive to understand how language-games are played in both the students' local culture and in the culture (or cultures) in which the target language is spoken. We have addressed discrepancies between the American and Vietnamese language-game of consoling, but, to be sure, there are countless other examples. Again, we are helping our students to enter a new form of life, namely the linguistic-cultural milieu in which the language they are learning is lived. As Wittgenstein writes, "to imagine a language means to imagine a form of life."[92] We do well then to take a step back and consider what language-games comprise a meaningful human life. Even more, we should look to how a proficiency in these language-games might enable students to modify them in a way that more strongly communicates one's intentions, thereby reflecting God's own departure from prescribed covenant procedures. However, in ignoring such matters, we, in a sense, are not preparing our students to be fully human in their target culture. Too often texts devote inordinate amounts of time to teaching students how to make complaints in hotel lobbies and give little to no attention to actions like forgiving, apologizing, confessing, or encouraging. The language-games of consuming take a tyrannical textual preeminence over those of contributing. In comprehensive contrast to Christ, we are equipping students, as they enter a new culture, to come not to serve but to be served, and to give their life for recreation in plenty.

Even more, we must also teach students to be proficient in the language-games that best prepare them to enter into that redeemed form of life known as the church, the communion of the saints. For example, if students dismiss how promises bind our words to a future course of action, then they will bring a certain skepticism to the biblical notion of the covenant. If words do not properly bind finite creatures, what claim could they ever make on the infinite creator? Similarly, if students fail to see the necessity of forgiving amid fallen human beings who regularly hurt one another, then they will certainly struggle to see their need to be forgiven by the God who, in their

---

92. Wittgenstein, *Philosophical Investigations*, 19.

minds, they have never wronged personally. We might also consider Lesslie Newbigin's reflection on learning the Tamil language. Amid his study, he was struck with the realization that he had never encountered a word for "hope." He then relates, "When I questioned my Hindu teacher about this, he asked me in turn what I meant by hope. Does hope mean anything? Things will be what they will be."[93] This is not to say, of course, that the Tamil language does or could not express the notion of hope. Rather I put it forward as an example of the intricate connection between language and worldview. Christianity, by contrast, places great emphasis on hope and, ultimately, hope serves as the most potent balm for the language-game of consoling. In effect, in facilitating a proficiency in consoling, we must aid our students in communicating hope.

And here we move from Christ's death to his resurrection. Because he is risen in the flesh, we can eagerly anticipate the coming consummation in which we will live in perfect relationship with our creator and all of his creation. Only Christ can hold out such hope. And, to be sure, short of this hope, all else is ultimately distraction from the definite destination of death. As such, we perform a spiritual service to our students in teaching them to console. For the deepest consolation needs hope, which awakens our hearts to the consolation that only God's hope can provide. Quite simply, "hope does not put us to shame, because God's love has been poured into our hearts through the Holy Spirit who has been given to us" (Rom 5:5). Teaching "Christianly" therefore demands that we impart proficiency in the language-games necessary for the creation and sanctification of the church, the very language-games that God himself has entered into. In so doing, we will enable our students to better interpret his intentions and better understand what he is doing with his words. May they then come to know that he uses words to save, to "communicate life itself."[94]

## Bibliography

Austin, J. L. *How to Do Things with Words*. Edited by J. O. Urmson and Marina Sbisà. 2nd ed. Cambridge, MA: Harvard University Press, 1975.

Bavinck, Herman. *Reformed Dogmatics, Vol. 1: Prolegomena*. Edited by John Bolt. Translated by John Vriend. Grand Rapids, MI: Baker Academic, 2003.

---

93. Lesslie Newbigin, *The Gospel in a Pluralistic Society* (Grand Rapids, MI: Eerdmans, 1989), 101.

94. Vanhoozer, *Remythologizing Theology*, 267–268.

Brown, Michael G. and Zach Keele. *Sacred Bond: Covenant Theology Explored.* Grandville, MI: Reformed Fellowship, 2012.

Carson, D. A. "Recent Developments in the Doctrine of Scripture." In *Collected Writings on Scripture.* Edited by Andrew David Naselli. Wheaton, IL: Crossway, 2010.

Drout, Michael D. C. *The Modern Scholar: Way with Words: Writing Rhetoric and the Art of Persuasion.* Prince Frederick, MD: Recorded Books, 2006.

Frame, John M. *The Doctrine of the Knowledge of God: A Theology of Lordship.* Phillipsburg, NJ: P&R, 1987.

Graham, Gordon. *Wittgenstein and Natural Religion.* Oxford: Oxford University Press, 2014.

Graves, Kathleen. "Syllabus and Curriculum Design for Second Language Teaching." In *Teaching English as a Second or Foreign Language.* 4th ed. Edited by Marianne Celce-Murcia, Donna M. Brinton, and Marguerite Ann Snow, 46–62. Boston: Heinle ELT, 2013.

Horton, Michael S. *Covenant and Eschatology: The Divine Drama.* Louisville, KY: Westminster John Knox, 2002.

———. *Introducing Covenant Theology.* Grand Rapids, MI: Baker, 2009.

Kenny, Anthony. *Wittgenstein.* Rev. ed. Malden, MA: Wiley-Blackwell, 2006.

Kerr, Fergus. *Theology after Wittgenstein.* 2nd ed. London: SPCK, 1997.

Kober, Michael. "Certainties of a World-Picture: The Epistemological Investigations of *On Certainty.*" In *The Cambridge Companion to Wittgenstein.* Edited by Hans D. Sluga and David G. Stern. Cambridge: Cambridge University Press, 1996.

Lash, Nicholas. "How Large Is a 'Language Game'?" *Theology* 87, no. 715 (1984): 19–28.

Mikulecky, Beatrice. *A Short Course in Teaching Reading: Practical Techniques for Building Reading Power.* 2nd ed. White Plains, NY: Pearson Education ESL, 2011.

Morgan, John and Mario Rinvolucri. *Vocabulary.* 2nd ed. Oxford: Oxford University Press, 2004.

Newbigin, Lesslie. *The Gospel in a Pluralistic Society.* Grand Rapids, MI: Eerdmans, 1989.

Robertson, O. Palmer. *The Christ of the Covenants.* Phillipsburg, NJ: P&R, 1981.

Searle, John R. *Speech Acts: An Essay in the Philosophy of Language.* Reprint ed. Cambridge: Cambridge University Press, 1970.

Stroud, Barry. "Mind, Meaning, and Practice." In *The Cambridge Companion to Wittgenstein.* Edited by Hans D. Sluga and David G. Stern. Cambridge: Cambridge University Press, 1996.

Thiselton, Anthony C. *New Horizons in Hermeneutics.* 20th Anniversary ed. Grand Rapids, MI: Zondervan, 1992.

———. *The Two Horizons: New Testament Hermeneutics and Philosophical Description.* Grand Rapids, MI: Eerdmans, 1980.

Vanhoozer, Kevin J. *The Drama of Doctrine: A Canonical Linguistic Approach to Christian Doctrine.* Louisville, KY: Westminster John Knox, 2005.

———. *Is There a Meaning in This Text?: The Bible, the Reader, and the Morality of Literary Knowledge*. Grand Rapids, MI: Zondervan, 1998.

———. *Remythologizing Theology: Divine Action, Passion, and Authorship*. Cambridge Studies in Christine Doctrine. Cambridge: Cambridge University Press, 2012.

Walls, Andrew F. *The Missionary Movement in Christian History: Studies in the Transmission of Faith*. Maryknoll, NY: Orbis, 1996.

Warfield, B. B. *The Plan of Salvation: Five Lectures Delivered at Princeton School of Theology: June, 1914*. Philadelphia: Presbyterian Board of Publication, 1915.

Webster, John. *Holiness*. Grand Rapids, MI: Eerdmans, 2003.

———. *Holy Scripture: A Dogmatic Sketch*. Current Issues in Theology. Cambridge: Cambridge University Press, 2003.

Wittgenstein, Ludwig. "On Certainty." In *Major Works: Selected Philosophical Writings*. New York: Harper Perennial Modern Classics, 2009.

———. *Philosophical Investigations*. Edited by P. M. S. Hacker and Joachim Schulte. Translated by G. E. M. Anscombe, P. M. S. Hacker, and Joachim Schulte. 4th ed. Chichester, West Sussex, UK: Wiley-Blackwell, 2009.

Wolterstorff, Nicholas. *Divine Discourse: Philosophical Reflections on the Claim That God Speaks*. Cambridge: Cambridge University Press, 1995.

# Section II

# Our Calling: Theology and the Teacher

# 4

# Seeing Clearly: My Role as a Humble, Worshiping Educator

*Kaylene Powell*

My eye itched, so I did what one often does when one has an itchy eye: I rubbed it. As hours passed, my eye became increasingly painful. Some friends dropped by for a visit; they quickly saw that I was uncomfortable, and one woman offered to wash her hands and take a look at my eye. After pulling back the eyelid and gazing intently for a moment, she pronounced in her heavily accented English, "Ah, yes, there is something there, something in your eye!" Yes, I had been able to feel that "something" for a few hours. "What is the *something*?" I asked her. She was not sure and urged me to seek professional medical care. We hailed a cab and rode several kilometers to one of the city's best hospitals, each passing car's headlights sending a wave of misery across my vision.

Once we were admitted to the emergency room and then to an eye doctor's station, the problem was quickly diagnosed. The something was a tiny, jagged chunk of coal dust; it had become embedded in my eyelid and was scratching the surface of my eye every time I blinked. Using a sterile swab, the doctor was able to extract the offending chunk before he washed and medicated my eye. He then carefully explained what I needed to do to make sure my eye would heal properly.

A corneal abrasion results when a foreign body in the eye scrapes the surface of the cornea; it is the most common of all eye injuries and is often disproportionately painful due to the rich concentration of nerve endings found in the cornea.¹ After experiencing the true depths of that pain firsthand, I never forgot the advice my friends fervently gave me during the ride home: "If you feel like you have something in your eye, never rub it!" In that area of northeast China, where coal is still the primary fuel burned for heating, it was an admonishment I would recall throughout many coming winters.

While the corneal abrasion is a physical malady, sometimes a speck in the eye is symbolic of something amiss in the heart or the spirit. A good example of this is portrayed in Hans Christian Andersen's tale, *The Snow Queen*. The devil creates a mirror which – to his sadistic delight – distorts images of everything reflected in it. Later, when the devil's helpers fly towards heaven with the intention of using the mirror to torment God and the angels, they drop the cumbersome object, and it falls to the earth, shattering into millions of tiny pieces that scatter over the earth like grains of sand. If a speck lands in a person's eye, everything the person sees becomes distorted; if a piece works its way into a person's heart, that heart becomes cold like a lump of ice. In the course of the story, a little boy named Kay is struck by a piece of the mirror. It first becomes embedded in his eye and then sinks down to take hold of his heart. From that point on, Kay is distracted and drawn away from his normal life by the dreaded Snow Queen, moving towards a fate of unending, frozen enslavement.²

Whether it is a literal abrasion or a figurative one, when our eyes are injured, we cannot see the world around us and our role in it as we should. The offending foreign body must be removed and the correct medicine must be applied so proper sight can be restored. As professional language educators, we may find our eyes tormented by specks of pride, perfectionism, cynicism, apathy, or over-commitment. The resulting scrapes and scratches disrupt the way in which we see many things including God, our students, and our work. Likewise, our hearts can become frozen to the point that we no longer properly fulfill our calling from God.

In such cases, new knowledge is generally not required; rather, we need a reminder of old and simple truths we can no longer see. With proper treatment and time, our vision can be completely restored so we once again see that all aspects of our work are meant to be a channel of worship and blessing, a

---

1. Catherine Harold, ed. *Professional Guide to Diseases*, 9th ed. (Philadelphia, PA: Wolters Kluwer, 2009), 669.

2. This summary is based on the tale as adapted from the 1872 translation by Mrs H. P. Paull, found in the following edition: Hans Christian Andersen, *The Snow Queen* (New York: Purple Bear Books, 2006).

reflection of God's glory for the promotion of his kingdom in our world. As we begin to view these things through healed eyes and hearts, our renewed viewpoint informs how we carry out every part of our job.

This is not simply an emotional matter. As Ricky Ricardo tells his wife, "Well, honey, it's a very nice thought, but as usual you have no logical 'splanation for doin' it the way you're doin' it."[3] We need a well-founded, logical plan for understanding the theological underpinnings for this endeavor, and we need practical application principles that will make daily progress more plausible, no matter how we may feel from one moment to the next. To that end, this essay contains biblically based definitions and explanations for the key ideas of glory, humility, and worship; a theoretical mapping of how these refreshed concepts relate to a proper view of our work; and an exploratory outline of how the aforementioned ideas can be directly applied to our professional lives.

## The Roots of the Abrasion

The symbolism in Andersen's story is not far off the mark. Various biblical passages tell us that one of God's angels developed his own distorted view, which resulted in prideful, rebellious actions and banishment from God's presence.[4] Later, he went looking for ways to tempt and ultimately destroy the crowning jewels of God's creative work, beginning his destructive domino effect with a seed of doubt, a question, and an invitation to disobey the one and only existing rule.[5] Just as the eyes of our earliest ancestors were opened to realize what they had done, their vision also became distorted, and their hearts began to freeze. This legacy would surround every member of the race who later entered into the fallen world: an unclear perception of God, self, and others, and a heart-soul that needed to be thawed and renewed.[6] Even after accepting salvation made available through the death of Jesus (the speck being removed), we must have a changed perspective on God's place, our place, and the convergence of the two (the medication being applied and the healing taking place).

---

3. "I Love Lucy: English Pronunciation." YouTube video, 5:24, posted by etorito1, 28 December 2012, https://www.youtube.com/watch?v=g10jFL423ho. (From *I Love Lucy*, Season 2, Episode 13, "Lucy Hires an English Tutor," written by Jess Oppenheimer, Madelyn Pugh, and Bob Carroll, Jr., originally aired on 29 December 1952.)

4. See Isa 14:12–15; Ezek 28:12–19; Luke 10:18; John 8:44; 2 Pet 2:4; Rev 12:9.

5. See Gen 1:26–27, 31; 2:15–17; 3:1–15.

6. See Isa 59:1–8; Matt 15:17–20; John 8:34; Rom 3:23; 5:12–14; Jas 1:13–15; 1 John 3:4–10.

## God's Place: Glory

To see God more clearly as our vision is restored, we must start with a deeper understanding of his essence in terms that we (in our limited sense) can comprehend. The Hebrew word for glory so often used in the Old Testament is *kabod* and comes from a root that means "heavy" or "weighty." This points to an inherent greatness or worth, so that there is an intimate connection between God's glory and his worth as displayed through his self-revelation.[7] This is the force and power of God's self-manifestation that makes him so impressive and awesome in our eyes.[8] His glory reveals something of him to us by both "the exhibition of his divine attributes (Ps 19:1)" and "the radiance of his presence (Luke 2:9)."[9] In fact, God's glory is so magnificent that any person who has ever interacted with him has had to do so indirectly (e.g. Exod 33:18–23). One author further defines it this way:

> . . . the glory of God is God's going public with his infinite beauty. As Jonathan Edwards taught, glory is not merely another one of God's attributes or characteristics (along with his holiness, love, power, and so forth). Rather, it is the "admirable conjunction of diverse excellencies *[sic]*." Glory is the dazzling, jaw-dropping, awe-inspiring showcase of God's character to a world darkened by sin.[10]

In the Old Testament, God's glory is objective, so that it is based on his very nature and not on the evaluation or opinion of others.[11] In other words, it doesn't matter what any particular person or group of people may say about him; God, without argument, exists and is infinitely greater than anyone or anything we could ever imagine. His infinite greatness extends into every aspect of his being (Father's wisdom, Son's grace, and Spirit's power), and is revealed just as much in his "self-giving love at the cross" as in every grand act that would strike godly fear into the hearts of people.[12] When we look

---

7. Lawrence O. Richards, *Expository Dictionary of Bible Words* (Grand Rapids, MI: Zondervan Regency Reference Library, 1985), 310.

8. Paul B. Duff, "Transformed 'from Glory to Glory': Paul's Appeal to the Experience of His Readers in 2 Corinthians 3:18," *Journal of Biblical Literature* 127, no. 4 (2008): 770.

9. John R. Kohlenberger III, ed., *NIV Nave's Topical Bible* (Grand Rapids, MI: Zondervan, 1992), 333.

10. Jeremy Treat, "The Glory of the Cross: How God's Power Is Made Perfect in Weakness," *Christianity Today* 57, no. 8 (2013): 58.

11. Richards, *Expository Dictionary*, 310.

12. Treat, "Glory of the Cross," 58–59.

at Christ and how he came to demonstrate a perfect blending of grace and truth, we can finally see a fuller view of God's glory as reflected in his supreme goodness.[13] After all, the crowning crescendo in the symphony of Christ's life was the "life-giving power of God as it has been manifested in the resurrection of Christ."[14] Sensibly and yet ironically, the guards standing watch when Jesus arose became like dead men (Matt 28:4) in the face of God's glorious power.

The Old Testament clearly teaches us that God is jealous of his glory and will not allow the honor that is due him to be given to anything else (i.e. idols).[15] Likewise, a proud person attempts to deprive God of his glory – something that God alone is truly worthy to receive. In essence, that person is committing "cosmic plagiarism."[16] In fact, it is when we study the attributes of God in an effort to know him more and grow closer to him that "we become increasingly aware of the indescribably vast distance between ourselves and God."[17] The Greek word used in the New Testament (*doxa*) carried over the meaning of *kabod* for an implication that was highly transformational in the Greco-Roman world. To the Greeks, individual honor, fame, and achievement made one worthy of praise from one's peers – and such praise was the goal everyone wanted to achieve. New Testament teachings further redefined greatness as allowing our human achievements and prominence to rightfully fade away when compared with the greatness of who God is and the magnificence of what he does, as he has actively expressed himself through his presence among his people.[18]

While more could be shared about God's glory, we can summarize this section by saying that God is the greatest of all that has been, is, and will be. He consistently demonstrates that greatness both through his very being and also his actions. A proper definition and understanding of God's glory will, therefore, cause us to see pursuit of our own gain and achievements as a very small and insignificant thing by comparison.

---

13. James Purves, "Pursuing 'Glory and Goodness,'" *Journal of European Baptist Studies* 5, no. 1 (2004): 41–42.

14. Duff, "Transformed," 771.

15. Eugene E. Carpenter and Philip W. Comfort, *Holman Treasury of Key Bible Words* (Nashville, TN: Broadman & Holman, 2000), 72.

16. C. J. Mahaney, *Humility: True Greatness* (Colorado Springs, CO: Multnomah, 2005), 32, 80–81.

17. Ibid., 89.

18. Richards, *Expository Dictionary*, 311. See also Matt 20:25–28; Mark 9:33–37; 2 Cor 12:7–10.

## My Place: Humility

The Hebrew term *anah* comes from a word family that can be synonymously translated as humble, humbled, humility, and humiliation. More specifically, *anah* may be translated as "gentle" and "humble" or as "poor" and "afflicted."[19] Indeed, the Old Testament posture of humility points to that of one who is weighed down or oppressed. This may include a forced submission from some external source, that is, an enemy or God, or an internal source, that is, one's own conscience that presses one to self-examination and confession.[20] This is a fitting thing: if God in his glory is great and exalted, then we in our limited and lowly state should acknowledge that we are poor in comparison and may very rightly feel weighed down by both an encounter with such overwhelming greatness and our pitiful efforts to carry on under the weight of our own imperfection.

Once again, the teachings of the Old Testament, carried over and redefined within the New Testament as teachings of Christ, point toward an abolishment of cultural norms. The word for humility (*tapeinos*) was contemptible to Greeks; whereas a successful man was seen as the highest standard for measuring what was honorable and glorious, a humble man would be viewed as a weakling and a failure.[21] However, this trait that was so despicable to the Greeks was the one that "Jesus made . . . the cornerstone of his character . . . [by which he] drew people to himself."[22] After all, our true measure of greatness is not found in the glory of man but the glory of God; we should, therefore, rightly view ourselves in the light of true humility and respond with submissive, obedient hearts.[23]

This great reversal was the core of Jesus's very life and mission on earth. He came among us as one who served (Luke 22:27), both to bring glory to his Father (John 12:23–28) and to give us an example of the kind of posture he wants us to assume in daily life (1 Pet 2:20–21). Thus, while some would assert that our humbling (by God's rod or by our own willing choice) is something that only hurts us and holds us back, the Bible teaches us it is actually one of the most freeing things we can ever experience, having a liberating effect on both our relationship with God and our relationship with others. It gives the

---

19. Ibid., 346.
20. Ibid.
21. Ibid., 347.
22. J. D. Douglas, *The New International Dictionary of the Bible, Pictorial Edition*, rev. ed. (Grand Rapids, MI: Zondervan, 1987), 455.
23. Richards, *Expository Dictionary*, 347.

Spirit of God free reign to fill us with the power of God so that, through our weakness, the glory of God might be further revealed.

> Humility is the soulmate of gratitude, and both are the heart expressions of people who have experienced the mercy of God. Humility is the acceptance of who we are – the grace to embrace our own identity and calling rather than to live by pretense. And this, of course, means that we refuse to envy others. Humility frees us to celebrate the gifts and abilities of others rather than feel diminished by them.[24]

This is one of the greatest paradoxes of the Christian faith: it is only through an unhindered view of God and oneself that the need of salvation is revealed and the way for salvation is made. In all actuality, the incarnate Jesus flipped the glory of God upside down and inside out so that such a full revelation and such a great salvation would be made possible. As Irenaeus said, "The Word of God, our Lord Jesus Christ, through his transcendent love, became what we are, that he might bring us to be even what he is himself."[25] Furthermore, when God gives grace to the humble, he helps us to change our minds so that he transforms us and uses us, in turn, as tools to transform the others and the world around us – once again with the ultimate intent of receiving the honor due him and drawing all people to himself.[26]

## The Meeting Place: Worship

When the greatness of God meets the lowliness of our hearts, the result of this intersection should be worship. As with the first two words we have explored, it is important to redefine this term according to its biblical use. Worship, at least in the minds of many contemporary English-speaking Christians, refers to a public, weekly gathering – and more specifically, to the music within that gathering. Hence, the concept of worship has become narrowly defined in terms of singing and listening to God's Word, generally within a corporate setting.

While there are many biblical examples of God-fearers gathering to pray, sing, study Scripture, and take part in related activities corporately, to focus

---

24. Gordon T. Smith, *Courage & Calling: Embracing Your God-Given Potential* (Downers Grove, IL: InterVarsity, 1999), 119.

25. Irenaeus of Lyons, *Against Heresies*, quoted in Tamara Grdelidze, "God, in Your Grace, Transform the World: Bible Study on 2 Corinthians 3:18," *Ecumenical Review* 56, no. 3 (2004): 328.

26. Grdelidze, "Transform the World," 333. See also John 12:32; Phil 2:9–11; Jas 4:6.

only on religious music or public performances neglects the deeper and broader scope of what worship entails. Both the Hebrew term (*shahah*) and the Greek term (*proskyneo*) most often used in Scripture to describe worship denote bowing down or lying prostrate before one who is superior and worthy of reverence (most often God, but also idols, angels, and people of high status). The modern English word is derived from the earlier form of "worthship," which pointed to how worthy of honor the object of worship is.[27] When God is the focus of our worship, it may include acknowledging his divine perfection in a wide number of ways including: adoration, thanksgiving, direct address, service, private meditation, and public displays.[28]

In the ancient world, in order to worship someone, a person simply had to show due respect by bowing to that deity or authority figure; it did not necessarily include doing other things such as offering a sacrifice. (It is important to note, however, that the Israelites were allowed to bow to leaders to show respect, but they were encouraged to bow *down* – fall on their faces – to God alone.) Likewise, the book of Proverbs uses this terminology to describe someone who is "stooping under a heavy load."[29] This is more than mere coincidence when we remember that God's glory is really the weight of his great worth and our humility is our weighed-down state of smallness, weakness, and poverty by comparison. Worship is, therefore, my acknowledgement of God day by day and moment by moment, as I bow my humble self toward his greatness, confessing my need for his grace and thanking him for his kindness.

Worship may be expressed via many different methods and activities,[30] but it should pervade every aspect of our self and daily life, including work.

> It is a gross error to suppose that the Christian cause goes forward solely or chiefly on weekends. What happens on the regular weekdays may be far more important, so far as the Christian faith is concerned, than what happens on Sundays . . . Most [people] ought to stay where they are and make their Christian witness in ordinary work rather than beyond it.[31]

---

27. Douglas, *Dictionary of the Bible*, 1070.
28. Ibid.
29. Carpenter and Comfort, *Key Bible Words*, 214.
30. For those who would like to further explore unique ways in which individuals may more fully experience joy in God's presence, see Gary Thomas, *Sacred Pathways* (Nashville, TN: Thomas Nelson, 1996).
31. Elton Trueblood, *Your Other Vocation* (New York: Harper & Brothers, 1952), 57–58.

Worship must involve the whole being: we have been called to love God with our entire heart, soul, mind, and strength (Mark 12:30); offer our body as a living sacrifice and our mind as a thought-transformation laboratory, all as a combined spiritual act of worship (Rom 12:1–2); and worship the Father in both Spirit and truth (John 4:24). Through justification in Christ and sanctification by the Holy Spirit, we are no longer limited to bowing our whole self before God in one place; we are now able – and are encouraged – to do that in any location, in the midst of whatever else we may be doing.[32] In sum, to worship God means to keep a constant, humble posture before God, aiming to acknowledge his glory in every part of our daily life (Job 42:4–6; Col 3:22–24).

## Work Seen Differently

Once we remember our main purpose in life and the mindset under which we must constantly live, we open our eyes and allow them to adjust to our newly prescribed lenses. Now we focus acutely on our work. What does it mean for us to view our educational work as an extension of our worship? Let us start by surveying the meaning of and purpose for work, according to a Christian worldview.

From the beginning of the biblical narrative, God is set apart from the supreme beings of other faiths because he does not remain aloof from his creation; instead, he draws near to them, working to create (and then recreate) them and their environment, sustaining them and remaining attentive to their cries.[33] Physical labor is viewed in a very positive light in the Bible, and those who unjustly avoid working are condemned. From this sprang the idea that work was ordained by God, and many Jews and early Christians held the conscious attitude that their work, no matter how menial, was an outlet through which they were to honor and obey God.[34] From the time of creation, the purpose of human beings has been to make something useful from the resources God has provided for them, and this is an idea that also carries over into the New Testament (Gen 1:28; 2:15; Col 3:22–23).[35]

Once again, however, the first disobedient act negatively impacted and skewed the perfect system God had created. "While God set Adam to work in

---

32. Carpenter and Comfort, *Key Bible Words*, 426.
33. Ibid., 424. See also Neh 1:4–11; Ps 130:1–2.
34. William L. Coleman, *Today's Handbook of Bible Times and Customs* (Minneapolis, MN: Bethany House, 1984), 116.
35. Ibid., 116–117.

the Garden of Eden as a way to participate and find satisfaction in the Lord's own meaningful labor, the fall introduced a dark aspect to work."[36] Now a Hebrew word (*amal*), which would not only mean "work" but also stand for "toil" and "trouble," entered the human vocabulary. This is the kind of work (especially in the context of work attempted apart from God) that Solomon later referred to in Ecclesiastes 2:10–11, when he complained that his efforts felt like empty and meaningless drudgery.[37] In essence, it reflects how the labor and efforts of fallen people are tainted by the presence of sin, and we will not experience a sense of complete fulfillment while we toil in temporary bodies within a fallen world.

Yet even in our present state, through other biblical examples, we see that work still maintains much potential for bringing joy to the worker and glory to God. For example, the Hebrew term *abad* means both to "work" and also to "serve," and it was used to refer to significant working acts that brought deep satisfaction, especially in the sense of religious significance and service to God.[38] Just as God made a way for creation to be redeemed and restored through the gift of his Son, so too was Jesus a supreme example of both working faithfully (John 5:16–18) and serving humbly (Mark 10:45) so that we might regain a proper perspective on God's view of work as we grow in our faith. Likewise, teachings of Jesus and his early followers found throughout the New Testament encourage us to take an even higher view of work and to work and serve with great diligence (Luke 10:2, 7; John 4:34–38; 1 Cor 15:58). New Testament words such as *kopos* demonstrate how God is, under the new covenant, continuing to redeem the ideas of "labor" and "toil" to be positive things, using them to encourage his people and draw attention to his glory (Eph 4:28; 1 Thess 1:3; 1 Tim 4:9–10).[39]

> Freed from relying on our inadequate and sinful actions to win God's acceptance, we are called to a life of grateful response to God's gracious acceptance of us through our faith in Jesus Christ. Our calling as Christians, our vocation in the world, is to devote ourselves to serving the good of the neighbor and the community

---

36. Richards, *Expository Dictionary*, 636.
37. Ibid.
38. Ibid.
39. Ibid., 637.

in every sphere of life, including family and personal relationships, our role as citizens, and our work.[40]

So while it remains that labor is not always the most enjoyable task in a person's life, we can still find satisfaction in our work as we do our best for God and influence the world around us positively in the process.[41] This is a key way in which our actions here can promote the restoration God has started and will complete at the end of time. Indeed, work was created by God as good, and he still wants to use it for good in our lives and in the lives of those we serve.

What, specifically, does this mean for us as educators? Though some of us may be teaching in settings where forthright Christian education is allowed or even encouraged, there are scriptural principles we can observe and apply, no matter our specific working context.

First, teachers were held in high esteem during Bible times, and it was a great honor to be known as a teacher. The word rabbi can also be translated as "master," and denotes a respect for learning and experience in general or in a particular area.[42] The ability to teach, in New Testament terms, is viewed as a divine gift, and those who receive the gift are called to accurately pass on the all-important truths they received from the Scriptures.[43] One author aptly notes that while the word "master" used to describe a person who was truly good in or exceptionally knowledgeable about some area, in today's educational world it often seems impossible to not feel like "we're all in over our heads," for just when we think we've "mastered our craft," the "circumstances and expectations [of our field] change."[44] We must remember that our work is a respectable and divinely appointed task while simultaneously looking for ways to continue our own learning and development, so that we might rightly recapture that title of master as we labor with focused diligence.

Second, we are reminded in Scripture that teaching is a difficult job, one that will require a higher standard of responsibility and accountability in God's eyes. Therefore, it is not something that every person should aspire to do (Matt 18:6; Jas 3:1). We must take each aspect of our work seriously and ask God to protect our students from any harm we would inadvertently bring them. This

---

40. David A. Krueger, *Keeping Faith at Work: The Christian in the Workplace* (Nashville, TN: Abingdon, 1994), 53.
41. Richards, *Expository Dictionary*, 638.
42. Coleman, *Today's Handbook*, 106–107.
43. Douglas, *Dictionary of the Bible*, 726.
44. Smith, *Courage & Calling*, 18.

is another reminder of why our correct view of God's glory and our humility are so important.

Third, we are compelled to teach, everything from essay writing and intensive reading skills to casual conversation practice, because we have experienced the transforming power of God's good news in our lives. God has started his transforming work in our lives, and, though that process is sometimes painful, it also drives us to serve as bold examples of Christ's love and redeeming power in our communication patterns, classroom management, attitude of service, and work ethic. "Because we need healing and have experienced God's amazing healing, we seek opportunities to teach, sharing God's good news with co-learners."[45]

Fourth, we must be "bilingual" in our work. This means being literate in two different types of language: the language of our faith and the language of our professional field. More than that, we want to look for ways in which we can bridge the gap between the two so that both languages are informing how we interact with and instruct our students.[46] In other words, our ultimate motivation as Christian language educators must be "to put a human voice to God's Word and a human model to God's ways."[47]

Finally, just as we remember that our teaching is an act of worship and an offering to God, we also consider and apply an adjusted awareness of learning. We strive to capture this historic attitude of Jesus's followers and help instill it in the lives of our students as much as we can:

> . . . for followers of Jesus, loving God with "all your mind" meant even more. They believed Jesus taught that God created everything, that God thought everything up. Therefore, anytime we learn something that's true, anytime we learn about how creation works or even about math or logic, we are actually thinking God's thoughts after him. We're getting to know God, and we do that because we love him. Learning can become an act of worship.[48]

I am not saying that Christian language educators should use their instructional time and classroom environments to preach to their students or

---

45. Jack L. Seymour, Margaret Ann Crain, and Joseph V. Crockett, *Educating Christians: The Intersection of Meaning, Learning, and Vocation* (Nashville, TN: Abingdon, 1993), 143–144.

46. Krueger, *Keeping Faith*, 73.

47. Steve Wamberg and John Conaway, *Faith Teaching: Teachers Like You Can Grow Faith Kids* (Colorado Springs, CO: Cook Communications, 1999), 88.

48. John Ortberg, *Who Is This Man?: The Unpredictable Impact of the Inescapable Jesus* (Grand Rapids, MI: Zondervan, 2012), 64.

force their students to discuss matters of life and theology that the students are not comfortable exploring – especially in non-religious educational contexts. I am saying, however, that when God began his work of regeneration in an educator's heart, that person should be so overwhelmed by a different perspective on God, life, their students, and their work that they will be unable to keep the transforming beauty of God's grace from spilling forth from their lives (Matt 5:16; Titus 2:9–10; 1 Pet 2:12). A deeper drive to work with excellence, a greater love and care for our students' well-being, an enhanced outlook that sees our work as eternally meaningful: these are not things we should be able to hide, nor are they things for which we should apologize. In fact, while we should not be obnoxious about displaying our faith-transformed lives, we have no reason to fear the scorn of non-Christian educators, since we are called to bow down to a higher authority (Rom 13:3; Gal 1:10; 5:23).

Figure 4.1 and the following explanatory notes serve as a summary of our discussion to this point:

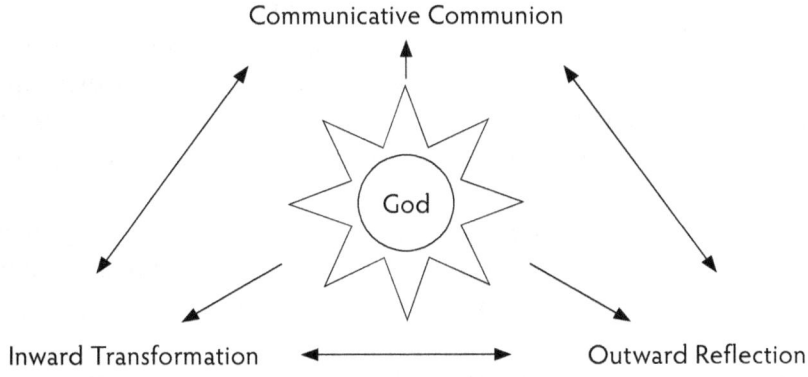

**Figure 4.1: Discussion Summary**

Communicative communion refers to our interaction with God. At the risk of sounding redundant, I use a term that is widely recognized in the current language education community. It might be argued that our communion (or time spent together) with God is not really communion without some sort of communication, but as language teachers, we know that meaningful communication does not occur without a balance of speaking and listening and contributions by both parties involved. When we spend time communing with God each day – and let there be no doubt that we must commune daily or we will begin to experience some degree of dissatisfaction in most or all areas of life – we need both to listen to him and to speak to him. If we want to improve in a skill or area, we must make a conscious effort to work at it every day; if we want a relationship to thrive and be disaster-resistant, we must devote quality time and energy to it. There is a direct connection between how deeply we commune with God, how effective we are in our work, and how much joy and fruit we reap from our labor.

Inward transformation refers to our ongoing renewal and the growth that occurs as we worship God. Recall that this worship is based on our humbly bowing down to God's wondrous glory, and that is a posture we are to assume in every part of our lives. This goes beyond worshiping God when we are communing with him in traditional "devotional" activities to humbly acknowledging God and working hand-in-hand with his Spirit as we accomplish every daily task. Referring to Romans 12:1–2 once more, ". . . in view of God's mercy . . . offer your bodies as living sacrifices, holy and pleasing to God – this is your spiritual act of worship. Do not conform any longer to the pattern of this world, but be transformed by the renewing of your mind . . ." We must continually invite the Holy Spirit to do this transforming work in our lives, especially in the realm of our thoughts. In our work, we regularly encounter such issues as struggling students, disgruntled or discouraged coworkers, and ambiguous communication from school administrators. These things are enough to drain our positive working energy if we rely on our own strength; yet, if we allow ourselves to be transformed as we assume and maintain our humble posture before God and draw from his glorious strength and wisdom, we can steadily take on more of his likeness so that we, in turn, become agents of transformation, helping to overcome evil with good in our teaching contexts.

Outward reflection refers to the glory of God that is naturally reflected from our lives into the lives of others when we have been (and continue to remain) in the presence of God's glory. Jesus reminded his students that when a lamp has been lit, it is foolish for someone to try to cover it with a basket; instead, the lamp is put on a stand so that it can give needed light to those occupying the dark room (Matt 5:15). In addition, when we see the moon shining in the sky, it is not really the light of the moon that we see but a reflection of the sun's light. If we regularly consider God's glory and our humble place in his presence, after we have bowed down to him and then lifted our faces, we will begin to absorb part of his essence. This is not to say that we will become gods, but that we will certainly be changed and affected in the most magnificent manner, coming away with a reflection of his glory radiating from our lives.

Let us pause for a moment to look at a couple of scriptural examples. First, there is the illustration of Moses found in Exodus 33:12–23 and 34:29–35. Moses experienced honest communicative communion with God on Mount Sinai; his previous encounters with God taught Moses how to respect the holiness of God's presence, and now the two of them are having a meaningful, two-way conversation. In the midst of their dialogue, God agrees to grant one of Moses's requests, right after which Moses boldly makes another request: "Now show me your glory" (v. 18). Clearly, his previous and present encounters have encouraged the process of inward transformation, and he is hungry for more. God agrees to grant that request, but in a modified way, since no mortal can bear to see the fullness of his glory and live. Yet, we read, even after catching a small glimpse of God's "back," Moses's face shines with a radiant brilliance (outward reflection), leaving the Israelites in awe of him. They are so afraid to approach him that Moses has to mask the radiance with a veil. Paul later refers to this illustration in 2 Corinthians 3:7–18. The wonder of Paul's contextual instruction is in the reminder that as those under the blood of Christ's sacrifice, we have an even greater degree of freedom to come into God's presence, to be transformed by his glorious power, and thereby to be even better and more permanent reflectors of his glory in our world.

Another example can be drawn from Isaiah 58:1–14. In the opening verses, God chastises the people of Israel for fasting with false motives and ungodly expectations. The people seem eager to know God's ways and to feel his presence (vv. 2–3), yet their actions speak louder than their words. God can see that their spoken promises do not reflect the true state of their hearts, since their communion is not honest or truly communicative. Yet, God goes on to promise that if the people will bow before his glory and outwardly demonstrate the humbled state of their hearts, he will transform them internally, resulting also in provision for the needs of many people (vv. 5–7). Finally, there is the guarantee that this true communion and transformation will naturally lead to a splendid display of God's glory through them (outward reflection), which will lead to an increase of their joy and the knowledge of God's glory throughout the world (vv. 8–14). This is a transformation we long to see take place in our own lives, so that our work might be more enjoyable, and our students and coworkers may benefit more completely from our labors, all to the chief end of glorifying the Lord.

## Applying the Diagram

Turning to daily application of these principles, we can explore starting points related to the most common areas of a typical language educator's work. Because work demands and contexts vary greatly, readers are encouraged to prioritize and adapt the following ideas as necessary to specific working situations. Under each work-related area are three bullet points with general suggestions connected to the respective points from the diagram: (1) communicative communion, (2) internal transformation, and (3) outward reflection. The concepts included here are by no means meant to be exhaustive, but rather a springboard from which a Christian language educator might regularly step in the name of personal evaluation and vision realignment.

### *Growing*

- We spend time listening to God and speaking with him, consciously paying attention to areas where we see we need to grow, both in a spiritual sense and also in a professional sense. We thank him for allowing us to approach him by the blood of Christ and for his ongoing patience and kindness towards us.
- We stop to honestly evaluate our strengths and weaknesses on a regular basis, seeking an outside, objective perspective as necessary. We lay our hearts bare before God's Spirit, inviting him to help us remain humble and see where we need to receive further transformation.
- We reflect both God's glory and our humble posture as we never stop learning in our own personal and professional lives. We prayerfully look for appropriate opportunities to share what God has been personally teaching us with our coworkers and students through words, body language, responses to various situations, and our overall working attitude.

### *Planning*

- We participate in ongoing dialogue with God about our lesson plans, which may include both praying as we work through a planning session as well as maintaining an open ear to change our plans after a planning session is completed, if needed. In this way, our lesson

plans are also a type of organic sacrifice spread out before the throne of God.
- We look for specific ways to apply what we have heard God say through his Word and his Spirit as we revisit helpful patterns from the past and explore new principles or methods for a fresher approach in our planning and teaching. We thank God for the wisdom and the good ideas he gives us to plan well, as he transforms us daily to conform more completely to his image.
- We make a conscious effort to include approaches, methods, and techniques that draw our students towards what is right and lovely (Phil 4:8) and help them consider deeper and more meaningful life topics and questions. We desire to see them develop in multiple aspects and levels through our lessons so that the fingerprints of God's glory and goodness might be seen on our lesson plans.

## *Texts and Supplementation*

- We ask God to guide us in the use of assigned materials and grant us wisdom in choosing and using additional materials. We tell him about any frustrations or inadequacies we face and listen for his voice guiding us in where to look for other helpful materials. We beseech God to plant his creative power in our mind at times when we must create our own materials from scratch, and we patiently listen.
- We humbly admit that even as every textbook and handout cannot be a perfect fit for every teaching context, so every teacher is not perfect and is daily in need of God's mercy and perspective. In this way, we remain objective, flexible, and relaxed as we evaluate, use, and adapt any assigned materials for our own contexts. We also ask God to mold and teach us, as needed, when we encounter materials based on a different approach or method than we would normally use.
- We evaluate any potential classroom materials through a spiritual-professional lens; we want any optional materials to reflect elements of goodness and redemption whenever appropriate. Likewise, we ask God to take required material that is seemingly dry or boring and illuminate it with the light of his presence so we might have joy in teaching it and our students might have joy in learning from it.

## *Lesson Presentation*

- We commune with God as we enter our classroom space before a lesson begins, and we consciously invite his glory to fill our classroom and inhabit the presentation of our lesson plan. We keep an open ear as we present our lesson, paying attention when God's Spirit tells us how to answer difficult questions or respond to spontaneous, teachable moments.
- We aim to use words, tone, body language, posture, and attitude that all reflect humility. No matter how much or how little our students may respect us, we try our best to be knowledgeable without being puffed up (1 Cor 8:1b). We look for ways to recycle old presentation methods and introduce new ones so that we grow in our ability to reach out to learners with a wide variety of learning styles and needs.
- No matter our natural personality and default presentation style, we hope to present material as clearly as possible so that students have the best possible chance of understanding the material. In this clear, orderly communication, God's peace-filled glory is likewise reflected (1 Cor 14:33).

## *Classroom Interactions*

- We often pray over our classroom interactions: we dedicate a class to God's glory before a lesson begins, we whisper brief prayers throughout the course of a class period, and we discuss specific interactions with God after class, as we reflect at the end of the day. We thank God for how he is at once both magnificently great and also intimately involved in the lives of our students and our interactions with them.
- When appropriate, we are not afraid to admit to individual students or a whole class that we have made a mistake in what we have taught them or confess that we do not know the answer to a question and need to seek it out after class is over. We constantly ask God to help us learn from past and current classroom interactions so that we might be better informed in handling future interactions, whether they are enjoyable or difficult. We ask for special grace to love and deal with students and situations that are particularly troublesome.
- Instances of and methods for error correction are guided by this ultimate desire to draw our students into the light of God's goodness.

We rejoice and thank God when struggling students show progress, difficult language points are successfully grasped, our approaches and explanations draw students closer to God's light and love reflected in our lives, and God grants us steady rapport with our students and favor with school administrators and coworkers.

## *Feedback/Assessment*

- We share our honest personal assessment of current work successes and failures with God and listen as he brings any insights to mind, showing us where things are truly flourishing and where they are honestly suffering. We steep ourselves in his Word as our ultimate source and example of truth and meaningful feedback.
- We provide our students with ongoing review and formative feedback and assessment opportunities so that their chances for successful learning and retention will increase. We continue to assume a learner's approach with a group of students, no matter how long we have taught them, so we can still adapt feedback and assessment methods to their class and individual situations as necessary.
- Any verbal or written feedback we give is tempered by the knowledge that our words are to reflect the very words of God (1 Pet 4:11). Any tests we personally write or help to create are produced with excellence and care, for the glory of God and for an honest assessment of our student's progress. By balancing fair grading with opportunities for leniency or extra credit when appropriate, we demonstrate a blend of God's higher standards for all that is good and right and his mercy.

## *After Class*

- We continually return to God's presence, listening to his feedback about how we have handled a lesson, a class, or an individual student's situation. We pour out our joys and frustrations to him. We further invite his glory to dwell in our office or any other space where we meet with coworkers and students for conferences after class.
- We confess to ourselves and to God that we are limited and know we can only do so much in one class period, week, semester, or year. We commit our students and the knowledge we have tried to pass on to

them into God's hands. Likewise, when we are finished teaching an individual or group of students, we ask God to continue the good work he has certainly begun in their lives, no matter how much or little we may influence them in the future (Phil 1:6).

- We never stop looking for after-class opportunities (in the hallway, in our office or home, etc.) to encourage our students, listen to their questions and concerns, and pray for them. Though we may not be able to pray with all of our students, coworkers, and administrators, we can and must certainly pray for them. Through these interactions, those we interrelate with in our working context see the glory of God radiating from us in a more consistent and long-term manner.

Two more noteworthy points should be included in the close of this application section. First, it is vital for us to always keep in mind the four dimensions of our students as we prepare to teach them and interact with them. Just as we have been called to love and serve God spiritually, emotionally, mentally, and physically, we should also love our students with our whole self just as we seek to teach and reach out to our students holistically. It is not enough for us to only consider a student's cognitive understanding of a lesson point, the comfortable level of their affective filter, or their physical ability to see visual aids and use classroom equipment. We must also keep an awareness of their soul at the forefront of our minds, for this fourth dimension is the least visible but the most important of all the dimensions with which we will interact.

Second, we are not meant to do all of this alone. Thanks be to God who has given us his Son as a mediator and his Spirit as a helper (Heb 4:14–16; John 14:26; Rom 8:26–27)! Beyond this, however, Scripture points to the beauty of communal support (Eccl 4:9–12). Each of us should establish a mutually encouraging relationship with a teaching mentor and/or an open-minded coworker. Ideally, such people will share your convictions and worldview; yet, even if they only hold us accountable to a high standard of excellence in our teaching, God can still use such a relationship to help us stay on track and maintain a focused perspective as we seek to implement an attitude of worship in our work. The appendix contains a schedule of suggested Scripture references that can serve as a starting point for reading, prayer, and meditation to be completed over the course of a month, alone or with a Christian mentor or partner-teacher.

## Conclusion

We left little Kay at the mercy of the Snow Queen, but that is not the end of his story. His faithful friend, Gerda, has searched far and wide to find him. When she finally arrives at the Snow Queen's palace, the only way Gerda can overcome the large and terrible guards is with prayer; as she prays, the words on her breath take the shape of angels, who form a wall of protection around her and help her advance. When she enters the palace (which the Snow Queen has temporarily left), Gerda finds her friend and is shocked at his frozen state. As Gerda embraces Kay, the hot tears that stem from her saddened but guileless spirit fall down onto Kay's chest and sink into his heart, thawing the ice and washing away the horrid chunk of glass that was lodged there. Then, as she sings a hymn over him, he weeps his own fresh tears, and the glass splinter is flushed from his eye. Gerda continues to promote Kay's healing by kissing his eyes, hands, and feet. Thus begins the conclusion of a tale that so meaningfully symbolizes both our initial salvation and our ongoing need for perspective renewal. We come to see our true state before God and depend on the blood of his Son to save us; later, we return time and time again to examine how we may have lost sight of his vision for us. In the end, as we see more clearly, we become less like Kay and more like Gerda, and we help to rescue others from their frigid and frustratingly unfruitful search for eternal life.

John Newton is most widely known and appreciated in our present day for his beloved hymn "Amazing Grace;" however, he wrote at least 280 other hymns[49] and completed numerous acts of service to advance the glory of God over the course of his life. When he was ordained as the curate at Olney Parish in Buckinghamshire, England, he soon began to apply a far-reaching philosophy; he was convinced that he should organize spiritual gatherings for both child and adult parishioners throughout the course of the week, so that every church member might be encouraged to adopt an ongoing, lifestyle-based attitude of worship.[50]

---

49. J. M. K. "How Sweet the Name of Jesus Sounds," *Bright Talks on Favorite Hymns* (Chicago, IL: John C. Winston Co., 1916). As reproduced by Wholesome Words Christian Biography Resources, retrieved from: http://www.wholesomewords.org/biography/bnewton4.html, paragraph 8.

50. Tim Challies, "Hymn Stories: How Sweet the Name of Jesus Sounds," Challies.com: Informing the Reforming (blog), June 23, 2013, http://www.challies.com/articles/hymn-stories-how-sweet-the-name-of-jesus-sounds.

One of Newton's lesser-known but still-cherished hymns is "How Sweet the Name of Jesus Sounds." A verse of that hymn beautifully sums up the thesis of this essay:

> Weak is the effort of my heart,
> And cold my warmest thought;
> But when I see Thee as Thou art,
> I'll praise Thee as I ought.[51]

It is interesting that this slave-transporter-turned-teacher should write the above words in addition to his famous personal description, "Was blind but now I see," as he would lose his physical vision to the point of near blindness in his old age. It seems that in his lengthy quest to bow before God and reflect God's glory, while he eventually lost his physical sight, Newton gained the most important and meaningful viewpoint of all: he saw what his true calling was and he sought to live out that calling in every aspect of his life, in light of who he was and who God is. Let us embrace his outlook and follow his example.

## Appendix for Chapter 4

### A Month of Suggested Readings for Further Reflection

|  | Week 1: Glory | Week 2: Humility | Week 3: Worship | Week 4: Combo |
|---|---|---|---|---|
| **Day 1** | Ps 105:1–7 | Mic 6:6–8 | Heb 12:18–29 | Phil 2:1–16 |
| **Day 2** | Ps 96:1–13 | Isa 65:24; 66:2 | Hag 1:2–9 | Rom 12:1–16 |
| **Day 3** | Isa 60:1–5; 18–20 | Ps 131:1–3 | John 4:19–24 | Isa 50:4–10 |
| **Day 4** | Ps 29:1–11 | Matt 20:25–28 | Isa 2:1–5 | 2 Cor 5:1–5, 16–21 |
| **Day 5** | 2 Cor 3:7–18 | 2 Cor 12:5–10 | Ps 95:1–7 | Ps 97:1–12 |
| **Day 6** | Ps 8:1–9 | Jas 4:1–12 | Rev 14:6–7 | Col 1:10–23 |
| **Day 7** | Ps 104:1–5, 24–35 | 1 Tim 1:15–17 | Rev 19:1–10 | 2 Cor 4:7–18 |

## Bibliography

Andersen, Hans Christian. *The Snow Queen*. New York: Purple Bear Books, 2006.

Carpenter, Eugene E., and Philip W. Comfort. *Holman Treasury of Key Bible Words*. Nashville, TN: Broadman & Holman, 2000.

---

51. *How Sweet the Name of Jesus Sounds*, n.d., http://cyberhymnal.org/htm/h/s/hsweetnj.htm.

Challies, Tim. *Challies.com: Informing the Reforming* (blog). http://www.challies.com/articles/hymn-stories-how-sweet-the-name-of-jesus-sounds.

Coleman, William L. *Today's Handbook of Bible Times and Customs*. Minneapolis, MN: Bethany House, 1984.

Douglas, J. D. *The New International Dictionary of the Bible, Pictorial Edition*. Rev. ed. Grand Rapids, MI: Zondervan, 1987.

Duff, Paul B. "Transformed 'from Glory to Glory': Paul's Appeal to the Experience of His Readers in 2 Corinthians 3:18." *Journal of Biblical Literature* 127, no. 4 (2008): 759–780.

Grdelidze, Tamara. "God, in Your Grace, Transform the World: Bible Study on 2 Corinthians 3:18." *Ecumenical Review* 56, no. 3 (2004): 327–333.

Harold, Catherine, ed. *Professional Guide to Diseases*. 9th ed. Philadelphia, PA: Wolters Kluwer, 2009.

"I Love Lucy: English Pronunciation." YouTube video, 5:24. Posted by etorito1. 28 December 2012. https://www.youtube.com/watch?v=g10jFL423ho.

J. M. K. "How Sweet the Name of Jesus Sounds." *Bright Talks on Favorite Hymns*. Chicago, IL: John C. Winston Co. 1916. As reproduced by Wholesome Words Christian Biography Resources, retrieved from: http://www.wholesomewords.org/biography/bnewton4.html.

Kohlenberger III, John R., ed. *NIV Nave's Topical Bible*. Grand Rapids, MI: Zondervan, 1992.

Krueger, David A. *Keeping Faith at Work: The Christian in the Workplace*. Nashville, TN: Abingdon, 1994.

Mahaney, C. J. *Humility: True Greatness*. Colorado Springs, CO: Multnomah, 2005.

Ortberg, John. *Who Is This Man?: The Unpredictable Impact of the Inescapable Jesus*. Grand Rapids, MI: Zondervan, 2012.

Purves, James. "Pursuing 'Glory and Goodness.'" *Journal of European Baptist Studies* 5, no. 1 (2004): 40–49.

Richards, Lawrence O. *Expository Dictionary of Bible Words*. Grand Rapids, MI: Zondervan Regency Reference Library, 1985.

Seymour, Jack L., Margaret Ann Crain, and Joseph V. Crockett. *Educating Christians: The Intersection of Meaning, Learning, and Vocation*. Nashville, TN: Abingdon, 1993.

Smith, Gordon T. *Courage & Calling: Embracing Your God-Given Potential*. Downers Grove, IL: InterVarsity, 1999.

Thomas, Gary. *Sacred Pathways: Discover Your Soul's Path to God*. Nashville, TN: Thomas Nelson Publishers, 1996.

Treat, Jeremy. "The Glory of the Cross: How God's Power Is Made Perfect in Weakness." *Christianity Today* 57, no. 8 (2013): 56–59.

Trueblood, Elton. *Your Other Vocation*. New York: Harper & Brothers, 1952.

Wamberg, Steve, and John Conaway. *Faith Teaching: Teachers Like You Can Grow Faith Kids*. Colorado Springs, CO: Cook Communications, 1999.

# 5

# Imitating the Humility of Christ in Language Teaching

## *Bradley Baurain*

*[H]ere is the path to the higher life. Down, lower down! This was what Jesus ever said to the disciples who were thinking of being great in the kingdom, and of sitting on His right hand and His left. Seek not, ask not for exaltation; that is God's work. Look to it that you abase and humble yourselves, and take no place before God or man but that of servant; that is your work; let that be your one purpose and prayer.*

Andrew Murray, Humility[1]

*If anyone would like to acquire humility, I can, I think, tell him the first step. The first step is to realise that one is proud. And a biggish step, too. At least, nothing whatever can be done before it.*

C. S. Lewis, Mere Christianity[2]

Christopher Marlowe's Renaissance drama, *Doctor Faustus*,[3] is based on the popular story of a man who sells his soul to the devil in exchange for

---

1. Andrew Murray, *Humility* (N.p.: World Invisible, 1895), 9.

2. C. S. Lewis, *Mere Christianity* (New York: Macmillan, 1952), 114.

3. Christopher Marlowe, *Doctor Faustus*, eds. David Scott Kastan and Norton Critical (New York: W. W. Norton & Co., 2005). This is the source for all following Act-Scene-line references.

power and pleasure. The tale is now a familiar one and has been employed (or satirized) everywhere from Goethe to opera to *The Simpsons*. The phrase "Faustian bargain" is idiomatic.

Whenever I read or teach this play, I am chilled by the fact that Faustus is a college professor filled with pride. Near the start of the drama,[4] he considers and arrogantly dismisses leading academic disciplines as pointless, including philosophy ("odious and obscure"), medicine and law ("for petty wits"), and theology ("unpleasant, harsh, contemptible, and vile").[5] Instead, he decides to take up the study of magic because it promises the greatest amount and extent of power: "A sound magician is a mighty god."[6]

Even this early in the play, pride blinds Faustus to the emptiness of his desires and the foolishness of his choice. When he "summons" Mephistopheles, the demon tells him directly that he came not because of the magic spells Faustus chanted, but because he was drawn to a soul in peril of damnation.[7] In addition, when Faustus inquires about Lucifer, Mephistopheles admits that Lucifer had fallen "by aspiring pride and insolence"[8] of exactly the sort Faustus himself has just been displaying. When Faustus makes his bargain and signs over the deed to his soul, then, it is a false bargain – not his eternal soul on one side of the scales, traded for power and pleasure on the other (Matt 16:26), but rather there is nothing at all on the other side of the scales. The power and pleasure are counterfeit, a charade, an absurdity. This is why the bargain is mocked in the comic scene immediately following, in which Robin jests about trading "My soul to the devil for a shoulder of mutton."[9]

In addition, the first request Faustus makes of Mephistopheles – to obtain a wife for him – is rejected as impossible, for both love and marriage are outside of Lucifer's domain. Only God can offer true pleasures. All Mephistopheles can provide are illicit sex and immoral, counterfeit pleasures.[10] Despite these and other interpretive clues, writ large onstage for the audience's moral and spiritual instruction, Faustus presses on in his pride and is carried off to hell at the end of the drama.

---

4. Act 1, Scene 1, lines 1–63.
5. Act 1, Scene 1, lines 106–109.
6. Act 1, Scene 1, line 62.
7. Act 1, Scene 3, lines 36–54.
8. Act 1, Scene 3, line 67.
9. Act 1, Scene 4, line 10.
10. Act 2, Scene 1, lines 135–154.

## The Temptation to Pride

My basic argument in this chapter is that all teachers, and especially Christian English language teachers (CELTs), are in constant danger of becoming Faustus and succumbing to the temptation of pride, with its full portion of blindness, emptiness, foolishness, self-deception, and self-importance. In response, we need to treat humility as an urgent moral and spiritual imperative.

Pride is a particular temptation for teachers in general. When we enter a classroom, we are almost always the most knowledgeable, experienced, or skilled person in the room in terms of the subject matter under consideration. Everyone there wants to learn what we know or become able to do what we can do. In such circumstances, it would be hard not to be tempted to impress, entertain, or show off to an audience predisposed to trust and admire us. We work in this environment not just occasionally but on a regular basis, and in some cases all day every day. The temptation to pride is therefore a powerful one. Even if we do not give in to outright arrogance, we are likely to ignore biblical warnings about the foolishness of many words (Prov 10:19; Eccl 5:2–3; Matt 6:7) and the importance of listening (Jas 1:19).[11] We somehow manage to "forget" that the wisdom of God is radically different from human learning (1 Cor 1:18–31). The tendency is to overestimate our knowledge and skill, or its worth, as well as to acquire an inflated valuation of our opinions or judgments on questions which the field continues to explore or about which experts continue to differ. Unchecked, this tendency pulls us to take small but sure steps toward pride and away from humility.

The teacher's temptation to pride is made even stronger by classroom dynamics. In addition to most likely being the most knowledgeable, experienced, or skilled person in the room, we are very likely also the person with the most authority or power. We lead, or try to lead, the pace, content, and direction of learning. We make judgments about whether learning has been successful and whether it is time to move on or not. We praise and encourage in order to instill higher levels of learner motivation. We assess constantly, and eventually hand out grades. These activities almost inevitably breed a feeling that whatever we do is right, or at least that we are the person best qualified to judge. "The teacher knows best," even if we give lip service to our fallibility and think of ourselves as "learner-centered."

---

11. See also Bradley Baurain, "Morality, Relationality, and Listening Pedagogy in Language Education," *International Journal of Listening* 25 (2011): 161–177.

This is part of the reason why so many teachers dislike or are made nervous or uncomfortable by classroom observations. To be observed in our classroom is to surrender a certain amount of authority and expertise. A colleague who offers advice for improvement – or worse, a supervisor who evaluates job performance – is telling us that we do not know as much as we think we do, that we are not as skilled as we think we are, that we did not make the best decision in a given situation, or even that we may have acted in an incorrect, oblivious, or unfair manner. Such things happen, and we should not find them surprising, given the complexity of our tasks coupled with our finitude and sinfulness as human beings, but occasions on which we as teachers are properly humbled in these ways are all too rare.

We as teachers can lead our students down the road of pride as well. While ostensibly learning critical thinking skills from us, for example, they often see all opinions as equally valid, feel entitled or pressured to find fault with all perspectives, or come to believe that the necessity of interpretation removes the possibility of surety. One Christian liberal arts college president summarizes this trend:

> Our highest calling as the university is to equip our graduates with a posture of suspicion about all claims of what is good and true. Postmodern intellectuals call this a hermeneutics of suspicion: our highest skills are interpretive, not declarative or formative. We come to the act of interpreting with extreme suspicion, if not cynicism; all texts (and people) are inherently deceitful. We who work in universities are the ones most capable of exposing those texts (and people) for what they really are. The writers of texts are motivated by power, the power of one gender or class over another, the power of the elite over the common person, the power of one faith over another, one culture over another. Therefore, we cannot trust, we are told, any proposed vision of human flourishing . . . This is the only intellectually credible posture, we are told, the only viable posture in postmodern culture.[12]

As the quote indicates, a lack of humility before texts easily becomes a lack of humility before persons. A mistrust is cultivated of all but oneself, that is, one reserves to oneself the right to judge all ideas, all values, and all interpretations. This is clearly pride, – the "hidden curriculum" in too many classrooms.

---

12. Philip W. Eaton, *Engaging the Culture, Changing the World: The Christian University in a Post-Christian World* (Downers Grove, IL: IVP Academic, 2011), 27.

These realities of teaching constitute a powerful temptation to pride. If we are not on guard, we will yield to temptation just by "doing our jobs" and going with the flow of the professional mainstream. Yet for those of us who not only teach but also pursue research or scholarship, the picture is even bleaker. In academic publishing, one of the most common opening moves, an expected component of academic discourse in the social sciences and elsewhere, is to articulate what previous scholars have missed or been mistaken about. A journal article is not worth publishing unless it displaces or supersedes previous work. A gap must be identified and then filled. This is so automatic we might have trouble envisioning alternatives. What would happen if our orientation was rather to demonstrate respect for tradition or to acknowledge that one was "standing on the shoulders of giants"? Instead, a premium is placed on what is new, accompanied by an assumption of "progress" despite the supposed lack of a "grand narrative" in postmodernism. One supporting, relatively small but telling, example: Replication studies are valuable for confirming and consolidating the findings of previous research, but a recent meta-review found that a mere 0.13 percent of articles in 100 leading education journals were replication studies.[13] There is little desire to conduct such studies, and little desire to publish them. They are "old news."

I am hardly the first to explore the problem of pride for teachers and scholars. Philip H. Phenix, a mainline Protestant academic of a previous generation, eloquently explains:

> No one in academic life can escape the temptation of academic pride. The ego of the scholar is inflated by the consciousness of his intellectual eminence. By sustained effort or natural brilliance he has become an expert. In his specialty he knows more than most other people and thus explicitly or covertly claims superiority to them. In his comprehension he grasps for himself the knowledge and skill pertaining to his sphere of competence. The student who works for an advanced degree looks fondly toward the day when he can be called "Master" or "Doctor." In these designations there is concrete evidence of one's prestige and worth. Through this recognition one feels justified in his own sight and in the eyes of others. And with what pride one looks upon journal articles and books which bear his name! What better proof of pre-eminence

---

13. Matthew C. Makel and Jonathan A. Plucker, "Facts Are More Important Than Novelty: Replication in the Education Sciences," *Educational Researcher* 43 (2014): 304–316.

than that one's words should thus be "made accessible to a wider audience"?[14]

Not only is pride a temptation for teachers in general, it is a strong temptation specifically for English language teachers. Our subject matter is at present a global language with nearly unrivaled political and economic power. In short, English teaching is an in-demand industry.[15] Learners want to know what we as TESOL professionals know and become able to do what we can do because very real and life-changing material rewards are associated with the ability to use English proficiently. English's privileged position is therefore a temptation to pride for those of us who teach it.

Furthermore, too many associate TESOL professionalism with a teacher's identity as a white "native speaker."[16] For example, British and North American accents are often seen as desirable and remain privileged in English-language teacher hiring despite the identification of English as an International Language (EIL), also called English as a Lingua Franca (ELF), as a variety of English in its own right, and despite the identification of intelligibility (not a specific accent) as a key phonological variable in communicative competence. This privileging also remains so despite the fact that the field in general opposes "native speakerism," a term indicating discrimination and prejudice based on "native speaker" identity.[17] Finally, this also remains so despite the many achievements of the NNEST (nonnative English-speaking teacher) movement.[18] One of the pioneers in the movement, in fact, specifically identifies hiring practices and inclusive environments as "unfinished business."[19] For those of us who fit the profile, therefore, the still-privileged position of white "native speaker" carries various temptations to pride. These temptations are embedded not only in identity or position but also in the ambient latticework of moral and spiritual issues. Pride might be as simple as passively accepting students' admiration of our "standard" accents, or it might be as complex as a self-congratulatory

---

14. Philip H. Phenix, "Religion and Academic Life: A Personal Interpretation," *Teachers College Record* 58 (1957): 418–424.

15. Ahmar Mahboob, "English: The Industry," *Journal of Postcolonial Cultures and Societies* 2.4 (2011): 4–61.

16. Robert Phillipson, *Linguistic Imperialism* (Oxford: Oxford University Press, 1992).

17. Adrian Holliday, *The Struggle to Teach English as an International Language* (Oxford: Oxford University Press, 2005).

18. George Braine, *Nonnative Speaker English Teachers: Research, Pedagogy, and Professional Growth* (New York: Routledge, 2010).

19. Lía D. Kamhi-Stein, "The Non-Native English Speaker Teachers in TESOL Movement," *ELT Journal* 70 (2016): 188.

sense of superiority for rejecting white "native speaker" privilege and working toward social justice in this area.[20]

Christian educators in general recognize the pervasiveness and insidiousness of all these various temptations to pride. For CELTs, the temptation might also take the form of a certain self-satisfaction or even smugness in helping those of lower socioeconomic status (as many refugees and immigrants are). Alter the moral and spiritual compass but a degree or two, and true servanthood is easily changed into self-centeredness. Instead of acting in humble obedience that brings God glory, we "give the gift of English" and become addicted to the role of benefactor as an ego-sustaining part of our teacher identities. As one Christian academic acknowledges, "I find the rip tide of self-promotion to be a powerful one, pulling me out to an eventual and certain ruin."[21] If indeed we inevitably teach who we are, then one of the consequences is such pride rippling out from us into the lives of our students. It is thus no surprise to find one student participant in a research study at a Christian college observing: "At the chance of sounding rude, but we learn what we see. A number of profs have a level of self-importance that is easy to mimic, and quite easy to see. There is more to it than just curriculum. Seeing how 'the learned' act is very influential."[22] Another consequence is that as we get caught up in what academia values, we can lose or displace the joy of learning, a joy I would argue flows from the fact that learning is something God created us to do. As another Christian professor notices:

> In academics emphasis is frequently placed more on how much one knows, rather than on the process of learning. An environment geared towards test-taking and preeminent reputations can easily take us far from humility, especially if a rigid certainty is elevated above inquiry . . . [T]he joy of our disciplines' exploring and sharing can also diminish. High standards and hard work are crucial to the learning process, but so is the freedom to *not* get it right on occasion and then try again. Sometimes I think we're

---

20. For one instructive response by an evangelical CELT to these issues and concerns, see the narrative by Timothy Mossman, "Unravelling Power and Privilege in the Academy: A Personal Account," *International Journal of Christianity and English Language Teaching* 2 (2015): 21–36.

21. Matthew J. Hall, "Christian Scholarship and the Distinguishing Virtue of Humility," *The Gospel Coalition Blog,* January 5, 2015, https://www.thegospelcoalition.org/article/christian-scholarship-and-the-distinguishing-virtue-of-humility.

22. Deborah C. Bowen, "'Blessed Are the Poor in Spirit': Imagining Excellence Otherwise," *Journal of Education & Christian Belief* 14 (2010): 14.

trying so hard to be right that we miss the journey of learning – more process than arrival.[23]

## The Imperative of Humility

In order to avoid becoming a Faustian teacher, humility is therefore a necessary and desirable virtue in education and English language teaching (ELT), as not only Christians have recognized. One contributor to *ESL Magazine,* for example, feels humbled as a teacher by her immigrant and refugee learners, who have endured so much, and by their courageous and creative willingness to start over in learning a new language and culture.[24]

Educational ethicists also occasionally attempt to recommend humility. A leading philosopher of education, David T. Hansen, for example, opposes "big ideals" such as social justice on the grounds that they "can become ideological or doctrinaire and can lead teachers away from their educational obligations and cause them to treat their students as a means to an end, whether the latter be political, social, or whatever."[25] A more appropriate orientation, by contrast, is one of "tenacious humility." What does this mean? For starters, "humility entails a refusal to treat students as less worthy of being heard than the teacher him- or herself."[26] Instead, teachers

> learn to see students for who they are – to listen, question, think, and wonder with them – rather than to see them solely through the lens or the terms of a big ideal. Their tenacious humility guides and disciplines their other ideals, keeping them in the service of teaching and learning.[27]

Therefore, "[t]enacious humility helps teachers hold at bay the tempting lure of ideals, theories, and ideologies which purport to 'explain' schools and students."[28]

---

23. Carmen Acevedo Butcher, "Scholar's Compass: Academics and Humility," *Emerging Scholars Blog,* February 15, 2015, http://blog.emergingscholars.org/2015/02/scholars-compass-academics-and-humility.

24. Stephaney Jones-Vo, "Reflections on Humility: What It Means to Be an ESL Teacher," *ESL Magazine* 47 (2004): 26-28.

25. David T. Hansen, *Exploring the Moral Heart of Teaching: Toward a Teacher's Creed* (New York: Teachers College Press, 2001), 188.

26. David T. Hansen, "The Place of Ideals in Teaching," *Philosophy of Education 2000* (2000): 47.

27. Hansen, *Exploring the Moral Heart of Teaching,* 188.

28. Hansen, "The Place of Ideals in Teaching," 47.

Such beliefs and ideologies close minds, oversimplify understandings, and short-circuit authentic learning processes. Tenacious humility, by contrast, "describes an ideal disposition, a moral ideal of character or personhood. Its pursuit constitutes a quest to become a better person and teacher."[29]

Another example of a secular attempt to recommend humility is *What the Best College Teachers Do*, by Ken Bain, who describes how the best college instructors cultivate trust between themselves and their students in part by rejecting power over them. That is, rather than attempting to wield their teacher authority to force students to learn, they speak and act as though learners are in charge of their own education.[30] Such teachers also manifest humility by being open about the ups and downs of their own intellectual journeys, thus giving their students encouragement to ask questions, make mistakes, and simply be curious. As one student put it: "When I heard my professor tell me how much difficulty she first had with chemistry, that gave me the confidence I needed to learn it. I used to think these people were just born with all this knowledge. That's the way a lot of them act."[31]

While these non-religious approaches have merit and can yield significant moral insights, in the end they fall short. Humility is surely linked to valuing students' perspectives, trust, openness, and ethical self-improvement, but these connections are spiritually inadequate to the challenge of actually resisting the temptation to pride. That is, these perspectives at best see the desirability of humility without indicating or providing the spiritual strength needed to pursue it.

A specifically Christian exploration of the imperative of humility is thus called for. What distinctives can eyes of faith perceive about this virtue? To begin, Christian thinking acknowledges the futility of all human work, including teaching and scholarship, apart from God. On this point, we turn again to Phenix, who observes:

> Religious faith begins by making manifest the futility and emptiness of this striving for recognition. It provides a perspective in which the struggle for eminence is seen in its true light as a pitiful search for reassurance and corroboration in the face of a gnawing anxiety and a desperate fear of dissolution . . . Religiously

---

29. Ibid., 49.
30. Ken Bain, *What the Best College Teachers Do* (Cambridge, MA: Harvard University Press, 2004), 74.
31. Ibid., 141–142.

transformed academic man understands that the way of pride is the way of death rather than of avoiding it, as he hopes to do by his struggle for recognition. He then discovers a new joy which lies not in his own vindication but in the loving consideration of ideas and in the self-forgetful service of others for their own sakes.[32]

Thomas Schreiner, reasoning from Ecclesiastes, likewise argues that since work gains meaning only under God's sovereignty and providence, fulfillment and joy from our work are possible only within a posture of proper humility: "Pride makes us want to be gods" – as Faustus and we teachers know better than most! – "but humility accepts the truth that we can't master time."[33] Instead, we humbly accept our place in the created order, including the fact that God's thoughts and ways are far above our own (Isa 55:8–9). Being a CELT is thus not only to be pursued according to mainstream standards of professionalism, but also and primarily to be accepted as a gift from God's hand:

> We give thanks to God for what he has called us to do. We thank him for the jobs we have. We don't master life, and we don't know what the days ahead will bring. But we put our trust in God, and eat and drink every day with joy.[34]

As a result, from a vocational standpoint Christian humility is linked with stewardship. One writer, speaking of the Christian artist in words that apply equally well to the Christian teacher, reflects that humility "takes seriously the responsibility that comes with the gift. Such humility and seriousness will lead to constant hard work, eager stewardship, and a readiness to learn from others. Without these all the gifts will bear no enduring fruit."[35]

Christian humility is connected not only with stewardship but with many other virtues as well. It can, for example, rightly be shown to be vocationally intertwined with service,[36] witness,[37] and reconciliation or

---

32. Phenix, "Religion and Academic Life."

33. Thomas Schreiner, "Stop and Enjoy the Ordinary," *Desiring God Blog*, 22 August 2015, http://www.desiringgod.org/articles/stop-and-enjoy-the-ordinary.

34. Ibid.

35. Jerram Barrs, *Echoes of Eden: Reflections on Christianity, Literature, and the Arts* (Wheaton, IL: Crossway Books, 2013), 56.

36. See Duane Elmer, *Cross-Cultural Servanthood: Serving the World in Christlike Humility* (Downers Grove, IL: InterVarsity, 2006), especially ch. 3.

37. See Bradley Baurain, "Christian Witness and Respect for Persons," *Journal of Language, Identity, and Education* 6 (2007): 213–215.

peacemaking.[38] In practice, it cannot be abstracted out but must be woven together with other qualities in a process of becoming godly or Christlike. Jonathan Edwards viewed humility as integrally connected to love, the chief Christian virtue. From his perspective, humility flows from a genuine love for God: "Love to God will dispose us to walk humbly with Him, for he that loves God will be disposed to acknowledge the vast distance between God and himself."[39] This in turn strengthens our faith:

> Humility also disposes one to be distrustful of himself, and to depend only on God. The proud man, that has a high opinion of his own wisdom, or strength, or righteousness, is self-confident. But the humble are not disposed to trust in themselves, but are diffident of their own sufficiency. It is their disposition to rely on God, and with delight to cast themselves wholly on Him as their refuge, and righteousness, and strength.[40]

What might change if we as CELTs walked into our classrooms thinking and acting as Edwards therefore advises?

> Distrust yourself. Rely only on God. Renounce all glory except from Him. Yield yourself heartily to His will and service. Avoid an aspiring, ambitious, ostentatious, assuming, arrogant, scornful, stubborn, willful, leveling, self-justifying behavior. And strive for more and more of the humble spirit that Christ manifested while He was on earth.[41]

How far do these connections and interrelationships go? Edwards asserted, "Humility is a most essential and distinguishing trait in all true piety."[42]

For the follower of Christ, then, humility is foundational. This is why Mark R. Schwehn, for example, identifies humility as a core intellectual virtue for Christians in academia.[43] In order to learn, one must give the other (person or text) the honor of believing they have something to teach. There must be a

---

38. See Donald B. Snow, *English Teaching as Christian Mission: An Applied Theology* (Scottdale, PA and Waterloo, ON: Herald Press, 2001), especially ch. 7.

39. Jonathan Edwards, *Charity and Its Fruits*, Kindle ed. (N.p.: Amazon, 1738), loc. 58–59.

40. Ibid., loc. 130–133.

41. Ibid., loc. 253–256.

42. Ibid., loc. 256–257.

43. Mark R. Schwehn, *Exiles from Eden: Religion and the Academic Vocation in America* (Oxford: Oxford University Press, 1993), 48–49.

posture of openness and respect – as opposed to the arrogance and suspicion described above by Eaton – that can only be grounded in humility.

Similarly, Matthew J. Hall contends that humility must be a distinctive for the Christian scholar because it is essentially countercultural.[44] Academic activities and professionalism tend to push us in the direction of pride, of feeling we know best and are in control, while humility "reminds us that our own work as scholars is a gift, a grace, a calling." It also pushes against the "siren song of self-promotion" that is so pervasive in academia, American culture, and even evangelicalism. In this context, he suggests three meanings for humility as an intellectual virtue: (1) Humility reminds us that we are lifelong students or learners (Rom 12:2). (2) Humility requires us to submit to the authority of God's Word. (3) Humility "compels" us to know and acknowledge our limitations and finitude.

> It's counterintuitive, but one of the most freeing things one can say as a Christian scholar is, "I don't know." But it's not only liberating, it's also stimulating. Being humble enough to admit our own limitations helps spark inquiry. If we're honest about what we don't know, we give an opening for intellectual curiosity to break through.[45]

Well and good, we are persuaded at this point in the essay of the substance and seriousness of the temptation to pride as well as of the necessity of Christian humility to guard us against this temptation. Pride has many ways to blind us to its power. We do not wish to take even one step down the road of Faustus. Humility must be cultivated; faith-based humility must be pursued. As CELTs, we should seek to set aside our privilege and power and "take up the basin and towel." In our professional and spiritual lives, we must aim to obey Paul's command: "Do not think of yourself more highly than you ought, but rather think of yourself with sober judgment, in accordance with the faith God has distributed to each of you" (Rom 12:3). We strive to enter our classrooms and stand before our students, not "wise in our own eyes" but in this spirit: "Trust in the Lord with all your heart and lean not on your own understanding" (Prov 3:5–7).

Just one more question: How?

---

44. Hall, "Virtue of Humility."
45. Ibid.

## Interlude

What keeps me humble? Limiting my answer to the professional side, I am presently on faculty at a seminary, yet what I teach appears to be far from the central disciplines of Bible and theology. I do not know Hebrew or Greek (yet). I have not been a pastor. I seldom preach. And what kind of seminary professor is that? My field of expertise is education. Yet this gains me little respect, for my colleagues in higher education believe themselves to be, by virtue of their experience, experts in this area as well. My discipline of specialization is English language teaching (ELT) or TESOL, which gains me nothing in a workplace in which my colleagues know and use English with a high level of proficiency. This may be part of why TESOL ends up at the bottom of most North American academic pecking orders, as every K–12 ESL teacher who has ever worked with her students in a repurposed maintenance closet already knows. What keeps me humble? What doesn't? The Lord is merciful.

What was I thinking? I must have been arrogant or delusional to propose this chapter. Surely at some level I must have known how convicting it would be to write about pride and humility. I must have known that if I write about pride too well, readers will know why. And that if I write about humility poorly, they will know why again. And that if I write about it too well, they will hold me to that impossible standard. The Lord is merciful.

Screwtape advised Wormwood to play a simple trick on his patient: "Catch him at the moment when he is really poor in spirit and smuggle into his mind the gratifying reflection, 'By jove! I'm being humble,' and almost immediately pride – pride at his own humility – will appear."[46] If the patient recognizes the pride, repeat as needed. Unfortunately, knowing this trick does not prevent it from working, though, as Screwtape recognized, laughter can break the cycle. So I am also thankful for an Inherit the Mirth cartoon[47] that captures the wry sense of helplessness and hopelessness that comes over me when I think about attempting humility in my own strength. The Lord is merciful.

If I were preaching, I could at this point give a self-deprecating chuckle and turn my listeners' attention to the biblical text. If we are to learn anything beyond the strength of temptation and the weakness of the flesh and the abstract characterization of a virtue, this is where this chapter must head. This is where this chapter was always heading. The Lord is merciful.

---

46. C. S. Lewis, *The Screwtape Letters* (New York: Macmillan, 1942), 63.
47. Used by permission. Copyright © 2012 Cuyler Black.

## The Imitation of Christ

In theological considerations of the virtue of humility, the doctrine of redemption is the hinge on which all turns.[48] That is to say, Christ's work of redemption in us must over time yield the fruit of humility, in our teaching and other academic endeavors as in every area of life. In light of this truth, "teacherly" humility is best sought through imitating Christ, or more precisely, through the process of learning to imitate Christ. As he instructed, being called "teacher" should not lead to pride, for we have only one Teacher, Jesus himself (Matt 23:8–11).

This essay therefore takes its cue from Keith L. Johnson:

> The discipline of theology proceeds rightly when it begins from the presupposition that all right thinking and speaking about God, reality and history takes it bearings from the life of the incarnate Jesus Christ. Our thinking about God has to follow after him, because our knowledge of God takes place in and through him. This starting point corresponds to Paul's instructions that we are to "seek the things that are above, where Christ is, seated at the right hand of God" (Col 3:1). Any right account of reality will begin with the person of Jesus; any true story of history will start with the history of what he has done; and wisdom and reason are called such only when they correspond to his own.[49]

To this end, this essay next examines and contemplates Philippians 2:1–11, and especially verses 5–8, as a crucial biblical text:

> In your relationships with one another, have the same mindset
>     as Christ Jesus:
> Who, being in very nature God,
>     did not consider equality with God something to be used to
>     his own advantage;
> rather, he made himself nothing
>     by taking the very nature of a servant,
>     being made in human likeness.

---

48. Mark A. Noll, *Jesus Christ and the Life of the Mind* (Grand Rapids, MI: Eerdmans, 2011), 61–63.

49. Keith L. Johnson, *Theology as Discipleship* (Downers Grove, IL: IVP Academic, 2015), 59.

> And being found in appearance as a man,
> > he humbled himself
> > by becoming obedient to death –
> > > even death on a cross!

These verses, possibly part of an early Christian hymn, describe the incarnation as an act of humility. Given that the incarnation was a unique event, the suggestion in verse 5 that it is an example or model for us to follow needs unpacking. In what ways can we "have the same mindset as Christ Jesus"? And what is at stake?

Within the structure of Paul's letter, it should be noted here that following Christ's example is the only path to unity, that is, the only way for the Philippian believers to live out in practice the unity they have in and through the gospel. This connection is seen more clearly in other renderings:

> Be so disposed toward one another as is proper for those who are united in Christ Jesus.[50]

> Think this way in your community which you also think in your union with Christ.[51]

> Let your bearing towards one another arise out of your life in Christ Jesus. (NEB)

Johnson explains: "A church living in a manner worthy of the gospel will be one whose members live in mutual self-sacrifice before one another in the pattern of Christ."[52] Commentator Moisés Silva well captures the epistle's flow of thought at this point:

> If the opposition being experienced by the Philippians calls for steadfastness, if steadfastness is impossible without spiritual unity, and if unity can come about only from an attitude of humility, then surely Paul must reinforce the critical importance of humility in the heart of believers. And what better way to reinforce this thought than by reminding the Philippians of the attitude and conduct of him to whom they are united in faith?[53]

---

50. Moisés Silva, *Philippians*, 2nd ed., Baker Exegetical Commentary on the New Testament series (Grand Rapids, MI: Baker Academic, 2005), 97.
51. G. Walter Hansen, *The Letter to the Philippians*, The Pillar New Testament Commentary series (Grand Rapids, MI: Eerdmans, 2009), 121.
52. Johnson, *Theology as Discipleship*, 138–139.
53. Silva, *Philippians*, 92.

It is also important to understand that, as F. F. Bruce notes, "Humility was not generally esteemed a virtue in pagan antiquity, in which the Greek word here translated *humility* bears the meaning 'mean-spiritedness.'"[54] The word can also be translated "low-mindedness," indicating a lack of generosity or a paucity of spirit. To the Greco-Roman mind, a "humble" person was a petty, limited person. The term "connoted lowliness, weakness, lack of freedom, servility, and subjection."[55] Pride or *hubris* was indeed a vice in Hellenistic culture, but humility was not the corresponding virtue; instead, it was nobility of spirit, that is, a persevering, humanistic ability to overcome challenges or difficulties. Humility was not desirable. Therefore, Paul's exhortation would have been rather surprising to his Gentile readers – an excellent example of how the wisdom of the gospel can appear foolish from a human perspective (1 Cor 1:18–25) – though in context it is clear that the apostle means humility to be the opposite of pride and self-centeredness (Phil 2:3–4).

Consequently, the word "attitude" (v. 5) is interpretively key in understanding Christlike humility. As Gerald Peterman explains:

> The English word **attitude** translates the Greek term *phroneo*, a theme-word in the book, appearing ten times (1:7; 2:2 [twice]; 3:15 [twice], 19; 4:2, 10 [twice]). Usually the word means "to employ one's faculty for thoughtful planning, with emphasis upon the underlying disposition or attitude."[56]

The term thus brings out both the inner and outer dimensions of humility. The inner dimension is the disposition or attitude or mindset – a desire or intention to live in a humble manner. The outer dimension is putting this desire or intention into practice – making actual choices in the real world so that it becomes a habit or a way of life. Though we can and will experience discontinuities between our inner intentions and outer actions, Jesus experienced no such friction. He perfectly lived out his perfect choices.

In verse 6, although Jesus was fully God, he did not consider that fact as "something to be used to his own advantage." His attitude, unlike the "selfish ambition" and "vain conceit" of verse 3, was entirely unself-centered:

---

54. F. F. Bruce, *Philippians*, New International Biblical Commentary series (Peabody, MA: Hendrickson, 1989), 62.

55. Hansen, *Philippians*, 115.

56. Gerald Peterman, "Philippians," in *The Moody Bible Commentary*, eds. Michael Rydelnik and Michael Vanlaningham (Chicago: Moody Publishers, 2014), 1861 (emphasis original).

> [H]e did not treat his equality with God as an excuse for self-assertion or self-aggrandizement; on the contrary, he treated it as an occasion for renouncing every advantage or privilege that might have accrued to him thereby, as an opportunity for self-impoverishment and unreserved self-sacrifice.[57]

As Jesus explained to the Jewish leaders, he did nothing on his own, but only as the Father directed (John 5:16–30). The purpose of his life was to fulfill the Father's will and plan. To act in any other way would be antithetical to his very nature, to the very character of God. He lived fully focused on his Father's glory.

In verse 7, Jesus "made himself nothing." What does this phrase mean? It has been a controversial one in theological history. The debates center around the Greek term *kenosis,* literally meaning "emptying." In the past, some have believed that Jesus emptied or divested himself of his divinity, including setting aside certain divine attributes. The "kenotic theory" suggests that he surrendered his divine power and glory during his earthly ministry. This view is reflected in the third verse of Charles Wesley's famous hymn, "And Can It Be?":[58]

> He left His Father's throne above,
> So free, so infinite His grace;
> Emptied Himself of all but love,
> And bled for Adam's helpless race.

Modern evangelical commentators, however, contend that a scriptural doctrine of God, the Trinity, and salvation makes this an untenable position. A biblical Christology simply cannot assert that the incarnation made Jesus less than he is (the Son of God). The "emptying" is therefore not literal but figurative, indicating the comprehensiveness or perfection of his unselfishness and self-sacrifice.

In what sense, then, did Jesus "empty himself"? Not by emptying himself *of* selected qualities or attributes, but simply by emptying *himself*, that is, by stepping down or choosing to take a lower position. As the verse goes on to explain, "By taking the very nature of a servant, being made in human likeness."

> This does not mean that he *exchanged* the nature (or form) of God for the nature (or form) of a servant: it means that he displayed the nature (or form) of God *in* the nature (or form) of a servant.

---

57. Bruce, *Philippians*, 69.
58. For complete hymn lyrics, see https://www.hymnal.net/en/hymn/h/296.

> An excellent illustration of this is provided by the account in John 13:3–5 of what took place at the Last Supper: it was in full awareness of his divine origin and destiny, in full awareness of the authority conferred on him by the Father, that Jesus washed his disciples' feet and dried them with the towel he had tied round his waist. The divine nature was displayed, and most worthily displayed, in the act of humble service.[59]

In other words, Jesus did not humble himself *despite* being God; he humbled himself *because* he is God. "Christ reveals God to be a God who acts in humility to serve others out of love."[60] "Crucial to Christ's story is the fact that he is equal with God and therefore that in his self-emptying and humbling himself to death on a cross, God's character is on display."[61] By doing what is described in this passage, the incarnate Son showed perfectly who God is and how God loves. One commentator calls this "divine selflessness: God is not an acquisitive being, grasping and seizing, but self-giving for the sake of others . . . From Paul's perspective this is how divine love manifests itself in its most characteristic and profuse expression."[62] Based on this understanding, Johnson offers a brief paraphrase of the flow of thought in this passage:

> Although Jesus has the status of God – and thus people expected that he never would humble himself in obedience like a human slave – Jesus confounded their expectations by humbly taking the form of a slave during his human life and death on the cross. God verifies that the humble and obedient Christ revealed the truth about his divine being by giving him the title Lord. Now everyone can see and know what God is truly like.[63]

In other words: "The true God must be seen not only as the all-powerful ruler over all things but also as the sovereign Lord who humbled himself in obedience to the point of death because of his great love for us."[64] Peterman summarizes:

> When emptying Himself the Son did not cease to be God nor did He give up His deity. He did not temporarily surrender the

---

59. Bruce, *Philippians*, 70.
60. Johnson, *Theology as Discipleship*, 145–146.
61. Gordon D. Fee, *Philippians*, The IVP New Testament Commentary series (Downers Grove, IL: IVP Academic, 1999), 36.
62. Ibid., 95.
63. Johnson, *Theology as Discipleship*, 137.
64. Ibid., 138.

independent exercise of His divine attributes (as if, with the Trinity, such a thing could happen). Indeed the verse does not say He gave up anything. Instead, One so glorious and powerful did the unexpected: He took on **the form** of **a bond-servant** (v. 7b). That is, *emptying* happens by *taking on* a new role.[65]

The incarnation made this possible!

From this perspective, the phrase "made himself nothing" indicates not one specific action but the entire trajectory of the gospel narrative and of the life of Christ. He voluntarily became a man, a slave, and a sacrifice. All are downward movements, the choosing of a lower position. This meaning is confirmed in the next verse, which marks Jesus's descent to the lowest point, "death – even death on a cross!" (v. 8).

This line of interpretation is further deepened and enriched by noticing that Paul (or the hymn) almost certainly has in mind here the Servant of the Lord in Isaiah 53:

> Jeremias claims that the expression *he emptied himself* is an exact translation of the Hebrew text of "he poured out his life." A comparison of the Servant Song in Isaiah and the hymn of Christ discloses other connections: the servant is highly exalted (Isa 52:13; Phil 2:9); the form of the servant (Isa 52:14; Phil 2:7); the humiliation of the servant (Isa 53:3–4; Phil 2:8); "therefore" God exalted the servant (Isa 53:12; Phil 2:9). The verbatim quotation of Isaiah 45:23 ("every knee will bow, every tongue will swear") at the end of the hymn (Phil 2:10–11) adds to the evidence that the line *he emptied himself, taking the form of a servant* is an allusion to the line in the Servant Song that the Servant of the Lord "poured out his life unto death."[66]

In verse 8, the humility of Christ is hand-in-hand with and climaxes in extreme obedience: "He humbled himself by becoming obedient to death – even death on a cross!" His obedience to his Father went as far as obedience could possibly go – to a humiliating, public death as a condemned criminal. He submitted perfectly to his Father's will and plan, despite the cost. Christ's humility, then, while it began as an inner attitude or disposition, a choice to step down into a servant's position, manifested itself as outer actions with real

---

65. Peterman, "Philippians," 1861 (emphasis original).
66. Hansen, *Philippians*, 149.

consequences, including suffering and death – and for us, salvation and eternal life. The narrative arc of the gospel continues (vv. 9–11):

> Therefore God exalted him to the highest place
>     and gave him the name that is above every name,
> that at the name of Jesus every knee should bow,
>     in heaven and on earth and under the earth,
> and every tongue acknowledge that Jesus Christ is Lord,
>     to the glory of God the Father.

Amen and amen!

## Lessons for Teachers

Based on this passage, how can we as language teachers follow the example and "have the same mindset as Christ Jesus" (v. 5)? How can we develop and practice Christlike humility with our students and colleagues, in our classrooms and professional lives? How can we fight the temptation to pride, embrace the imperative of humility, and pursue the imitation of Christ?

TESOL teacher educator Kitty B. Purgason points the way in her applied paraphrase of this passage:

> [A]lthough you may be in a position of power because of your citizenship in a powerful nation, your higher education, your proficiency in English, or your role as a teacher, don't take that for granted or try to hold on to that power; instead, be like Jesus who relinquished power and who came to serve.[67]

### *Stepping Down*

First, we can imitate Christ's humility by choosing to step down. "Jesus deliberately stripped himself of the rights and privileges of his divine majesty as Lord and took the form of a slave to serve the needs of others."[68] In the same way, we can strip ourselves of the rights and privileges of being a teacher, especially an English language teacher, and choose to take the position of a

---

67. Kitty B. Purgason, "Classroom Guidelines for Teachers with Convictions," in *Christian and Critical English Language Educators in Dialogue: Pedagogical and Ethical Dilemmas*, eds. Mary Shephard Wong and Suresh Canagarajah (New York: Routledge, 2009), 188.

68. Hansen, *Philippians*, 151.

servant or even a slave in order to serve the needs of others. These others are likeliest to be our students, but might also be our colleagues or members of the community. We do not serve a lesson plan, a curriculum, or a program (much less a spreadsheet!). As the saying goes, "Teach the students first, the material second."

Grace, a participant in one of my research projects, provides a concrete example of stepping down. She perceived classroom management as an area calling for this kind of humility:

> I have a personal aversion to top-down authoritarian teaching . . . I find that as I walk with God in humility and a heart to serve, I don't feel good about a "command" style of teaching. So, I find that my Christian faith causes me to spend more time talking through things with my students and setting boundaries and challenging them in gentle, firm, and more relational ways.[69]

A second example applies specifically to overseas Christian English language teachers (CELTs), whom Snow exhorts to learn the local language.[70] English's status as a global language is a temptation to use that for self-centered advantage. By learning the local language, however, CELTs can "elevate those around them to the teacher role."[71] This "is one of the best ways for Western Christian English teachers to really step out of our position of power, not to mention our comfort zone, and humble ourselves as we also take on the role of students."[72] Michael, in another study of mine, found this to be true in his own experience.[73] His learning Vietnamese while teaching English created empathy with his students, "that realization, you know, that we're both learning, we both have so far to go." It also encouraged his students to take more risks: "When you really goof up in Vietnamese, I feel like it gives them more confidence to goof up [in English]."

---

69. Bradley Baurain, "Beliefs into Practice: A Religious Inquiry into Teacher Knowledge," *Journal of Language, Identity, and Education* 11 (2012): 324.

70. Donald Snow, "Peacemaking, Reconciliation, and the Role of Christian English Teachers in TESOL," (plenary presentation at the Christians in English Language Teaching Conference, Long Beach, CA, 30 March 2004).

71. Snow, *English Teaching*, 63.

72. Snow, "Peacemaking." See also Donald Snow, "English Teachers, Language Learning, and the Issue of Power," in *Christian and Critical English Language Educators in Dialogue: Pedagogical and Ethical Dilemmas*, eds. Mary Shephard Wong and Suresh Canagarajah (New York: Routledge, 2009), 173–184.

73. Bradley Baurain, *Religious Faith and Teacher Knowledge in English Language Teaching* (Newcastle, UK: Cambridge Scholars Publishing, 2015), 107–110.

The choice to step down implies the choice to be a lifelong learner, not only of our academic subjects but also of our learners and their contexts. Learner is a lower position than teacher, so to choose a learner's attitude or orientation is to step down. Though this is merely a platitude or cliché in many teacher education circles, it can be a significant aspect of Christian humility. This is an incarnational choice: instead of seizing our rights and privileges as experts and teachers, we take the unexpected step of becoming or remaining students ourselves. Our students might be encouraged by our "coming alongside" them in this sense. Additionally, doing so demonstrates a respect for the complexities of truth and knowledge and our limitations as finite human beings. The best reason for stepping down in this way, however, is that doing so imitates Christ's humility. Stan Guthrie explains that the humanity of Jesus means he did not always have a "divine trump card" in his pocket for avoiding the hardships that can accompany learning.[74] Jesus truly "learned obedience from what he suffered" (Heb 5:7–10). This suggests a Christian orientation for learning alongside students while at the same time remaining "above" them in terms of exercising "teacherly" responsibility and authority.

### *Stepping Away*

Second, we can imitate Christ's humility by choosing to step away from the center. We teachers sometimes discuss whether our work is or should be teacher-centered, learner-centered, or learning-centered. The real issue lies deeper. Serving our students does not mean they occupy the center, any more than the fact that we benefit from Jesus's service means that we take center position in his choices and actions. That position belongs to God alone. In his incarnation and mission of redemption, Jesus did everything in obedience to his Father. In our teaching, interactions with students, and other professional activities, we should strive to do the same. At the center of our calling to language teaching is God himself, the giver and creator of all language and all learning. He is the one who provides the purpose and strength to serve.

This aspect of humility dovetails well with a recent essay by educational philosopher Gert Biesta, who urges a recovery of the idea of "being taught by" as opposed to the contemporary emphasis on "learning from." This emphasis, he believes,

---

74. Stan Guthrie, *All That Jesus Asks: How His Questions Can Teach and Transform Us* (Grand Rapids, MI: Baker Books, 2010), 60. Chapter 4 discusses "His Humanity."

has radically changed common perceptions of what teaching entails and of what a teacher is. Constructivist thinking has, on the one hand, promoted the idea of teaching as the creation of learning environments and as facilitating, supporting or scaffolding student learning. On the other hand it has, in one and the same move, discredited the "transmission model of teaching" and thus has given lecturing and so-called "didactic teaching" a really bad name. Constructivism seems, in other words, to have given up on the idea that teachers have something to teach and that students have something to learn from their teachers.[75]

In a note, he explains: "[F]or a teacher to be a teacher he or she needs to teach something, that is, needs to bring something new to the situation and this, as I aim to demonstrate, is radically different from just facilitating the process of learning."[76] This "something new" is a "gift" that comes from "outside" and "transcends" the knowledge and experience students already have.

As a result of Biesta's argument (which is more complex and substantial than my brief summary here), in my opinion, humility – but not the loss of authority[77] – is required of teachers because this "gift" and "transcendence" are beyond our ability to engineer. Though our pedagogical activities matter, no lesson plan can include "transcendent truths" as an objective. No professional skill can guarantee that this kind of teaching and learning will occur. "[T]he experience of being taught, the experience of receiving the gift of teaching, is not an experience that can be produced by the teacher."[78] Seen through eyes of faith, this argument points to God as the true center of education.

## *Stepping Forward*

Third, we can imitate Christ's humility by choosing to step forward in obedience. In a sense, this should not be anything unusual. The Christian life we seek to walk inside the classroom should be the same as the one we seek to walk outside the classroom. Praying continually, worshiping in all we do, pursuing spiritual disciplines and growth, and so on should not be left at the

---

75. Gert Biesta, "Receiving the Gift of Teaching: From 'Learning From' to 'Being Taught By,'" *Studies in Philosophy and Education* 32 (2013): 451.

76. Ibid., 451, n. 2.

77. See ibid., 459, where Biesta argues that "teacherly" humility and authority can and must coexist.

78. Ibid., 457.

door of the classroom. Professional excellence is not achieved by displacing faith, which is or should be at the foundation of all we are and do.

Are we willing to obey to the uttermost and lowest point, as Jesus did? To endure humiliation? Even to be misunderstood and condemned about humility itself? This is what happens to Purgason in critical pedagogue Brian Morgan's response to her recommendation of humility (above).[79] He objects to it as a merely tactical move on her part, done in order to make her religious discourse more palatable to the TESOL mainstream. Morally, he evaluates her conception of humility as lacking. From his perspective, humility needs to be characterized by a dialogical openness to change, that is, doubt or vulnerability even at the level of core beliefs and commitments.[80] This, however, does not describe the humility of Christ and so it need not describe ours either. Jesus carried out his mission of redemption in complete obedience to his Father. This submission of his will was a foundational commitment, not open for negotiation or change in the name of "humility." Similarly, as CELTs engage in teaching, we are open to learning and change, but not at the bedrock level of faith in and obedience to God. These are not open for negotiation or change in the name of "humility." We approach teaching as learners and strive to remain open to reflection, criticism, and discovery while simultaneously believing that we have something good and true and eternal which we must try to live out and to which we must bear witness. This should not beget pride, because our confidence in this area is not in or from ourselves but in and from God. In the end, Morgan's critique of Purgason comes across as a straightforward demand to conform to postmodern assumptions concerning the nature of morality – a demand which, curiously, does not appear to be open to dialogue or change. His position also perhaps suggests that genuine humility is no more considered a virtue in contemporary academic culture than it was in the Greco-Roman culture of Paul's day.

---

79. Purgason, "Classroom Guidelines."

80. Brian Morgan, "The Pedagogical Dilemmas of Faith in ELT: A Dialogic Response," in *Christian and Critical English Language Educators in Dialogue: Pedagogical and Ethical Dilemmas*, eds. Mary Shephard Wong and Suresh Canagarajah (New York: Routledge, 2009), 198–199.

## Conclusion

In their recent book, *Teaching and Christian Imagination,* David Smith and Susan Felch describe a centuries-old image of a "tower of wisdom."[81] This is a visual metaphor for a classical liberal arts education and its ultimate purpose, a virtuous life. The width of the tower is "charity" or Christian love. Its height is "perseverance in the good." Various virtues, spiritual disciplines, and good deeds are placed as bricks or building blocks in the tower. "By practicing what each block teaches," or learning each spiritual subject in proper order and with right attitudes and actions, "the diligent learner will build up a tower of wisdom in his or her soul." This process of growth and edification represents "climbing toward lived wisdom and building an inner tower to protect against the onslaught of temptations and vice." Tellingly, the foundation of this tower, that on which all else rests and depends, is "humility, the mother of all virtues."

What might change if we conceived of our teaching and professionalism in terms of this metaphor? What might be transformed, in our lives and in the lives of our students, if we sought more faithfully and actively to imitate the humility of Christ throughout the entirety of our teaching and learning endeavors?

## Bibliography

Bain, Ken. *What the Best College Teachers Do.* Cambridge, MA: Harvard University Press, 2004.

Barrs, Jerram. *Echoes of Eden: Reflections on Christianity, Literature, and the Arts.* Wheaton, IL: Crossway Books, 2013.

Baurain, Bradley. "Beliefs into Practice: A Religious Inquiry into Teacher Knowledge." *Journal of Language, Identity, and Education* 11 (2012): 312–332.

———. "Christian Witness and Respect for Persons." *Journal of Language, Identity, and Education,* 6 (2007): 201–219.

———. "Morality, Relationality, and Listening Pedagogy in Language Education." *International Journal of Listening* 25 (2011): 161–177.

———. *Religious Faith and Teacher Knowledge in English Language Teaching.* Newcastle upon Tyne, UK: Cambridge Scholars Publishing, 2015.

Biesta, Gert. "Receiving the Gift of Teaching: From 'Learning From' to 'Being Taught By.'" *Studies in Philosophy and Education* 32 (2013): 449–461.

Bowen, Deborah C. "'Blessed Are the Poor in Spirit': Imagining Excellence Otherwise." *Journal of Education & Christian Belief* 14 (2010): 7–17.

---

81. David I. Smith and Susan M. Felch, *Teaching and Christian Imagination* (Grand Rapids, MI: Eerdmans, 2016), 171–173.

Braine, George. *Nonnative Speaker English Teachers: Research, Pedagogy, and Professional Growth.* New York: Routledge, 2010.
Bruce, F. F. *Philippians.* New International Biblical Commentary Series. Peabody, MA: Hendrickson, 1989.
Butcher, Carmen Acevedo. "Scholar's Compass: Academics and Humility." *Emerging Scholars Blog,* 15 February 2015, http://blog.emergingscholars.org/2015/02/scholars-compass-academics-and-humility.
Eaton, Philip W. *Engaging the Culture, Changing the World: The Christian University in a Post-Christian World.* Downers Grove, IL: IVP Academic, 2011.
Edwards, Jonathan. *Charity and Its Fruits.* Kindle ed. N.p.: Amazon, 1738.
Elmer, Duane. *Cross-Cultural Servanthood: Serving the World in Christlike Humility.* Downers Grove, IL: InterVarsity, 2006.
Fee, Gordon D. *Philippians.* The IVP New Testament Commentary Series. Downers Grove, IL: IVP Academic, 1999.
Guthrie, Stan. *All That Jesus Asks: How His Questions Can Teach and Transform Us.* Grand Rapids, MI: Baker Books, 2010.
Hall, Matthew J. "Christian Scholarship and the Distinguishing Virtue of Humility." *The Gospel Coalition Blog,* 5 January 2015, https://www.thegospelcoalition.org/article/christian-scholarship-and-the-distinguishing-virtue-of-humility.
Hansen, David T. *Exploring the Moral Heart of Teaching: Toward a Teacher's Creed.* New York: Teachers College Press, 2001.
———. "The Place of Ideals in Teaching." *Philosophy of Education 2000* (2000): 42–50.
Hansen, G. Walter. *The Letter to the Philippians.* The Pillar New Testament Commentary Series. Grand Rapids, MI: Eerdmans, 2009.
Holliday, Adrian. *The Struggle to Teach English as an International Language.* Oxford: Oxford University Press, 2005.
Johnson, Keith L. *Theology as Discipleship.* Downers Grove, IL: IVP Academic, 2015.
Jones-Vo, Stephaney. "Reflections on Humility: What It Means to Be an ESL Teacher." *ESL Magazine* 47 (2004): 26–28.
Kamhi-Stein, Lía D. "The Non-Native English Speaker Teachers in TESOL Movement." *ELT Journal* 70 (2016): 180–189.
Lewis, C. S. *The Screwtape Letters.* New York: Macmillan, 1942.
———. *Mere Christianity.* New York: Macmillan, 1952.
Mahboob, Ahmar. "English: The Industry." *Journal of Postcolonial Cultures and Societies* 2, no. 4 (2011): 46–61.
Makel, Matthew C., and Jonathan A. Plucker. "Facts Are More Important Than Novelty: Replication in the Education Sciences." *Educational Researcher* 43 (2014): 304–316.
Marlowe, Christopher. *Doctor Faustus.* Edited by David Scott Kastan and Norton Critical. New York: W. W. Norton & Company, 2005.
Morgan, Brian. "The Pedagogical Dilemmas of Faith in ELT: A Dialogic Response." In *Christian and Critical English Language Educators in Dialogue: Pedagogical*

*and Ethical Dilemmas*. Edited by Mary Shephard Wong and Suresh Canagarajah, 193–204. New York: Routledge, 2009.
Mossman, Timothy. "Unravelling Power and Privilege in the Academy: A Personal Account." *International Journal of Christianity and English Language Teaching* 2 (2015): 21–36.
Murray, Andrew. *Humility*. N.p.: World Invisible, 1895.
Noll, Mark A. *Jesus Christ and the Life of the Mind*. Grand Rapids, MI: Eerdmans, 2011.
Peterman, Gerald. "Philippians." In *The Moody Bible Commentary*. Edited by Michael Rydelnik and Michael Vanlaningham, 1857–1865. Chicago: Moody Publishers, 2014.
Phenix, Philip H. "Religion and Academic Life: A Personal Interpretation." *Teachers College Record* 58 (1957): 418–424.
Phillipson, Robert. *Linguistic Imperialism*. Oxford: Oxford University Press, 1992.
Purgason, Kitty B. "Classroom Guidelines for Teachers with Convictions." In *Christian and Critical English Language Educators in Dialogue: Pedagogical and Ethical Dilemmas*. Edited by Mary Shephard Wong and Suresh Canagarajah, 185–192. New York: Routledge, 2009.
Schreiner, Thomas. "Stop and Enjoy the Ordinary." *Desiring God Blog*, 22 August 2015, http://www.desiringgod.org/articles/stop-and-enjoy-the-ordinary.
Schwehn, Mark R. *Exiles from Eden: Religion and the Academic Vocation in America*. Oxford: Oxford University Press, 1993.
Silva, Moisés. *Philippians*. 2nd ed. Baker Exegetical Commentary on the New Testament Series. Grand Rapids, MI: Baker Academic, 2005.
Smith, David I., and Susan M. Felch. *Teaching and Christian Imagination*. Grand Rapids, MI: Eerdmans, 2016.
Snow, Donald B. *English Teaching as Christian Mission: An Applied Theology*. Scottdale, PA and Waterloo, ON: Herald Press, 2001.
———. "English Teachers, Language Learning, and the Issue of Power." In *Christian and Critical English Language Educators in Dialogue: Pedagogical and Ethical Dilemmas*. Edited by Mary Shephard Wong and Suresh Canagarajah, 173–184. New York: Routledge, 2009.
———. "Peacemaking, Reconciliation, and the Role of Christian English Teachers in TESOL." Plenary presentation, Christians in English Language Teaching Conference, Long Beach, California, 30 March 2004.

# 6

# Transformational Teaching: Engaging in a Pneumatic Teaching Praxis

*Robert L. Gallagher*

As I left high school to attend college, I told my father, "Dad, I am not going to be a teacher. You are a teacher, mum is a teacher, and my brother and sister are teachers. But, I am never going to be a teacher." However, the stress of moving from home to my first full-time job as a metallurgist in a steel plant south of Sydney, Australia, together with four nights a week of part-time studies at the regional university, took its toll. After four long years, I received a letter in the mail from my employer that read, "Your services are no longer required." My boss fired me! It was a shock! I was unsure of my next move since I had found material engineering so difficult, had no skill-set to earn money or network to foster career opportunities, and was only halfway through my degree with a long transcript of failed science courses. Having recently received the filling of the Holy Spirit, I prayed, and asked God for guidance.[1]

---

1. "The filling of the Holy Spirit" is the concept of God giving his Spirit to indwell believers enabling them to live the Christian life pleasing to him. This happens through the Spirit's power of birthing a new spiritual creation in those who come to faith in Christ. J. D. G. Dunn states, "It is important to realize that for the first Christians the Spirit was thought of in terms of divine power clearly manifested by its effect on the life of the recipient; the impact of the Spirit did not leave individual or onlooker in much doubt that a significant change had taken place in him

After praying for a number of weeks, into my mind bubbled the desire to teach. At first, I was resistant to the idea since it opposed everything I had told my family. Yet, the thought kept reoccurring – why don't you teach? Late one Friday afternoon, six weeks into the academic year, I ran my finger down the list of schools and colleges in the phone book and dialed, "Edmund Rice College," without any knowledge of what the institution was about, or where it was located. On receiving a phone connection, I inquired if the college had any teaching opportunities. The answer was encouraging. I then quickly informed the speaker that it was only a few years since I graduated from high school, I had never taught before or taken an education course, and I was struggling to complete my part-time Bachelor of Science degree at the University of Wollongong. I was more than surprised when the man on the other end of the phone said, "That's alright. Can you come up now for a job interview?" Three days later I found myself standing before 49 fourteen-year-old students at a Catholic Boys High School, five minutes' walk from my home, and with a pile of textbooks, teaching them mathematics, commerce, geography, art, and physical education.

Our God is a God of surprises. Sometimes we do not know the purposes of God for our lives. Yet, as we pray, full of his Spirit, he orchestrates and guides his people to fulfill his mission in our world. I learned how to teach over the next eight years (grades 7 to 12), not merely transmitting academic content, but developing an effective educational method. I loved teaching with the Irish Congregation of Christian Brothers. There I learned my instructional ethos that has shaped my life's vocation, which has evolved into teaching the Bible in educational establishments, para-church organizations, and churches around the world over the last fifty years. From my early twenties there has remained an awareness of the necessity of a relationship with God's Spirit in order to have my life filled with prayer, guidance, and teaching ability. The thesis of this essay is that through prayer, the Holy Spirit fills, guides, and empowers God's teachers in their journey towards accomplishing his mission in the world. The essay will first consider the significance of the role of the Holy Spirit in all of Christian life and ministry before describing the main ministry tapestries of Jesus's teaching. The life of the Lukan Jesus serves as my model of transformation with an understanding that the Spirit's presence enabled him to have a prayer-filled walk, guided by God, and empowered in speech

---

[or her] by divine agency." J. D. G. Dunn, "Spirit, Holy Spirit," in *New Bible Dictionary*, 3rd ed., D. R. W. Wood, ed. (Downers Grove, IL: InterVarsity, 1999), 1128.

and behavior. Lastly, I will consider the implications of what Luke, the gospel writer, is saying to his audience and future generations, including Christian teachers of the twenty-first century.

## Toward a Pneumatic Teaching Praxis

To begin, I need to construct a pneumatic teaching praxis for followers of Christ that will be transformational for both student and teacher. I start my quest by anchoring my reflections in Scripture and affirming the oral tradition behind the Bible as being uncorrupted, reliable, and authentic, as well as being mindful of the importance of carefully defining concepts. The term "praxis" refers to the act of engaging or applying ideas. Coupled with the word "pneumatic," which incorporates the person and works of the Holy Spirit, this phrase suggests that God's Spirit may empower a teaching career. Although I should bring an appreciation of the history of Christian teaching into the discussion and give an account of my approach to biblical interpretation, the limited scope of my paper hinders such ventures.[2] Before exploring the guiderails of Spirit-filled teaching in ministry contexts, it is fundamental to my praxis to highlight the person and attributes of the Holy Spirit. Throughout the journey, the teacher should make space and time for movements of reflection and action constantly returning to the Word of God, and always reliant upon the Spirit's outworking.[3]

In this practice of pneumatic teaching, the role of God's Spirit is essential. As a Christian teacher, I am always prayerfully conscious of my dependence on the Spirit of Jesus. I need him to fill me afresh with his empowering presence

---

2. For a history of the expansion of the Christian faith, see Robert L. Gallagher, "Pentecost to Protestantism," 87–106, "Protestantism to the Present," 107–127, and "Present to Potential Prospect," 129–142 in *Changing Worlds*, Nathan Bettcher, Robert L. Gallagher, and Bill Vasilakis, eds. (Adelaide, SA: CRC Churches International, 2005); Robert L. Gallagher, "Engaging in Pneumatic Mission Praxis," in *Transforming Teaching for Mission: Educational Theory and Practice*, Association of Professors of Missions Series, eds. Robert A. Danielson and Benjamin L. Hartley (Wilmore, KY: First Fruits Press, 2014), 132–135. Regarding the history of Christian education, see Robert L. Gallagher, "Historic Perspectives on Teaching Mission," in *Teaching Christian Mission in an Age of World Christianity*, Association of Professors of Missions Series, Angel Santiago Vendrell, ed. (Wilmore, KY: First Fruits Press, 2017); and Robert L. Gallagher and John Mark Terry, *Encountering Missions History*, Encountering Missions Series, No. 8 (Grand Rapids, MI: Baker Academic, 2017). For my approach to biblical interpretation see Robert L. Gallagher, "Missionary Methods: St. Paul's, St. Roland's, or Ours?" in *Missionary Methods: Research, Reflections, and Realties*, eds., Craig Ott and J. D. Payne, 3–22. Evangelical Missiological Society Series, No. 21 (Pasadena, CA: William Carey Library, 2013).

3. See an example of the process in Robert L. Gallagher, "'Me and God, We'd Be Mates:' Towards an Aussie Contextualized Gospel," *International Bulletin of Missionary Research* 30, no. 3 (2006): 127–132.

and to guide me in my preparations – before the course begins, during class sessions (whether residential or online/hybrid), and in my post-engagements – asking God that he will enable me to speak and behave according to his will (Luke 22:42).[4] Figure 6.1 shows this sequence of teaching praxis involving thought and deed, and serves as a framework for the chapter.

ENGAGING IN PNEUMATIC TEACHING PRAXIS

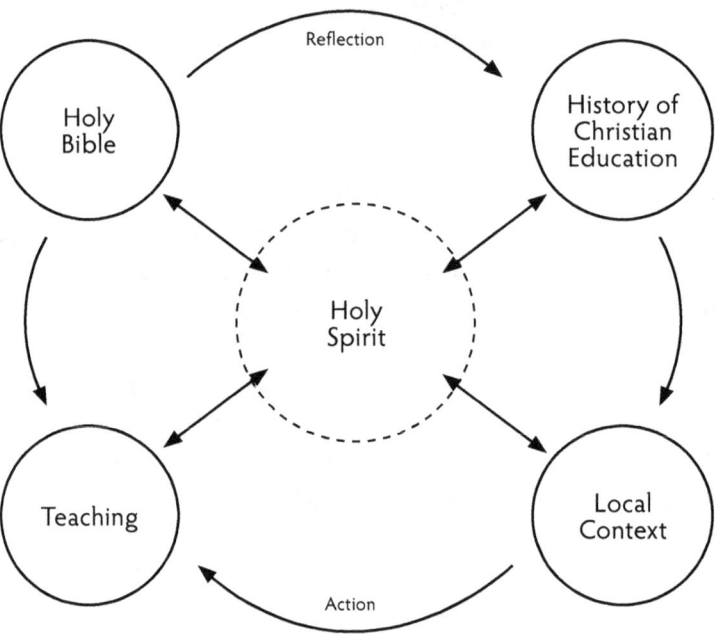

**Figure 6.1**

## Believing in the Spirit

Central to this method of teaching praxis is the intertwining of the Holy Spirit throughout our lives. From my perspective, the contemporary church might have a theology of the Spirit, yet it has little awareness of his presence and

---

4. In writing this paper, which is an extension of my teaching, I am constantly praying for God's strength and wisdom.

power. The Spirit played a vital role, however, in the first-century church. For instance:

> A reading of the book of Acts reveals two main categories. The Holy Spirit worked in the disciples of the early church to bring: joy in the midst of persecution (5:41), paradigm shifts from monocultural to cross-cultural perspective (1:6–8; 2:21; 3:25; 4:24; 8:14–25; 9:43; 10:44–48; 11:15–18; 15:6–11), boldness in preaching (4:29–31), contextualization of the message (2:14–40; 3:12–26; 13:16–41; 14:15–17; 17:22–31), selection and training of leadership (6:1–7; 13:1–4; 20:28), planning and development of the church (15:28; 16:6–7), and deep spirituality (1:14; 3:1; 4:31; 6:4; 8:15; 10:1; 13:3). On the other hand, the Spirit also worked in non-Christians through the gifts of the Spirit to empower the weak and lowly (1:13–14; 2:17–18; 9:32–42; 16:14–15, 25–34), as well as to create a sense of awe and wonder (2:6–7, 12; 3:10–11) through the fear of God (5:5, 11), and the joy of the Gospel (8:8).[5]

Christians can have a theology, yet without the experience of the Holy Spirit, their faith is dead. Signs of the weakening of the contemporary church abound with its lack of prayer and divine utterance, all the while attending to study, yet devoid of revelation.[6] The creative act of the Spirit of illumination has lost its hold on intellect and heart.[7] J. Hudson Taylor claims, "Since the days before Pentecost, has the whole church ever put aside every other work and waited upon him for ten days that [the Spirit's] power might be manifested? We give too much attention to method and machinery and resources, and too little to the source of power."[8] Lesslie Newbigin concurs:

> What I have called the Pentecostal Christian has the New Testament on his side when he demands first of all of any body of so-called Christians, "Do you have the Holy Spirit?" For without

---

5. Robert L. Gallagher, "The Forgotten Factor: The Holy Spirit and Mission in Protestant Missiological Writings from 1945–95," in *Footprints of God: A Narrative Theology of Mission*, eds. Charles E. Van Engen, Nancy Thomas, and Robert L. Gallagher (Monrovia, CA: MARC, 1999), 208–209.

6. In 2 Timothy 3:5a, Paul states that in the last days, people will be "having a form of godliness but denying its power."

7. The terms "utterance," "revelation," and "illumination" refer to the various ways the Spirit speaks to his people such as preaching, Scripture, and Christian doctrine, together with other creative methods (e.g. audible voice, dreams, visions, nature, and angels).

8. J. Hudson Taylor, "The Source of Power for Christian Missions," in *The Missionary Review of the World* 53 (New York: Missionary Review Publishing, 1930), 516.

that all your creedal orthodoxy and all your historic succession avails you nothing. To quote again the blunt words of St. Paul: "If any man hath not the Spirit of Christ, he is none of his."[9]

In the Western church, we need to repent of two related errors. First, we need to repent of undervaluing that the Holy Spirit can empower our teaching through his word, history, and any other circumstance he chooses.[10] Second, we need to stop overestimating the significance of our own ministry in strengthening God's kingdom. These assumptions imply that we are more proficient in teaching than the Holy Spirit. This results in a reliance on human wisdom rather than the wisdom of God. François Fénelon, the seventeenth-century mystic, acknowledges,

> It is certain from the Holy Scriptures (Rom. viii; John xiv) that the Spirit of God dwells within us, acts there, prays without ceasing, groans, desires, asks for us what we know not how to ask for ourselves, urges us on, animates us, speaks to us when we are silent, suggests to us all truth, and so unites us to him that we become one spirit (1 Cor. vi 17). This is the teaching of faith, and even those instructors who are farthest removed from the interior life, cannot avoid acknowledging so much.[11]

The Holy Spirit is a person. He is not a power or energy. He has a will, intelligence, and knowledge. He has the ability to love, see, and think.[12] The Spirit is the teacher, a constant presence, which we cannot be. He is the One who leads us to God.[13] David Platt warns,

---

9. Lesslie Newbigin, *The Household of God* (London: SMC Press; New York: Friendship Press, 1954), 100–101.

10. See Robert L. Gallagher, "The Holy Spirit in the World: In Non-Christians, Creation, and Other Religions," *Asian Journal of Pentecostal Studies* 9, no. 1 (2006): 17–33; Robert L. Gallagher, "Spirit-Guided Mission," *Evangelical Missions Quarterly* 42, no. 3 (2006): 336–341; and Robert L. Gallagher, "Holy Spirit: Missions Guide," *Bible Advocate* 141, no. 7 (2007): 8–9.

11. François Fénelon, *Christian Counsel, Spiritual Progress: or Instructions in the Divine Life of the Soul*, ed. James W. Metcalf (New York: M. W. Dodd, 1853), 89.

12. The Holy Spirit is a Person as shown in the following scriptures: the Spirit speaks (Luke 4:18–19; Acts 1:16, 20; 4:25–26; 28:25); teaches (Luke 12:12; Acts 1:2); decides (Acts 15:28); discerns (Acts 13:9–11); directs (Acts 13:2, 4); guides (Luke 2:27; 4:1, 14); gives joy (Luke 10:21; Acts 13:52), wisdom (Acts 6:3, 10), strength (Acts 9:31), and faith (Acts 6:5; 11:24); reveals (Luke 2:26; Acts 7:55); appoints leaders (Acts 20:28); and empowers (Luke 4:14; 24:49; Acts 1:8; 8:14–24; 10:38).

13. The Holy Spirit is the Gift (Luke 11:13; Acts 2:38; 5:32; 8:20; 10:45; 11:17; 15:8) and Promise of God (Luke 24:49; Acts 1:4; 2:33, 39). He is deity, as shown in the following scriptures: Trinitarian God (Luke 4:18; Acts 5:3–4, 9; 10:38; 16:6–7; 20:28); omnipotent (Luke 1:35);

> Let us not, then, be so foolish as to confine the work of the Spirit to one professional, speaking in one place, at one time of the week. Let us not be so unwise as to bank the spread of the gospel on a certain person at a certain place when all week long the Spirit of God is living in every single man and woman of God, empowering each of us to advance the kingdom of God for his glory.[14]

Christ lives in his people through the Spirit as a living presence. Christian faith reproduces Christ in us as God sanctifies, possesses, and transforms our lives by the power of the Spirit. J. I. Packer declares,

> Think of it this way. It is as if the Spirit stands behind us, throwing light over our shoulder on to Jesus who stands facing us. The Spirit's message to us is never, "Look at me; listen to me; come to me; get to know me," but always, "Look at him, and see his glory; listen to him and hear his word; go to him and have life; get to know him and taste his gift of joy and peace." The Spirit, we might say, is the matchmaker, the celestial marriage broker, whose role it is to bring Christ and us together, and ensure that we stay together.[15]

We must always be dependent on the Holy Spirit through prayer.[16] The Spirit is the activity of our prayer as we speak to God. In this cyclical way, God can use us daily in the power of his Spirit.[17] For instance, "The pattern of the people of God praying and the filling of the Holy Spirit propelling people into mission is a Lukan motif that begins at the baptism of Jesus and continues throughout Luke-Acts (Luke 4:1, 14, 18)."[18] As Pope Francis affirms,

---

witnesses (Acts 5:32); can be blasphemed against (Luke 12:10), lied to (Acts 5:3), tested (Acts 5:9), and resisted (Acts 7:51); and the Trinitarian call of Paul (cf. Acts 9:15; 13:1–4; 22:10; 22:13–15).

14. David Platt, *Radical Together: Unleashing the People of God for the Purpose of God* (Colorado Springs, CO: Multnomah Books, 2011), 70.

15. J. I. Packer, *Keep in Touch with the Spirit: Finding Fullness in Our Walk with God* (Grand Rapids, MI: Baker Books, 2005), 57.

16. Robert L. Gallagher, "Praying for Mission," *The Pneuma Review* 9, no. 1 (2006): 19–20.

17. Robert L. Gallagher, "Receiving the Holy Spirit's Power for Missions," *Stulos Theological Journal* 12, no. 1 (2004): 21–33.

18. Robert L. Gallagher, "From 'Doingness' to 'Beingness': A Missiological Interpretation of Acts 4:23–31," in *Mission in Acts: Ancient Narratives in Contemporary Context*, edited by Robert L. Gallagher and Paul Hertig, American Society of Missiology Series, No. 34 (Maryknoll, NY: Orbis, 2004), 54.

> In every activity of evangelization, the primacy always belongs to God, who has called us to cooperate with him, and who leads us on by the power of his Spirit. The real newness is the newness which God himself mysteriously brings about and inspires, provokes, guides, and accompanies in a thousand ways. God asks everything of us, yet at the same time, he offers everything to us.[19]

The Spirit of God supplies the resources of ministry in the church. The Spirit is more than the Comforter. He is the Spirit of truth and revelation. The church needs to be open and available to the reserves of the Holy Spirit. The abilities of the world and the church are futile and inadequate to serve the overall purposes of God. Only the fullness of the Spirit will give the church an abundance of wisdom and power.[20]

## Argument So Far and Continuing

The argument so far has attempted to construct a system of Christian teaching that riveted in Scripture, produces Spirit-filled speech. Essential to this practice of reflection and action is the awareness of the necessity of the Holy Spirit to empower all that we do and say (in Christian life and ministry), returning to the Word of God in prayerful reflection. I believe that Luke projects the Messiah as a pattern of what individual followers should imitate through the filling of God's Spirit.

> The author of the gospel of Luke stresses the characteristics that true disciples of Jesus must have on their journey to arrive at the heavenly destination in the kingdom of God. Similarly, in Acts, Luke underscores the characteristics that a true Christian community must have on its journey to arrive at the final destination that God has for it in the kingdom.[21]

Since the Lukan Messiah is an archetype of what believers should imitate, the remaining section of this chapter will view the work of God's Spirit in Christ's calling. The entwining of Jesus's filling of the Spirit, prayer rhythms,

---

19. Pope Francis, *Evangelii Gaudum* (Rome: Vatican Press, 24 November 2013), 12.
20. See Robert L. Gallagher, "Mission from the Inside Out: An Integrative Analysis of Selected Latin American Protestant 'Writings' in Spirituality and Mission," *Missiology: An International Review* 40, no. 1 (2012): 9–22.
21. Robert L. Gallagher and Paul Hertig, "Introduction: Background to Acts," in *Mission in Acts: Ancient Narratives in Contemporary Context*, eds. Robert L. Gallagher and Paul Hertig, American Society of Missiology Series, No. 34 (Maryknoll, NY: Orbis, 2004), 12.

vocational guidance, and empowerment of speech produces transformational teaching that will advance my claim that through prayer, the Holy Spirit fills, guides, and empowers God's teachers in their journey towards accomplishing his mission in the world.

## God's Spirit in Christ's Calling

All that Jesus accomplished was through the power of the Holy Spirit (Luke 3:19–21; Luke 4:1, 14). At the beginning of Christ's ministry, Luke weaves together the coming of the Spirit, divine affirmation, and prayer (Luke 3:21–23a; 4:1, 14, 18–19; cf. Acts 1:2, 4–5, 8; 2:1–4, 17–18, 33, 38–39). Filled with the Spirit at thirty years of age, Jesus began displaying the kingdom of God on earth. His gospel intertwined the Spirit, word, and deed, similar to the strands of a rope. Christ used all the strands to function as God intended so that Jesus's preaching interconnected with his social activism and vice versa. To achieve God's plan, the Son taught and performed miracles by the power of the Spirit. Jesus's declaration of God's kingdom involved the proclamation of the good news together with miracles of healing and deliverance that met the physical and psychological needs of the people of first-century Palestine. Jesus went from village to village preaching the kingdom of God and healing the sick and demonized (Luke 4:15, 40, 43–44; 6:6; 7:21; 8:1–2; 13:10; 16:16; Acts 10:38; cf. Acts 20:25; 28:31). J. D. G. Dunn maintains, "The Evangelists . . . were in no doubt that Jesus's whole ministry had been in the power of the Spirit from the beginning (Matt 12:18; Luke 4:14, 18; John 3:34; also Acts 10:38)."[22]

### *Jesus's Filling of the Spirit*

It is critical to analyze Jesus's connection with the filling of the Spirit, prayer, guidance, and teaching in the Gospel of Luke with the conviction that this interlacing is an example for all believing generations. "The promise [the gift of the Holy Spirit] is for you and your children and for all who are far off – for all whom the Lord our God will call" (Acts 2:39). Festooned throughout the birth narratives is the repetition of being Spirit-filled. After four hundred years of silence between Malachi and Matthew, this chorus is startling. Once again, God is revealing himself to Israel at the celebration of his Son coming to earth to herald God's kingdom. John the Baptist (Luke 1:14–15), Mary (Luke 1:35),

---

22. Dunn, "Spirit, Holy Spirit," 1127.

Elizabeth (Luke 1: 41), Zechariah (Luke 1:67–68), and Simeon (Luke 2:25–27), all received "the Holy Spirit upon" them to teach God's truth: to proclaim the news of God's only begotten Son entering human history to bring salvation to all humanity, both to the Jews and to the Gentiles (Luke 2:30–32).

This sequence of fillings of the Spirit is climaxed when Jesus prayed at his water baptism, and "the Holy Spirit descended on him in bodily form like a dove," God declaring his love and pleasure of his Son, even before Christ began his earthly ministry (Luke 3:21–23a). The intensity of the Spirit's action continues in Luke 4 when "Jesus, full of the Holy Spirit, left the Jordan, and was led by the Spirit into the wilderness" (Luke 4:1; cf. Acts 10:38); he returned to "Galilee in the power of the Spirit" (Luke 4:14a); and then there is the finale in the synagogue at Nazareth where Jesus declared,

> *The Spirit of the Lord is on me*, because he has anointed me *to proclaim* good news to the poor. He has sent me *to proclaim* freedom for the prisoners and recovery of sight for the blind, to set the oppressed free, *to proclaim* the year of the Lord's favor. (Luke 4:18–19, emphasis mine; cf. Isa 61:1–2)

In the first four chapters of Luke's Gospel, he records that the power of the Most High came upon the son of a priest while still in his mother's womb, a wife from the daughters of Aaron, an engaged virgin, a priest of the division of Abijah, a righteous city dweller, and the One who is mightier than all who is the baptizer in the Holy Spirit and fire (Luke 3:15–17; cf. Acts 1:5; 2:1–4; 10:44–48; 11:15–18).[23]

If Jesus the divine needed the fullness of the Spirit to fulfill God's purposes, how much more should we, his followers, need the Spirit to live and minister? We need the Spirit to abide in God's blessing and teach his truth. The highpoint of Luke's episode of the Lord's prayer is the exhortation to ask, seek, and knock so that the believer might receive, find, and open the gift of the Spirit given to the children of God (Luke 11:1–13). "If you then, though you are evil, know how to give good gifts to your children, how much more will your Father in heaven give the Holy Spirit to those who ask him" (Luke 11:13; cf. Acts 5:32).

---

23. Why does the filling of the Spirit disappear so early in Luke's Gospel, and only resurface in his second volume? I believe that the author employs the principle of first allocation thereby implying that the belief (i.e. the infilling of the Spirit upon the faithful) continues throughout the remaining text even though not specifically mentioned. What Luke establishes in the first section of his gospel he infers in the other parts of his first book. In other words, as Jesus's human birth was conceived by the Spirit (Luke 1:35), and his public preaching and healing began empowered by the Spirit (Luke 3:22–23a; 4:1, 14, 18–19), so the Messiah continued to be "full of the Holy Spirit" since "the Spirit of the Lord was upon him."

God promises his Spirit to those who ask him. As Christians, we need the Spirit in order to teach to our full potential (Acts 4:29–31). Ask God for his Spirit's empowerment to enable you to continue Jesus's teaching ministry.[24]

In examining the case study of the Lukan Jesus, I am interested in his relationship with the Holy Spirit that informs my current teaching. In God's vocation, I need to pray for the Spirit's help before a course starts (pre-presence), during class sessions (presence), and after the course finishes (post-presence). Regarding the pre-presence mode of teaching, how did Jesus prepare for his role as a teacher of the kingdom of God? Jesus in his humanity received revelation from three sources, which are also available to us: study, synagogue, and Spirit.

First, through study, Jesus's parents taught him about the history of his family, tribe, and nation regarding the heroes of the faith (see Jesus's genealogy from Joseph to Adam in Luke 3:23–38). This involved the person and attributes of God since the Lord revealed himself within the history of his people. Mary and Joseph taught Jesus the salvation history of God's covenant people (Luke 2:51; see Luke 2:21–24, 33–35). "And Jesus [the child] grew in wisdom and stature, and in favor with God and man" (Luke 2:52). We also need to study and understand the history of our family, culture, and Christian faith to be fully equipped to teach.

Second, the synagogue instructed Jesus. At twelve years of age, he interacted with the scribes in the temple at Jerusalem. "After three days they found him [Jesus] in the temple courts, sitting among the teachers, listening to them and asking them questions. Everyone who heard him was amazed at his understanding and his answers" (Luke 2:46–47). Following Jesus as our model, let us imitate him by becoming lifelong learners via informal, non-formal, and formal ways.

Finally, study and the synagogue together with God's Spirit prepared Christ for his teaching ministry. Jesus used life situations in first-century Palestine to instruct people about the kingdom. The Holy Spirit quickened these occasions to reveal truth in everyday terms. For instance, Jesus told stories about farmers sowing seed, people finding buried treasure, and merchants trading pearls, as well as illustrating his narratives with fig trees, mustard seeds, sheep, and

---

24. In the book of Acts, Luke records the empowerment of the Holy Spirit upon Christ's followers to enable the continuance of Jesus's ministry in teaching and miracles: Pentecost Christians, men and women (Acts 2:1–4); Peter (Acts 4:8); early church (Acts 4:31); seven Hellenistic servers (Acts 6:3–5); Stephen (Acts 6:5, 9–10; 7:55); Samaritans (Acts 8:15–20); Cornelius, family, and friends (Acts 10:24, 44–47; 11:15–16; 15:8); Jesus (Acts 10:38); Barnabas (Acts 11:24); Saul/Paul (Acts 9:17; 13:9–10); disciples at Pisidian Antioch (Acts 13:51–52); and the disciples of John the Baptist at Ephesus (Acts 19:1–6).

goats because the Spirit exposed these metaphors to him (see Luke 13:18–21). Pray that the Spirit would show you images for your teaching to give meaning to your message.

In addition to a pre-presence preparation, Christian teachers should pray during class sessions for God's presence and insights. In Jesus's vocation, he understood his audience beyond his natural abilities. On a number of occasions, the gospel writer states that "Jesus knew their [his audience] thoughts," which often appears before he began his teaching (Luke 6:8; 9:47; 11:17; also Matt 9:4; 12:25). The presence of the Spirit gave Jesus perceptions of the present needs of his audience that he would then address in his teaching.

During a leaders' conference in Colombo, Sri Lanka, last summer, I was teaching on biblical interpretation by encouraging the pastors to read the Bible as a whole, and not chop the Scriptures into theological, moral, or ethical bits and pieces. As I spoke along these lines, into my imagination came a picture of eating in a restaurant the night before where they were preparing the food by chopping up vegetables into tiny pieces and making a huge hubbub in the process. Using drama, I shared this metaphor as our normal approach to Bible study. The scene was so familiar to the audience that they immediately understood the lesson with accompanying smiles and laughter.

Lastly, it is equally important to pray post-presence after a class or course for clarity and multiplication of the teaching. One of the tasks of the Holy Spirit is to remind us of truth and show us the future. Before Jesus's resurrection, he taught his disciples about the function of the Spirit, saying, "All this I have spoken while still with you. But the Advocate, the Holy Spirit, whom the Father will send in my name, will teach you all things and will remind you of everything I have said to you" (John 14:25–26). Again, Jesus said, "I have much more to say to you, more than you can now bear. But when he, the Spirit of truth, comes, he will guide you into all the truth. He will not speak on his own; he will speak only what he hears, and he will tell you what is yet to come" (John 16:12–13).

Before teaching in Sri Lanka, the conference director listened to one of my sermons in a graduate school chapel on the Internet concerning the contemporary application of forgiveness from the life and teaching of Jesus. He then adapted the lesson for his church the Sunday before his daughter was to leave for Europe with conflict hanging in the air between her and a church leader. After the message, there was reconciliation between the two parties; and a visiting pastor at the church on that Sunday, likewise, took the topic of forgiveness to his church to preach. Jesus still proclaims the importance of forgiveness and multiples the fruit of his teaching (Matt 5:21–26 [cf. Luke 12:57–59]; 6:9–15 [cf. Luke 11:1–4]; 18:15–35).

## *Jesus's Prayer Rhythms*

In the previous section, I suggested the effect of prayer in the connection of Jesus's service with the filling of the Spirit.

> When all the people were being baptized, Jesus was baptized too. And as he was praying, heaven was opened, and the Holy Spirit descended on him in bodily form like a dove. And a voice came from heaven: "You are my Son, whom I love; with you I am well pleased" [see Ps 2:7 coupled with Isa 42:1]. Now Jesus himself was about thirty years old when he began his ministry. (Luke 3:21–23a)

I will now develop this Lukan concept of prayer and the purposes of God to highlight the repeated pattern in the gospel narrative.

The Gospel of Luke speaks about prayer, Jesus's prayers, and his teaching on prayer, more than any of the gospel writers. This interest in prayer continues in the book of Acts with the first Christian church. "In Acts, the apostolic church puts into effect our Lord's teaching on prayer."[25] Prayer saturates every significant event in the life of Jesus and the believing community. P. T. O'Brien states, "Prayer is a significant motif in the Lukan writings as both the terminology and the contexts make plain."[26] For instance, forms of the Greek verb "to pray" (*proseuchomai*) occur in the following texts in the Gospel of Luke: 1:10; 2:37; 3:21; 5:16; 6:12; 9:18; 11:1; 18:1, 10, 11.[27] Three representative passages are as follows:

- Yet the news about him spread all the more, so that crowds of people came to hear him and to be healed of their sicknesses. But Jesus often withdrew to lonely places and prayed (Luke 5:15–16);
- One of those days Jesus went out to a mountainside to pray, and spent the night praying to God. When morning came, he called his disciples to him and chose twelve of them, whom he also designated apostles (Luke 6:12–13);

---

25. J. G. S. S. Thomson, "Prayer," in *New Bible Dictionary*, 3rd ed., ed. D. R. W. Wood (Downers Grove, IL: InterVarsity, 1999), 949.

26. P. T. O'Brien, "Prayer in Luke-Acts," *Tyndale Bulletin* 24 (1973): 126.

27. *Proseuchomai* and its cognate noun *proseuche* appear 47 times in Luke-Acts compared to 17 in Matthew, 12 in Mark, 0 in John, and 16 times in other New Testament writings.

- Then Jesus told his disciples a parable to show them that they should always pray and not give up (Luke 18:1).

This Greek verb is also found in texts such as Luke 6:28 (cf. Matt 5:44), Luke 11:2 (cf. Matt 6:9), Luke 20:47 (cf. Matt 23:14; Mark 12:40), Luke 22:41 (cf. Matt 26:36), and Luke 22:44 (cf. Mark 14:39).[28]

Second, Luke records the words of a number of prayers, many of which we find in no other gospel. The Gentile writer presents the content of Simeon's prayer (Luke 2:29–32), Jesus's prayer upon the return of the seventy disciples (Luke 10:21–22; cf. Matt 11:25–27), the Lord's Prayer (Luke 11:2–4; cf. Matt 6:9–13), the prayers offered at the temple (Luke 18:9–14), Jesus's prayer at the Mount of Olives (Luke 22:42; cf. Matt 26:39; Mark 14:36; Ps 40:8), and Jesus's death prayers from the cross (Luke 23:34, 46; cf. Matt 27:46; Ps 22:1).[29] These last two prayers occurring at the Crucifixion have no parallel text in the Synoptics: "Jesus said, 'Father, forgive them, for they do not know what they are doing.' And they divided up his clothes by casting lots" (Luke 23:34; cf. Ps 22:18); and "Jesus called out with a loud voice, 'Father, into your hands I commit my spirit.' When he had said this, he breathed his last" (Luke 23:46; cf. Ps 31:5; Matt 27:50; Mark 15:37; John 19:30).

Compared with the gospels of Matthew and Mark, only Luke records the following accounts of prayer: the worshipers praying outside the temple (Luke 1:10) with Zechariah in prayer (Luke 1:13); Anna, the prophet, praying night and day at the temple (Luke 2:36–38); Jesus praying at his water baptism (Luke 3:21–22; cf. Matt 3:13–17; Mark 1:9–11); Jesus praying at the selection of the twelve apostles (Luke 6:12–16; cf. Matt 10:1–4; Mark 3:13–19); Peter's revelation of Jesus the Messiah after Jesus prayed (Luke 9:18–20; cf. Matt 16:13–16; Mark 8:27–29); Jesus praying at his Transfiguration (Luke 9:28–31; cf. Matt 17:1–3; Mark 9:2–4); and Jesus praying before the teaching of the Lord's prayer (Luke 11:1–2; cf. Matt 6:9). Concerning Jesus's Transfiguration, for example, Luke 9:28–31 states,

> About eight days after Jesus said this [the Messiah, the Son of God must be killed and raised on the third day], he took Peter, John, and James with him and went up onto a mountain to pray. As he was praying, the appearance of his face changed, and his

---

28. In addition, Luke uses the verb "to pray" in Acts 1:24; 6:6; 8:15; 9:11; 10:9, 30; 11:5; 12:12; 13:3; 14:23; 16:25; 22:17; 28:8.

29. Furthermore, the book of Acts records the prayer of the selection of Matthias (Acts 1:24–25), the prayer offered by the community upon the release of Peter and John from prison (Acts 4:24–31), and Stephen's death prayers (Acts 7:59–60).

clothes became as bright as a flash of lightning. Two men, Moses and Elijah, appeared in glorious splendor, talking with Jesus. They spoke about his departure, which he was about to bring to fulfillment at Jerusalem.

Luke begins his gospel with God's people praying outside the temple (Luke 1:10), and closes his gospel with the followers of Jesus joyfully blessing God inside the temple (Luke 24:52–53).

Why does Luke include the prayer motif at key junctions of his story? Luke associates prayer with the most important events of Jesus's life. Jesus prays at his baptism (Luke 3:21) and after a day of working miracles (Luke 5:15–16). Before choosing the Twelve, Jesus spends the night on a mountain in prayer (Luke 6:12). Jesus prays alone before the first prediction of his Passion and before Peter's confession of faith (Luke 9:18; cf. Luke 5:16). Jesus goes to the Mount of Transfiguration to pray (Luke 9:29). He prays with gladness and thanksgiving after the mission of the seventy because of his Father's revelation to his little children (Luke 10:17–24). Jesus's example of praying leads the disciples to ask him to teach them how to pray (Luke 11:1). Finally, Jesus prays during his agony on the Mount of Olives (Luke 22:39–46) and during his Crucifixion (Luke 23:34–46).

Luke alone relates two special parables about persevering prayer: the friend at midnight (Luke 11:5–8) and the unjust judge (Luke 18:1–8). He alone presents the story of the pharisee and the tax collector at prayer in the Jerusalem temple (Luke 18:9–14), and states that Jesus exhorted his disciples to pray during his agony at Gethsemane (Luke 22:40). Additionally, Jesus gave direction in how to pray: "Bless those who curse you, pray for those who mistreat you" (Luke 6:28); "When you pray, say: 'Father, hallowed be your name, your kingdom come...'" (Luke 11:2); and "He told them, 'The harvest is plentiful, but the workers are few. Ask the Lord of the harvest, therefore, to send out workers into his harvest field'" (Luke 10:2).

The Lukan Gospel teaches that God always answered Jesus's prayers. For example, he receives the Holy Spirit at his baptism (Luke 3:22), the twelve apostles, after spending "the whole night in prayer to God" (Luke 6:12–16), and Peter's confession of faith after his prayer (Luke 9:20). Other examples include: his glorification at the Transfiguration (Luke 9:29), the disciples learning to pray the Lord's Prayer after watching him pray (Luke 11:1), the repentance of Peter (Luke 22:62) because Jesus had prayed that his faith would not fail (Luke 22:32), and the apostles preaching the forgiveness of sins to the people of Jerusalem (Luke 24:47; Acts 2:38; 5:31; 10:43; 13:38; 20:32; 26:18; cf. Luke

23:39–43), which Jesus had requested of his Father at the Crucifixion (Luke 23:34). Luke implies that what follows upon Jesus's prayer is the answer to his prayer and the sign of its effectiveness.[30]

Luke not only gives importance to the role of prayer, but prayer for him serves a particular purpose. It is the means whereby God directs and guides his mission of salvation to "lost" humanity. That is why Jesus exhorts his disciples to ask, seek, and knock to receive, find, and open the good gift of the Holy Spirit (Luke 11:9–11). Contrary to the actions of the Pharisees (Luke 5:30–35), his followers would give blessing to God for his provision (Luke 9:16; 24:30, 50–51; cf. Luke 24:36; Acts 15:33), and, in watchful prayer standing before the Son of Man (Luke 21:34–46), become a joyful house of prayer for the nations (Luke 19:43–50; cf. Isa 56:6–8). Luke, a Gentile of the nations, underscores this point at the garden of Gethsemane on the Mount of Olives (Luke 22:39–46), connecting prayer and God's plan of redemption. Jesus could have frustrated salvation history, yet Luke records him in "prayer" five times (Luke 22:40, 41, 44, 45, 46). The episode is book-ended by Jesus exhorting the disciples, "Pray that you may not fall into temptation," and, in the middle, Jesus kneels in earnest prayer, asking, "Father, if you are willing, take this cup from me; yet not my will, but yours be done."

In the segment above, I expanded the concept of prayer in the Lukan narrative to show the weight of the recurring prayer motif. Why is this important? Maybe there are too many scriptural references with no story weaving them together, and I need to select the most important ones. Perhaps it reads as a list without a pertinent point. Yet, the sheer volume of the repetition at every significant episode in Jesus's life highlights that prayer was essential. Luke intended this thread to run through time even unto today and our vocational call. The prayer life of Jesus is an example for all followers of Christ. As believing teachers, it is essential for us to surrender our responsibilities to God via prayer in order to fulfill his will.

---

30. Luke records the prayer life of the early church in his second volume such as the following: while praying the disciples receive the Spirit that empowers them to speak the Word of God with great courage and affect (2:42; 4:31). Prayer is the special obligation of the Twelve (6:4). It accompanies the ordination of the church's ministers and commissioning of its missionaries (6:6; 13:3; 14:23). Through prayer the Samaritans receive the Spirit (8:15, 17), and Cornelius, family, and friends are converted (10:2, 4, 9, 31; 11:5). Prayer precedes the miracles of the apostles (9:40; 12:5; 27:29; 28:8). Through prayer are communicated the divine power, inspiration, and guidance of the Holy Spirit in community (16:13, 16; 20:36; 21:5). Like Jesus, the church prayed at the decisive moments of its life (1:14; 4:23–31).

In summary, through the Lukan prayer theme, God guides the exploits of Jesus, and applies the dynamic power of the Spirit for salvation history. O'Brien confirms, "Luke's central concern in his presentation of this theme [prayer in Luke-Acts] is to show that it had an important supporting role in his account of redemptive history, for by it God had guided his people."[31] Luke conceives of prayer as a means by which God guides the course of redemptive history (*Heilsgeschichte*), using prayer to serve as a way in which he makes known the divine plan of salvation.

During a lunch break from my job at the Wollongong steel works, I was walking on a nearby beach praying and thinking about 1 John 1:9: "If we confess our sins, he is faithful and just, and will forgive us our sins and purify us from all unrighteousness." As I walked along the shore, with the waves breaking and receding, I stopped and turned around. Looking back across the yellow sands, I observed my footprints. A wave crashed and rushed to the beach, and quickly retreated. Suddenly I was aware that the marks of my steps had disappeared. They were completely gone. It was as if I had never walked along that beach. There I stood in the middle of the pristine sand facing the direction I had tramped without any evidence that I had ever taken that path. All around was clean ground. At that moment came the thought that this is a picture of 1 John 1:9. As we tread life's passage in the way we want to go and how we want to do it, we move away from God. Yet, when we decide to stop heading in that direction, and turn and face our Creator, acknowledging the trodden mess before us, and asking for his cleansing, his waves of grace and mercy roll into our lives and wash away all our strident steps. During that lunch break, God's Spirit used my prayers to serve as a means to make known his divine plan of salvation.

### *Jesus's Vocational Guidance*

Through prayer, the Holy Spirit transforms and equips us on our journey towards accomplishing God's mission in the world (*missio Dei*). Life's pilgrimage is not alone. Through prayer, the Holy Spirit not only fills and empowers us, but also directs us. In Luke's Gospel, for example, we see the Spirit guiding

---

31. O'Brien, "Prayer in Luke-Acts," 127. Contra Max Turner, "Prayer in the Gospels and Acts," in *Teach Us to Pray: Prayer in the Bible and the World*, ed., D. A. Carson (Grand Rapids, MI: Baker, 1990), 75, who states, "The texture of Luke's portrait of prayer is too exotic to sum up in any epigram; for him prayer is not a technique for achieving some object or goal; it is man relating every aspect of his life . . . to God."

Simeon, a righteous person seeking the messianic hope. The writer underscores the role of the Spirit three times in Luke 2:25–27a:

> Now there was a man in Jerusalem called Simeon, who was righteous and devout. He was waiting for the consolation of Israel, and the Holy Spirit was on him. It had been revealed to him by the Holy Spirit that he would not die before he had seen the Lord's Messiah. Moved by the Spirit, he went into the temple courts . . .

The Spirit came upon Simeon to reveal Jesus the Messiah; and the Spirit guided him into the Jerusalem temple "when the parents brought in the child Jesus to do for him what the custom of the Law required." Likewise, the Spirit directed the Son of God: "Jesus, full of the Holy Spirit, left the Jordan and was led by the Spirit into the wilderness" (Luke 4:1); and "Jesus returned to Galilee in the power of the Spirit, and news about him spread through the whole countryside" (Luke 4:14).[32] Moreover, if Jesus needed the Spirit's filling and leading to fulfill his life's mission, then how much more do we need the Spirit to teach? Jesus is the pathfinder of how to live according to the fullness of God's blessing.

How does this work practically? How does God's Spirit guide our vocational call transforming and equipping us towards the *missio Dei*? There are three categories of talents that God develops in our teaching ministry: innate abilities, acquired skills, and spiritual gifts.[33]

First, innate abilities are those talents that we are born with. My family was a family of elementary teachers. They were also leaders in the community, which required oral and written communication skills. When I was a little boy, dinner discussions often centered around *Robert's Rules of Order* in how to conduct business meetings and make group decisions. In elementary school, my class teacher chose me as the lead actor in plays as I was a proficient reader. Every semester each student had to go to the headmaster's office to read a book passage. Even though I was a good reader, it was a nerve-racking experience that I dreaded, more so, because the principal was my father.

---

32. Luke advances the practice of the Spirit's guidance by illustrating how the early church experienced direction such as Philip and the Ethiopian (Acts 8:29, 39), Peter to Cornelius' home (Acts 10:19–20; 11:12), Agabus and the famine (Acts 11:28), the church at Syrian Antioch (Acts 13:1–4), the Jerusalem Council (Acts 15:28), Paul's second mission journey (Acts 16:6–7), Paul to Jerusalem and Rome (Acts 19:21), Paul to suffer (Acts 20:22–23), and Paul to suffer in Jerusalem (Acts 21:4, 11–12).

33. See J. Robert Clinton and Richard W. Clinton, *Unlocking Your Giftedness: What Leaders Need to Know to Develop Themselves and Others* (Altadena, CA: Barnabas Publishers, 1998).

Next, through prayer God guided my fledgling innate talents by enabling me to acquire communication skills. At nineteen, the founding minister of our church invited me to give my first sermon, only months after my change of allegiance to Christ. The topic I chose was the call of God, and my message lasted for over sixty minutes. After nearly fifty years, my memory of the sermon is fuzzy, yet I remember that the congregation was extremely encouraging and gracious of such a long message during a Sunday night service. To improve my preaching, I began to analyze sermons by American Pentecostals such as Jack Hayford, Bob Mumford, and T. L. Osborne, and British charismatic preachers such as David Pawson, Derek Prince, and Malcolm Smith. By listening to their speeches hour-after-hour on reel-to-reel tapes and then cassettes, I studied their sermon structure, content, and illustrations while detailing the timing of each segment. In the meantime, I practiced my sermon delivery by preaching to trees in an isolated forest and then from there progressing to small home groups and youth meetings.

Furthermore, in developing a teaching ministry, not only are there our innate abilities and acquired skills that God uses, but also the Spirit's gift of teaching (see Acts 2:42; 13:1; Rom 6:17; 12:7; 1 Cor 12:28; 14:6, 26; 2 Tim 1:13). The gift is the Holy Spirit himself, yet at times, as he wills, he manifests himself to reveal God's omnipresence, omniscience, and omnipotence (1 Cor 12:11).

Until a few months ago, my wife, Jayna, and I were co-pastors of an English congregation at an ethnic church in our hometown. During one summer, our Christian community studied the Gospel of Mark; and to prepare for the sermon series I began reading and listening to the gospel six months before we started. The following illustration shows how all three categories of teaching talents (i.e. innate abilities, acquired skills, and spiritual gifts) come together when God desires to speak.

In my prayer and study of the fourth chapter of Mark's Gospel, I experienced two interventions of the Spirit. I had been reflecting on the parable of the sower for a Sunday sermon (Mark 4:1–34), yet without a precise message. During the night before I was to preach, I awoke conscious of two separate expressions related to the parable. The first awakening instantly brought to my mind the phrase, "God has designed his seed to produce a crop." Without getting out of bed, I immediately wrote the words on a paper pad beside my bed and went back to sleep. One and half hours later I again was awake with another clear thought that I wrote down – "And, it is our responsibility to protect God's seed." In the morning, I unscrambled the scribble on the writing pad, and used it as a biblical foundation to preach my sermon, emphasizing the two phrases that I believe the Spirit gave me during the night. God has designed his Word (the living Scripture) to produce his desired fruit such as Christlike character. Yet, our responsibility is to protect God's Word (his seed) that the Spirit has planted in our lives. For the congregation that Sunday morning, the warning was especially true concerning the thorns of life's worries, the deceitfulness of riches, and the desires for other things that can grow around our Christian soul and choke the Word of God, making it unfruitful (Mark 4:18–19).

## *Jesus's Empowerment of Speech*

Looking to Jesus as the Lukan model of a person's fullness of life, we see the nature of the Spirit's residing to work out God's teaching intentions by way of our natural talents, learned skills, and gifts of the Spirit. For Luke, the Spirit fills and guides God's people because of prayer to manifest the Lord's presence and dispense his love and grace. The Gospel of Luke underscores the vitality of the first believers in both Spirit enabled speech and action, yet because of the limited scope of my paper, I will focus only on speech. Among the followers of the Way, Luke makes a decisive union between the Spirit and speech from the beginning of his gospel all the way to the last chapter of his second book.

In Luke's first volume, the Holy Spirit gives both women and men the ability to speak about the matters of God. For example, Elizabeth exclaimed in a loud voice the revelation of Mary being the bearer of the God Child – "When Elizabeth heard Mary's greeting, the baby leaped in her womb, and Elizabeth was filled with the Holy Spirit. In a loud voice she exclaimed: 'Blessed are you among women, and blessed is the child you will bear'" (Luke 1:41–42); Zechariah prophesied the coming of the messianic kingdom – "His [John the Baptist] father Zechariah was filled with the Holy Spirit and prophesied: 'Praise be to the Lord, the God of Israel, because he has come to his people and redeemed them'" (Luke 1:67–68); Jesus proclaimed his messiahship – "The Spirit of the Lord is on me, because he has anointed me to proclaim good news to the poor. He has sent me to proclaim freedom for the prisoners and recovery of sight for the blind, to set the oppressed free, to proclaim the year of the Lord's favor" (Luke 4:18–19; cf. Isa 61:1–2a); and before rulers, the disciples of Jesus were not to worry about what to say in their defense, – "for the Holy Spirit will teach you at that time what you should say" (Luke 12:11–12; also Luke 21:12–15).

Jesus the Messiah, Spirit-filled from his birth (Luke 1:35) and Spirit-empowered from the beginning of his ministry (Luke 3:22), taught with divine anointing because of the Spirit's enabling (Luke 4:15; 6:6; 13:10) – "God anointed Jesus of Nazareth with the Holy Spirit and power, and how he went around doing good and healing all who were under the power of the devil, because God was with him" (Acts 10:38; also Luke 4:16-21). In Luke's mind, Jesus's Sermon on the Mount (Luke 6:20–49) and his teaching parables (concentrated in Jesus's journey from Galilee to Jerusalem [Luke 9:51–19:45; cf. Acts 1:1–2]),[34] were Spirit-inspired.[35] R. H. Mounce, commenting on the Sermon on the Mount, describes the teaching as the quality of ethical life expected of believers who have already entered the kingdom. He observes, "Imagine a man [or woman] outside of Christ, without the empowering aid of the Holy Spirit, trying to exceed the righteousness of the scribes and Pharisees."[36] I would parallel this rhetorical statement with another: imagine Christ himself trying to teach the possibility of such a quality of ethical life without the empowering aid of the Holy Spirit.

Even after Jesus's resurrection, he gave "instructions [about the kingdom of God] through the Holy Spirit to the apostles he had chosen" (Acts 1:1–2). Jesus still taught in the power of the Spirit after his Father had raised him from the dead. Jesus, empowered by the Spirit, began and continued his teaching ministry ("seated at the right hand of God") by way of the first-century Christian church.[37] Should not this relationship also be true of believing teachers today?

---

34. Some examples of the Lukan parables of Jesus are: the good Samaritan (Luke 10:25–37); the persistent man (Luke 11:5–8); the rich fool (Luke 12:16–21); the great supper (Luke 14:16–24); the lost sheep (Luke 15:1–7); the lost coin (Luke 15:8–10); the lost son (Luke 15:11–32); the shrewd manager (Luke 16:1–9); the unjust judge (Luke 18:2–8); the Pharisee and the tax collector (Luke 18:9–14); and the ten minas (Luke 19:11–27).

35. See Robert L. Gallagher, "Discourse Analysis of Luke-Acts," in *Luke, the Holy Spirit, and Mission: An Integrative Analysis of Selected Protestant 'Writings' in Theology, Mission, and Lukan Studies*, PhD diss. (Pasadena, CA: Fuller Theological Seminary, 1998), 10–15, 245–252.

36. R. H. Mounce, "Sermon on the Mount," in *New Bible Dictionary*, 3rd ed., ed. D. R. W. Wood (Downers Grove, IL: InterVarsity, 1999), 1078.

37. There is a pronounced link between speech and the Holy Spirit in the believers of the first-century church whether it is teaching, preaching, prophecy, speaking in tongues, or witnessing to the resurrection of their Lord Jesus. For instance: Jesus, after his Resurrection, speaking to his followers of the kingdom of God (Acts 1:2); Jesus pronouncing the relationship between the Spirit, his disciples, and witnessing (Acts 1:8); David foretelling in the Psalms (Acts 1:16, 20; cf. Pss 69:25; 109:8; and Acts 4:25–26; cf. Ps 2:1–2) together with Isaiah speaking in his book of Isaiah (Acts 28:25; cf. Isa 6:9–10); Pentecost Christians speaking a missional language (Acts 2:4); both women and men of the early church prophesying (Acts 2:17–18); Peter speaking to the Sanhedrin Council (Acts 4:8); the first believers witnessing boldly (Acts 4:31, 33–34a); Stephen speaking with wisdom (Acts 6:3, 10); Cornelius, family, and friends speaking in tongues and praising God (Acts 10:44–46); Paul speaking to Elymas the sorcerer (Acts 13:9–10); the disciples of John the Baptist speaking in tongues and prophesying (Acts 19:6); and the giving

How much more should we as teachers allow the Spirit of Jesus to enable our speech?[38]

Speeches inspired by the Spirit are similarly prominent in Acts. Jesus declared in Acts 1:8, "But you will receive power when the Holy Spirit comes on you; and you will be my witnesses in Jerusalem, and in all Judea and Samaria, and to the ends of the earth." As in the Old Testament, no longer was the Spirit's sporadic presence restricted to a handful of male leaders to achieve God's specific tasks. The coming of the Spirit at Pentecost gave women and men, young and old, powerless and powerful, the capability to contribute to God's mission and the competence to speak about the Lord Jesus. Peter commenting to his Jewish audience in Jerusalem about the Pentecostal phenomenon of fire, wind, and languages, interpreted Joel 2:28–32, pronouncing:

> This is what was spoken by the prophet Joel: "In the last days, God says, I will pour out my Spirit on all people. Your sons and daughters will prophesy, your young men will see visions, your old men will dream dreams. Even on my servants, both men and women, I will pour out my Spirit in those days, and they will prophesy." (Acts 2:16–18)

In this pericope, Peter mentions twice that the coming of the Spirit will embolden women to prophecy, which in Lukan terms, is the ability to speak under divine inspiration. The Apostle even underscores the point by adding a phrase not found in Joel: "and they [men and women] will prophecy."[39]

---

of warning prophecies by Agabus (Acts 11:28; 21:11–12), and the churches of Macedonia (Acts 20:22–23) and Tyre (Acts 21:4).

38. Compare Acts 16:6 with 16:7 where Luke speaks of the Holy Spirit and the Spirit of Jesus being the same; once again underscoring his Trinitarian view. Cf. Acts 5, and Peter's questions to Ananias and Sapphira regarding their lying hypocrisy: v. 3 (Holy Spirit), v. 4 (God), and v. 9 (the Spirit of the Lord [Jesus]).

39. See the biblical role of women in leadership that follows. Women's leadership in the Old Testament – Prayers: Rebekah (Gen 25:22); Rachel (Gen 30:22–24); Hannah (1 Sam 1:12–18); Prophets: Miriam (Exod 15:20–21); Deborah (Judg 4:4–10); Isaiah's wife (Isa 8:3); Huldah (2 Kgs 22:3–20 [22:14]; 2 Chr 34:22); Theologians: Miriam (Exod 15:1–21); Deborah the judge (Judg 5:2–31a); Hannah (1 Sam 2:1–10); Abigail (1 Sam 25:3–42 [25:23–31]); wise woman (2 Sam 14:2); mothers (Prov 1:8; 6:20; cf. Prov 31:26); Nazirites (Num 6:2); Influencers: Sarah (Gen 21:1–2, 12); Jael (Judg 4:19–21; 5:24–27); Ruth (Ruth); Naomi (Ruth); Bathsheba (1 Kgs 1:11–2:25); Queen of Sheba (1 Kgs 10:1–10, 13; cf. 2 Chr 9:1–9, 12); widow of Zarephath (1 Kgs 17:1–24; cf. Luke 4:25–26); Esther (Esth); Tamar, Rahab, Ruth and the wife of Uriah (Matt 1:1–7); and Missionaries: Naaman's servant (2 Kgs 5:2–4; cf. Luke 4:27–28). Women's leadership in Luke-Acts – Prayers: Anna (Luke 2:37); women praying (Acts 1:14); Prophets: Anna's prophecy (Luke 2:36–38); Mary the first evangelist (Luke 24:10–12); women witnessing (Acts 1:8; 2:1–4; 17–18); cf. Num 11:29; Joel 2:28–32); Philip's four daughters (Acts 21:9); Theologians: Mary's song (Luke 1:46–55); Priscilla (Acts 18:2, 18); and Influencers: women patrons (Luke 8:2–3); Martha and

In Luke's second volume, the outworking of this prophecy highlights the correlation between the Spirit and witness. Peter has seven speeches or sermons and Paul has eleven[40] with one homily from Stephen before the Sanhedrin Council after he was arrested in Jerusalem (Acts 7:2–53), and one from James at the Jerusalem church council (Acts 15:13–21).[41]

The record of such an explosion of speeches in Luke-Acts is an indicator of the prime function of the church in the new age of the Spirit. Energized by the Holy Spirit, the community of believers talks about Jesus. If the Spirit of God comes upon a person or community, they are going to speak about the Lord, whether it is witnessing, worshiping, prophesying, proclaiming, praising, sermonizing, or speaking in tongues (see Acts 4:31; 10:44–46; 19:6).

This is an important concept since many Protestant denominations base their foundational dogma on the relationship between the Spirit and speech from Luke-Acts. An essential ingredient in recovering the intended message of the Bible, however, is to treat the Bible as a whole. In Wellington, New Zealand, I had the opportunity to facilitate a Pentecostal leadership conference based on the book of Acts with a request to emphasize the Holy Spirit. Rather than give a pneumatological treatise challenging the group's expertise of this topic, I handed out a list of the seventy-three documented Scriptures in Luke-Acts that speak of the Spirit. Dividing the sixty leaders into small groups, I asked the question, "What is the author's understanding of the role of the Holy Spirit in Luke-Acts?" I withheld my opinion, and gave the Spirit room

---

Mary at Bethany (Luke 10:38–42); Galilean women witnesses of the resurrection (Luke 23:55; 24:1–4); Tabitha (Acts 9:36–41); Mary the mother of Mark (Acts 12:12); Lydia (Acts 16:13–15, 40); "leading Greek women" (Thessalonica, Acts 17:4; Berea, Acts 17:12; Athens, Acts 17:34).

40. The sermons and speeches of Peter and Paul in Acts are: Peter: selection of a successor to Judas, Jerusalem, 1:16–22; Peter: signs on the day of Pentecost, Jerusalem, 2:14–36; Peter: healing of the lame man in the temple, Jerusalem, 3:12–26; Peter: before the Sanhedrin for preaching the resurrection of Christ, Jerusalem, 4:8–12; Peter: at Cornelius' house, to present the gospel to Gentiles, Caesarea, 10:34–43; Peter: defense to the church about what had happened in Caesarea, Jerusalem, 11:4–17; Paul: Sabbath sermon to Jews in the synagogue at Antioch of Pisidia, 13:16–41; Paul (and Barnabas): to the crowd who wanted to worship them, Lystra, 14:15–17; Peter: church council, Jerusalem, 15:7–11; Paul: Athenians on Mars' Hill, Athens, 17:22–31; Paul: gathering of the Ephesian elders, Miletus, 20:18–35; Paul: mob of people who tried to kill Paul, Jerusalem, 22:1–21; Paul: defense before the Sanhedrin Council, Jerusalem, 23:1–6; Paul: defense before Felix, Caesarea, 24:10–21; Paul: defense before Festus, Caesarea, 25:8, 10–11; Paul: defense before Herod Agrippa II, Caesarea, 26:1–23; Paul: to shipmates in a violent storm, Mediterranean Sea, between Crete and Malta, 27:21–26; and Paul: testimony to Jewish leaders, Rome, 28:17–20, 25–28.

41. In addition, there is one speech from Gamaliel before the Sanhedrin Council at Jerusalem regarding the apostles (Acts 5:35–39), Demetrius speaking to the workers who were disturbed at Paul's preaching at Ephesus (Acts 19:25–27), and the Ephesian town clerk appeasing the rioters in Ephesus (19:35–40).

to reveal his thoughts. Forty-five minutes later, the pastors began to share their findings group-by-group with bullet-point facts written on large sheets of butcher paper. It took over sixty minutes to complete the exercise. Not one of the groups mentioned the expression, "speaking in tongues." Yet, this belief is foundational to the movement's creed: when the Spirit fills a believer, the immediate, initial evidence of the Spirit's indwelling is the ability of that person to speak with other tongues (Acts 2:4; 10:46; 19:6).[42] How did this consequence happen at a Pentecostal leaders' conference? Instead of defaulting to the seven biblical verses supporting their doctrinal stance, the exercise positioned the Pentecostal influencers to consider the unabridged message of God, which took into account the author's repeated theological patterns.[43] They prayerfully considered over seventy Lukan verses on the works of the Spirit and did not confine themselves to those Scriptures that fed their denominational bias.

My theological tradition is Australian Pentecostalism, and I do exercise the gift of a prayer language to edify my spirit (1 Cor 14:2). Nonetheless, I am encouraging a broader approach to biblical exegesis that includes studying whole books of the Bible rather than truncated portions that we squeeze into molds of our religious custom. If people support this vision of a bigger reading of the Bible, Glenn R. Paauw "envisions groups of people regularly reading whole books of the Bible. I see them gaining a basic understanding of the major movements of the biblical story; a basic understanding of genre. They would be thinking of the Bible in terms of story. They are thinking, how can I authentically continue Jesus's story of restoration in my world?"[44]

---

42. Luke refers to "the baptism with the Holy Spirit" (Acts 1:5) that the early church experienced at Pentecost by different expressions such as "the promise of my Father upon you" (Luke 24:49), "clothed with power from on high" (Luke 24:49), "the promise of the Father" (Acts 1:4 cf. Luke 24:49), "the Holy Spirit comes upon you" (Acts 1:8), "filled with the Holy Spirit" (Acts 2:4), "poured forth this" (Acts 2:33), "Holy Spirit fell upon" (Acts 10:44), "the gift poured out upon" (Acts 10:45), "received the Holy Spirit" (Acts 10:47), "Holy Spirit fell upon" (Acts 11:15), and "baptized with the Holy Spirit" (Acts 11:16). Furthermore, the Holy Spirit came through the laying on of hands of Peter and John to the Samaritans (Acts 8:17–19), Ananias of Damascus to Saul (Acts 9:12, 17), and Paul to the followers of John the Baptist at Ephesus (Acts 19:6). Compare Acts 6:6; 13:3.

43. For further theological patterns concerning the Spirit consider the following: the apostle Peter received the Holy Spirit (John 20:22), yet was subsequently filled with the Spirit in Acts 2:4, 14, 38 and Acts 4:8, 31. Likewise, Stephen was full of the Spirit and wisdom (Acts 6:3), full of faith and the Holy Spirit (Acts 6:5), full of wisdom and the Spirit (Acts 6:10), and even at his stoning, was again full of the Holy Spirit (Acts 7:55).

44. Glenn R. Paauw, "Stop Snacking on 'Scripture McNuggets,'" in *Christianity Today* (16 September 2016), 7, http://www.christianitytoday.com/ct/2016/september-web-only/stop-snacking-on-scripture-mcnuggets.html.

What I claim in this last section of my chapter is that the Gospel of Luke portrays Jesus Christ as the model of how believers should live. Jesus's filling of the Spirit, dedication to prayer, and yielding to God's guidance, enabled him to teach transformationally to the people of first-century Palestine that accomplished God's mission in the world. My engagement in a pneumatic teaching praxis should follow Jesus as a missional paradigm that has relevancy for today.

## Implications

If I believe what Luke is telling me in his Gospel (and the book of Acts), then as a Christian teacher I know that God loves everyone equally, and I should allow the Spirit to teach and empower me to witness. In that process, I need to be open to the Spirit's transformation as I follow my teaching vocation in word and deed for the kingdom of God. As well, I need to live a life of prayer, using my innate abilities, acquired skills, and spiritual gifts for witness in submission to the guidance of the Holy Spirit. In witnessing to the Crucifixion, Resurrection, and Ascension of Jesus Christ, I will seek to participate in God's mission in the world through the empowering of the Spirit as a witness of God's saving grace in Jesus Christ. All of the above implications are in fulfillment of my calling as a teacher in submission to God.[45]

## Conclusion

In this essay, I attempted to move towards engaging in a pneumatic teaching praxis that showed the importance of the Holy Spirit in my ministry of teaching. By using the Lukan Jesus as my case study of transformation, I presented the argument that the work of God's Spirit in Christ's calling to teach involves the interweaving of the filling of the Spirit, prayer rhythms, vocational guidance, and empowerment of speech. Through the continuous practice of prayerful, biblical reflection and action, the Spirit infuses, directs, and enables God's teachers in their journey towards accomplishing God's mission in the world.

---

45. I am indebted to Charles E. Van Engen for his seminal teaching on biblical theology of mission. See Charles E. Van Engen, "Seeking Ways Forward in Mission Theology," in *Contemporary Mission Theology: Engaging the Nations*, Robert L. Gallagher and Paul Hertig, eds. Essays in Honor of Charles E. Van Engen, American Society of Missiology Series, No. 53 (Maryknoll, NY: Orbis, 2017), 289–296.

## Bibliography

Clinton, J. Robert and Richard W. Clinton. *Unlocking Your Giftedness: What Leaders Need to Know to Develop Themselves and Others*. Altadena, CA: Barnabas Publishers, 1998.

Dunn, J. D. G. "Spirit, Holy Spirit," in *New Bible Dictionary*. 3rd ed. Edited by D. R. W. Wood. Downers Grove, IL: InterVarsity, 1999.

Fénelon, François. *Christian Counsel, Spiritual Progress: or Instructions in the Divine Life of the Soul*. Edited by James W. Metcalf. New York: M. W. Dodd.

Gallagher, Robert L. "Discourse Analysis of Luke-Acts." In *Luke, the Holy Spirit, and Mission: An Integrative Analysis of Selected Protestant 'Writings' in Theology, Mission, and Lukan Studies*, PhD diss. Pasadena, CA: Fuller Theological Seminary, 1998.

———. "From 'Doingness' to 'Beingness': A Missiological Interpretation of Acts 4:23–31." In *Mission in Acts: Ancient Narratives in Contemporary Context*. Edited by Robert L. Gallagher and Paul Hertig, 45–58. American Missiological Series, No. 34. Maryknoll, NY: Orbis, 2004.

———. "Engaging in Pneumatic Mission Praxis." In *Transforming Teaching for Mission: Educational Theory and Practice*, Association of Professors of Missions Series. Edited by Robert A. Danielson and Benjamin L. Hartley, 132–135. Wilmore, KY: First Fruits Press, 2014.

———. "The Forgotten Factor: The Holy Spirit and Mission in Protestant Missiological Writings from 1945–95." In *Footprints of God: A Narrative Theology of Missions*. Edited by Charles Van Engen, Nancy Thomas, and Robert L. Gallagher, 199–214. Monrovia, CA: MARC, 1999.

———. "Historic Perspectives on Teaching Mission." In *Teaching Christian Mission in an Age of World Christianity*, Association of Professors of Missions Series. Edited by Angel Santiago Vendrell. Wilmore, KY: First Fruits Press, 2017.

———. "Holy Spirit: Missions Guide," *Bible Advocate* 141, no. 7 (2007): 8–9.

———. "The Holy Spirit in the World: In Non-Christians, Creation, and Other Religions." *Asian Journal of Pentecostal Studies* 9, no. 1 (2006): 17–33.

———. "Missionary Methods: St. Paul's, St. Roland's, or Ours?" In *Missionary Methods: Research, Reflections, and Realities*. Edited by Craig Ott and J. D. Payne, 3–22. Evangelical Missiological Society Series, No. 21. Pasadena, CA: William Carey Library, 2013.

———. "Mission from the Inside Out: An Integrative Analysis of Selected Latin American Protestant 'Writings' in Spirituality and Mission." *Missiology: An International Review* 40, no. 1 (2012): 9–22.

———. "'Me and God, We'd be Mates': Toward an Aussie Contextualized Gospel." *International Bulletin of Missionary Research* 30, no. 3 (2006): 127–132.

———. "Pentecost to Protestantism." In *Changing Worlds*. Edited by Nathan Bettcher, Robert L. Gallagher, and Bill Vasilakis, 87–106. Adelaide, SA: CRC Churches International, 2005.

———. "Praying for Mission." In *The Pneuma Review* 9, no. 1 (2006): 19–20.

———. "Present to Potential Prospect," In *Changing Worlds*. Edited by Nathan Bettcher, Robert L. Gallagher, and Bill Vasilakis, 129–142. Adelaide, SA: CRC Churches International, 2005.

———. "Protestantism to the Present." In *Changing Worlds*. Edited by Nathan Bettcher, Robert L. Gallagher, and Bill Vasilakis, 107–127. Adelaide, SA: CRC Churches International, 2005.

———. "Receiving the Holy Spirit's Power for Missions." *Stulos Theological Journal* 12, no. 1 (2004): 21–33.

———. "Spirit-Guided Mission." *Evangelical Missions Quarterly* 42, no. 3 (2006): 336–341.

Gallagher, Robert L., and John Mark Terry. *Encountering Missions History*, Encountering Missions Series, No. 8. Grand Rapids: Baker Academic, 2017.

Gallagher, Robert L., and Paul Hertig. "Introduction: Background to Acts." In *Mission in Acts: Ancient Narratives in Contemporary Context*. Edited by Robert L. Gallagher and Paul Hertig, American Society of Missiology Series, No. 34. Maryknoll, NY: Orbis, 2004.

Harris, Lindell O. "Prayer in the Gospel of Luke." *Southwestern Journal of Theology* 10 (1967): 59–69.

Mounce, R. H. "Sermon on the Mount." In *New Bible Dictionary*. 3rd ed. Edited by D. R. W. Wood. Downers Grove, IL: InterVarsity, 1999.

Newbigin, Lesslie. *The Household of God*. London: SMC Press; New York: Friendship Press, 1954.

O'Brien, P. T. "Prayer in Luke-Acts." *Tyndale Bulletin* 24 (1973): 111–127.

Paauw, Glenn R. "Stop Snacking on 'Scripture McNuggets.'" *Christianity Today*, 16 September 2016, http://www.christianitytoday.com/ct/2016/september-web-only/stop-snacking-on-scripture-mcnuggets.html.

Packer, J. I. *Keep in Touch with the Spirit: Finding Fullness in Our Walk with God*. Grand Rapids, MI: Baker, 2005.

Peterson, Eugene H. *Eat This Book: A Conversation in the Art of Spiritual Reading*. Grand Rapids, MI: Eerdmans, 2006.

Platt, David. *Radical Together: Unleashing the People of God for the Purpose of God*. Colorado Springs, CO: Multnomah, 2011.

Pope Francis. *Evangelii Gaudum* 12. Rome: Vatican Press, 24 November 2013.

Taylor, J. Hudson. "The Source of Power for Christian Missions." *The Missionary Review of the World* 53. New York: Missionary Review, 1930.

Thomson, J. G. S. S. "Prayer." In *New Bible Dictionary*. 3rd ed. Edited by D. R. W. Wood. Downers Grove, IL: InterVarsity, 1999.

Turner, Max. "Prayer in the Gospels and Acts." In *Teach Us to Pray: Prayer in the Bible and the World*. Edited by D. A. Carson. Grand Rapids, MI: Baker, 1990.

Van Engen, Charles E. "Seeking Ways Forward in Mission Theology." In *Contemporary Mission Theology: Engaging the Nations*. Edited by Robert L. Gallagher and Paul Hertig, Essays in Honor of Charles E. Van Engen, American Society of Missiology Series, No. 53. Maryknoll, NY: Orbis, 2017.

Wright, Christopher J. H. *The Mission of God: Unlocking the Bible's Grand Narrative*. Downers Grove, IL: IVP Academic, 2006.

———. "Reflections on Moving Beyond the Bible to Theology." In *Moving Beyond the Bible to Theology*. Edited by Stanley N. Gundry and Gary T. Meadors, 320–346. Grand Rapids, MI: Zondervan, 2009.

Wright, N. T. *Scripture and the Authority of God: How to Read the Bible Today*. New York: HarperOne, 2011.

# Section III

# Our Classroom: Theology and Practice

# 7

# Exploring Method as Metaphor: A Historical Perspective for Second Language Educators

*Cheri Pierson*

### A Classroom Scenario

Ms Kim greets her adult ESL students and asks them about their weekend. They respond in short phrases such as, "I went to work" or "I went to church." After taking attendance, she projects a short conversation on the whiteboard about replying to an invitation for the class party, instructing the students to listen as she and an assistant model the conversation. She then asks the whole class to repeat the conversation after her. Students move into pairs to practice the conversation. After ten minutes, Ms Kim calls on several volunteers to role play the conversation in front of the class. To conclude this segment of the lesson, she has students answer various comprehension questions about the conversation. Satisfied that they understand, she transitions to the next phase of the lesson.

When reflecting on this classroom scenario, Ms Kim uses a range of techniques to help students comprehend and rehearse the model conversation. Oxford calls this process recycling because it serves as a metaphor for the cyclical nature of language learning in the classroom.¹ Ms Kim chooses to incorporate recycling into her introduction because she understands that her students will never learn the conversation if it is only presented just once. She views each segment of the lesson as part of a carefully woven tapestry with repeated designs. She considers what was taught previously and what needs to be taught when guiding students to accept or decline an invitation. She also knows that recycling helps students to internalize the language so it becomes an automatic process.

Language teaching is full of questions as to how people learn a foreign language successfully. Historically, various theories and methods have been proposed in order to answer these questions. For example, behaviorists claimed that dialogues and drills were critical to successful language learning. Obviously, Ms Kim integrates a short dialogue and practice into the opening phase of her lesson. She modifies the choral repetition drill into a short whole-class practice because she believes that practicing the conversation orally provides a model that students can use when producing their own conversations later in the lesson.

Herron suggests that what we choose to teach and how we teach are intimately linked to metaphor. She states that a metaphor may be "conscious or unconscious, but in either case we must understand what it is in order to comprehend what we are doing."² I would add that these decisions are also intimately linked to our experience as Christ-followers, so there is a need for an extension of these metaphors to include this experience. Therefore, the purpose of this essay is to explore some well-known methods in second and foreign language education as metaphor and then to offer some scriptural reflections for second language educators to consider as they think more deeply about the process of teaching in the classroom.

## Method as Metaphor: A Review of the Literature

Recent publications in the discussion of method and metaphor are helpful in laying the groundwork for why metaphor is important in the language classroom. Smith and Carville suggest that metaphors help educators see things

---

1. Rebecca Oxford, *Language Learning Strategies: What Every Teacher Should Know* (New York: Newbury House, 1990), 42, 67.
2. Carol Herron, "Foreign Language Learning Approaches as Metaphor," *The Modern Language Journal* 66, no. 3 (1982): 235.

differently by "illuminating one thing in terms of another."[3] Metaphors shed light on a subject and bring into focus dimensions and features otherwise unclear or even unnoticed. They state, "A metaphor is more suggestive than definitive and has expansive explanatory power. It guides, shapes, and organizes our views, practices and choices in a certain direction."[4]

Nattinger expands on this, suggesting that metaphors provide us with a framework for organizing our knowledge and giving shape to the unknown. The more similarities shared between two entities, the better the metaphor works. He states, "Any model, any theory, any description is a metaphor of a sort, so most of the explaining and learning we do takes place metaphorically."[5]

Lakoff and Johnson observe that metaphors are a fundamental mechanism of mind that allows individuals to use what they know about their physical and social experience to provide understanding of countless other subjects.[6] Such metaphors structure the most basic understandings of each individual's experience, and thus can shape perceptions and actions without awareness.

Herron makes a similar observation that a metaphor is intuitive in its origins. "It is an apprehension of affinities; although it may become totally rational; the purpose of metaphor is to shed light on the common elements of two realities."[7] She suggests that "what we teach . . . and how we teach, along with the complementary perceptions of value, are intimately linked to metaphor."[8] Smith and Carvill claim that metaphors orient our ways of teaching and provide coherence and meaning. Further, they also suggest that we naturally live and teach by metaphors.[9]

Brown agrees, stating that "Metaphor is a pervasive and profound characteristic of human language."[10] He provides a few examples, stating that both journey metaphors ("I'm on the road to success") and war metaphors ("The Yankees battled the Red Sox") are characteristic of metaphors used in

---

3. David Smith and Barbara Carvill, *The Gift of the Stranger: Faith, Hospitality, and Foreign Language Learning* (Grand Rapids, MI: Eerdmans, 2000), 83.

4. Ibid.

5. James R. Nattinger, "Communicative Language Teaching: A New Metaphor," *TESOL Quarterly* 18, no. 3 (1984): 392.

6. George Lakoff and Mark Johnson, *Metaphors We Live By* (Chicago, IL: University of Chicago Press, 2003).

7. Herron, "Foreign Language Learning," 235.

8. Ibid., 241.

9. Smith and Carvill, *Gift of the Stranger*, 83.

10. H. Douglas Brown, *Principles of Language Learning and Teaching*, 6th ed. (White Plains, NY: Addison Wesley Longman, 2014), 88.

the English language.[11] Certain phrases may have previously been distinctive metaphors, but have become so ingrained that we don't think of them as metaphor anymore, and therefore are dead metaphors. However, whether we realize it or not, they still have strong implications for how we teach and how we manage the classroom.

Smith and Carvill then extend the relationship of metaphor to include spiritual virtues. Citing Mark Schwehn, they remark that a basic set of spiritual virtues developed within the context of religious commitment and community is integral to healthy learning.[12] Virtues such as charity, justice and humility "should inform and shape learning." Schwehm claims that to "teach these virtues" means first to exemplify them, second to order life in the classroom and throughout the academic community in such a way that their exercise is seen and felt as an essential aspect of inquiry.[13]

For the purposes of this essay, we will use metaphor as the essence of making a connection between understanding and experiencing one thing in terms of another and this includes not just language, but also how we perceive the world and act on those perceptions. It explains, describes and then guides our perceptions and our actions in the creative ways that we use them. These perceptions shape the way we think and live. One common understanding of metaphor deems it as a mere linguistic ornament whose meaning can be fully translated (and better expressed) in more straightforward language.[14] We however are saying something stronger. Metaphors generate new connections and insights. We believe that the writers of Scripture understand and use metaphor in a similar manner to help us understand realities of the Christian life.

---

11. Ibid.

12. Smith and Carvill, *Gift of the Stranger*, 83.

13. Ibid.

14. This understanding dates back at least to Aristotle. See Kevin J. Vanhoozer, *Is There a Meaning in This Text?: The Bible, the Reader, and the Morality of Literary Knowledge* (Grand Rapids, MI: Zondervan, 1998), 116, 128. For an extended treatment on the nature of metaphors see Paul Ricoeur, *The Rule of Metaphor: Multi-Disciplinary Studies of the Creation of Meaning in Language,* trans. Robert Czerny, Kathleen McLaughlin, and John Costello, SJ (Toronto: University of Toronto Press, 1977).

## What Are Some Common Assumptions in Metaphors?

There are a number of assumptions in regard to teaching and learning which are represented in metaphorical terminology.[15] Smith and Carvill suggest metaphors such as nurture, cultivation, production and liberation are common in education. Whichever metaphor we choose tends to influence teaching and learning methods as well as curricular choices. They state, "It makes a difference whether we think of foreign language learners as plants to be cultivated or as production sites within measureable input and output."[16]

According to Ward, three common metaphors seem to account for the current thinking and planning in higher education.[17] Each of these will be associated with a specific methodology in this essay. Two of these metaphorical representations he likens to a production site and filling a container:

> These two [approaches] are closely related, though they use different symbolism. They are both faulty. One of the key problems in both of these concepts of education is their rooting in the *tabla rasa* view of childhood . . . This view of the learner as an empty slate to be written on by 'those who know' is even applied to the teaching of adults.[18]

In a previous article, I suggest that metaphorical assumptions have influenced teaching and learning in higher education, but more specifically, they have influenced the teaching and learning of English to speakers of other languages for decades.[19]

Metaphors prove useful when examining different approaches to teaching and learning.[20] Postman and Weingartner claim that many educators conceptualize teaching and learning through the use of metaphors.[21] Young offers the following perspective:

---

15. Ted W. Ward, *Evaluating Metaphors of Education* (Monrovia, CA: MARC Publications, 1996).
16. Smith and Carvill, *Gift of the Stranger*, 83.
17. Ward, *Evaluating Metaphors of Education*, 7–26.
18. Ibid., 45–46.
19. Cheri Pierson, "Reflection on Educational Metaphors for Teaching English as a Second Language to Adult Learners," *PAACE Journal of Lifelong Learning* 17 (2008): 53.
20. J. Apps, "Metaphors in Education," Unpublished lecture notes (LEPS/ACE Department, Northern Illinois University, DeKalb, Illinois, 1995).
21. Pierson, "Reflection on Educational Metaphors," 52.

Metaphors form visual constructs through which we associate, interpret and organize thought. They dominate and delimit our consideration of experience and phenomena. Because one's metaphor of teaching and learning interacts with fundamental issues such as the nature of knowledge and the nature of persons, it impinges directly on the way pedagogical decisions are made.[22]

Accordingly, if metaphors do represent an educator's fundamental notions, such as the nature of knowledge, it is not only important to capture and align a proper metaphor for the learning structure, but essential for educators to investigate the advantages and disadvantages of these metaphors. In doing so, an appropriate concept of teaching and learning can be forged to create deeper success for educators and students.[23]

## Grammar Translation Method: The Mind-Body Metaphor

Like a bucket ready to be filled,[24] the transmission of knowledge from teacher to learner is viewed as a unidirectional act in the filling metaphor.[25] The teacher transmits what she knows most often through lecture directly to the students. Freire characterized this cognitive approach to teaching and learning as "banking." He states,

Instead of communicating, the teacher issues communiqués and makes deposits, which the students patiently receive, memorize and repeat . . . The scope of the action allowed to the students extends as far as receiving, filing and storing the deposits.[26]

Since this model is teacher-directed, the experiences and skills of the learners may not be seen as important.[27] Smith suggests that the filling approach assumes that learners understand the content in the same way it is

---

22. M. Young, "Planning Theological Education in Mission Settings," in *With an Eye on the Future,* eds D. Elmer and L. McKinney (Monrovia, CA: MARC, 1996), 79.
23. Pierson, "Reflection on Educational Metaphors," 53.
24. Young, "Planning Theological Education," 79.
25. Pierson, "Reflection on Educational Metaphors," 53.
26. Paulo Freire, *Pedagogy of the Oppressed* (New York: Seabury, 1970), 58.
27. R. Wicket, *Models of Adult Religious Education Practice* (Birmingham, AL: Religious Education Press, 1991), 139.

understood by the teacher.[28] Ward argues that the filling orientation tends to encourage learner passivity, which diminishes their creativity and skills of critical thinking.[29]

This approach to education may have legitimacy if, as Young suggests, the active role of the learner is included, and critical and independent thinking are encouraged. But Joyce and Weil,[30] and Habermas and Issler,[31] point out that even with the student taking an active role, learning within this model remains restricted to the cognitive domain.[32]

For centuries, the Grammar Translation Method, also known as the Classical Method, represented the filling metaphor in language education. According to Brown, foreign language education in schools in the Western world was synonymous with the learning of Latin or Greek.[33] In the Classical Method era, focus was devoted to academic study and reading texts but not to oral communication. During the nineteenth century, the Grammar Translation Method dominated foreign language education and it is still practiced in modified forms in foreign language classrooms today.[34] In these settings, language learners memorize vocabulary lists and grammar rules in order to translate texts into the target language.[35] Richards and Rogers summarize,

> . . . the Grammar-Translation Method is still widely practiced, it has no advocates. It is a method for which there is no theory. There is no literature that offers a rationale or justification for it or that attempts to relate it to issues in linguistics, psychology or educational theory.[36]

---

28. David L. Smith, *A Handbook of Contemporary Theology: Tracing Trends and Discerning Directions in Today's Theological Landscape* (Wheaton, IL: Bridge-Point/Victor Publisher, 1992), 50.

29. Ward, *Evaluating Metaphors of Education*, 46.

30. Bruce R. Joyce and Marsha Weil, *Models of Teaching*, 4th ed. (Needham Heights, MA: Allyn & Bacon, 1992).

31. Ronald T. Habermas and Klaus Issler, *Teaching for Reconciliation: Foundations and Practice of Christian Education Ministry* (Grand Rapids, MI: Baker, 1992).

32. Pierson, "Reflection on Educational Metaphors," 53–54.

33. H. Douglas Brown and Heekyeong Lee, *Teaching by Principles*, 4th ed. (White Plains, NY: Pearson Education, 2015), 17.

34. Jack C. Richards and Theodore S. Rodgers, *Approaches and Methods in Language Teaching*, 2nd ed. (Cambridge: Cambridge University Press, 2001), 4–5.

35. Ibid., 6.

36. Ibid., 7.

They suggest that since this method has little support in the literature of linguistics, psychology, and education, it should be enough for teachers to reexamine its prominence in language education.[37]

However, Herron expands our understanding of the classical method in a positive light by connecting it to a mind-body or gymnastics metaphor. She suggests that the mind-body metaphor is embedded in the theory of mental discipline. She explains, "The mental disciplinarians of the nineteenth century asked us to think of the mind as if it were a muscle of the body which could be trained and strengthened through certain academic exercises."[38] Thus, the idea of training one's cognitive muscles develops stronger language learners. The role of the teacher in this model is described as a physical trainer who shapes his students' minds and provides exercises that train their language muscles. Rather than students being passive learners as the filling metaphor implies, learners are actively engaged in academic exercises that help them to become skilled readers and translators of texts from the original language to the target language.

## *Scriptural Reflection*

Isn't it interesting that New Testament authors like Paul and the author of Hebrews use a mind-body metaphor to describe the Christian life? In 1 Corinthians 9:26–27 Paul states, "Therefore I do not run like a man running aimlessly; I do not fight like a man beating the air. No, I beat my body and make it my slave so that I may preach to others." According to Paul, Christian service requires a rigor of both mind and body. Training, exercise and commitment are needed to fight against sin. Hebrews offers a similar metaphor:

> Everyone who competes in the games goes into strict training. They do it to get a crown that will not last; but we do it to get a crown that will last forever. Therefore I do not run like a man running aimlessly. Therefore, since we are surrounded by so great a cloud of witnesses, let us also lay aside every weight, and sin which clings so closely, and let us run with endurance the race that is set before us. (Heb 12:1–2 ESV)

In the section of Hebrews just prior to these verses the author sketches out the lives of Old Testament witnesses – from Abel through Noah, Abraham and

---

37. Pierson, "Reflection on Educational Metaphors," 54.
38. Herron, "Foreign Language Learning," 235.

Moses, to many unnamed men and women who remained faithful to God throughout their earthly journeys despite great difficulties and challenges. The rigor of mind and body are demonstrated in the lives of these "witnesses."

A more recent example of a "witness" who showed commitment in training both his body and mind is the Scottish Olympian runner Eric Liddle, winner of the gold medal for the 400 meters at the 1924 Olympics in France. In the 1981 film "Chariots of Fire" he is quoted as saying, "I believe that God made me for a purpose, but He also made me fast. When I run I feel his pleasure."

Eric physically trained his mind and body in preparation for the 100 meters for months before he discovered that the heat for his event was on a Sunday. He refused to run, causing an international stir. Yet an opportunity came for him to instead compete in the 400 meters, which he ran and actually won. His intensive training helped him to spontaneously compete, and even succeed in a different event. A week later he returned to Scotland as a hero and was asked to speak at many events. At one such event he concluded his speech with these words, revealing a spiritually trained mind:

> It has been a wonderful experience to compete in the Olympic Games and to bring home a gold medal. But since I have been a young lad, I have had my eyes on a different prize. You see, each of us is in a greater race than any I have run in Paris, and this race ends when God gives out the medals. It has always been my intention to be a missionary . . . and I will be putting my energy in preparing for that race.[39]

In the moments that followed Liddle's announcement "it's reported that the room was completely silent and people stared at Eric with open mouths; the impact of what he said was slowly sinking in. The greatest athlete (of Scotland) was giving up running to go to China."[40]

Eric Liddel and the other unnamed witnesses that are listed in Hebrews 11 that represent the mind and body metaphor knew the prize that awaited them. It wasn't just learning a language successfully or getting a wreath for a race won. It was far greater. What they won was an eternal prize – heaven itself.

---

39. Janet Benge and Geoff Benge, *Eric Liddell: Something Greater Than Gold* (San Diego, CA: YWAM Publishing, 1998), 67.

40. Ibid.

## Audiolingual Method: The Production Metaphor

According to Herron, the production metaphor implied a shift from "changing the powers of the mind towards training for specific, future, social and personal living."[41] Therefore, the production model views the learner as a product to be molded by the supervisor (teacher) and learning as an object of conditioning with an emphasis on quantification of learning. Although the student is actively involved in the learning process, administrators, curriculum developers and educators determine educational goals and objectives – a process that leaves the learners' needs largely ignored. Educational strategies that emerge from behaviorists such B. F. Skinner, include both programmed instruction and behavioral modification techniques.[42]

The Audiolingual Method (ALM) stems directly from the production metaphor. Along with this method, compatible teaching materials for English as a foreign language are still used in language classrooms throughout the world.[43] In the mid-twentieth century the Audiolingual Method developed as a reaction to the Grammar Translation paradigm and was prompted by the movement toward positivism and empiricism.[44] According to Brown and Lee, ALM was built on the foundations of structural linguistics, contrastive analysis, aural-oral teaching techniques and behavioral psychology.[45]

Proponents claim that learners are able to master a foreign language more effectively and efficiently using audiolingual techniques than with earlier grammar-based approaches. This method was widely adapted in North American higher education and provided the methodological framework for university-level foreign language curricula and teaching resources for more than three decades.

Nattinger suggests that the implications of this production metaphor are that it links language teaching to the development of marketable and useable skills.[46] In order for skills to be useable, the concept of recycling material is essential. In our opening scenario, Ms Kim uses recycling in her teaching of a conversation. As stated previously, this technique acts as a metaphor describing the cyclical nature of language learning in a classroom. Just as we recycle

---

41. Herron, "Foreign Language Learning," 238.
42. Pierson, "Reflection on Educational Metaphors," 54.
43. Richards and Rodgers, *Approaches and Methods*, 67.
44. Ibid., 54.
45. Brown and Lee, *Teaching by Principles*.
46. Nattinger, "Communicative Language Teaching," 392.

aluminum cans on a regular basis, teachers recycle newly learned vocabulary and structures. It is important for teachers to remember that students never learn vocabulary when it's presented just once. Teachers have to consider what has been taught and to consciously work in practice of previous forms, words, skills and tasks.[47]

Chomsky's theory of universal "deep structures" in language caused audiolingual approaches to decline in popularity in the 1960s and 1970s.[48] Other factors contributing to this decline include psychologists' recognition of the affective and interpersonal nature of human learning,[49] as well as the limited roles available to learners being seen as stimulus-response mechanisms.[50]

In spite of these difficulties, Knowles suggests that there is a place for this model in higher education. He writes,

> I believe each of these models describes part of our reality. In some circumstances we, indeed, do behave like machines. When I learned to type, it seemed appropriate that behaviorist strategies be used to teach my fingers to hit the right keys. But most learning, and certainly most significant learning, seems far more complex than either of these models [mental gymnastics and manufacturing] takes into account.[51]

## *Scriptural Reflection*

Jesus used a production metaphor when he talked to his disciples about wise and foolish builders. He said,

> As for everyone who comes to me and hears my words and puts them into practice, I will show you what they are like. They are like a man building a house who dug down deep and laid the foundation on rock. When a flood came, the torrent struck that house but could not shake it, because it was well built. But the

---

47. Cheri Pierson, "TESOL Classroom Dynamics Practicum Course Notes" (Wheaton College, 2016), 36–37.
48. Noam Chomsky, *Syntactic Structures* (The Hague, Netherlands: Mouton, 1957).
49. Brown, *Principles of Language Learning*, 104.
50. Richards and Rodgers, *Approaches and Methods*, 62.
51. Malcolm Knowles, "Contributions of Malcolm Knowles," in *The Christian Educator's Handbook of Adult Education*, eds. K. Gangel and J. Wilhoit (Wheaton, IL: Victor Books, 1993), 95.

> one who hears my words and does not put them into practice is like a man who built a house on ground without a foundation. The moment the torrent struck the house, it collapsed and its destruction was complete. (Luke 6:46–49)

Some key words in this passage relate to our metaphor of production. Jesus is teaching his listeners that they must first hear and then put into practice what he teaches. The fact that we can listen without practicing is often the case of poor production. Jesus is saying that how we build and on what foundation we build is going to help us when the challenges come, and come they will. So hearing what the teacher says, modeling it and practicing it helps strengthen our ability in the language learning process. Even though a dialogue is not particularly useful by itself, when placed together with practice and other elements we find that it is useful in building confidence and foundations for the learners.

What seems relevant to the production metaphor in this passage is the idea of a wise builder who puts into practice what Jesus has taught. He likens it to a well-built house. Brick by brick a house is built on a sure foundation rather than on a foundation of sand. Practice seems to imply good results. Knowing the basics of building a solid house is inferred here and some parts of life are like that. They may seem routine, but these routines lead to disciplines that are essential to the Christian. Thus, the building metaphor that we see in this story may have implications for the language learner who needs to practice and recycle basic conversations or functions used within the production model of language learning.

## Humanistic Methods: The First Language Acquisition Metaphor

The post-audiolingual methods that appeared in the 1970s are usually referred to as the designer era. In these methods second-language learners are equated with children learning their first language. Students acquire language best when a focus is put on meaning and function rather than on memorizing rules and dialogues. Students' linguistic, cognitive and affective needs are considered important and the language they learn is communicative rather than form focused. These methods served as a bridge to the communicative approaches that followed.

Herron suggests that the metaphor of first language acquisition is interesting but it has some serious limitations.[52] For example, adults are not children who are introduced to language acquisition for the first time. Rather, adults are experienced language users and have a great deal of linguistic competence in their first language.

## *Scriptural Reflection*

In Luke 9:46–48, an argument breaks out among Jesus's disciples as to who is the greatest. Jesus sees a little child and begins his teaching.

> Jesus knowing their thoughts, took a little child and had him stand beside him. Then he said to them, "Whoever welcomes this little child in my name welcomes me; and whoever welcomes me welcomes the one who sent me. For he who is least among you all – he is the greatest."

Jesus uses a little child to help his adult followers understand who is the greatest in his kingdom. What can we learn from a young child in language acquisition? We learn about their curiosity, their innocence and their ability to learn from others. We also see that there is a lack of pretention or embarrassment. They want to learn and they acquire knowledge by having open hearts and open ears. Jesus isn't saying we have to be childish but we can be childlike in the way we learn to trust in him. I think this is a great picture of what learning can be like and how difficult it can be when we consider the humbling task of learning a language as an adult.

## Communicative Methods: The Journey Metaphor

In contrast to the mind-body, production, and first language acquisition metaphors discussed above, Ward offers the metaphor of the journey or "life-walk."[53] According to Ward, this educational approach suggests both the journey and the final destination.[54] In essence, the learning experiences of the language learner are as important as the destination. With an emphasis on both process and destination, this model is organic and dynamic. Kliebard explains,

---

52. Herron, "Foreign Language Learning," 241.
53. Ward, *Evaluating Metaphors of Education*.
54. Pierson, "Reflection on Educational Metaphors," 56.

> The curriculum is the route over which students travel under the leadership of an experienced guide and companion. Each traveler will be affected differently by the journey since its effect is at least as much a function of the predilections, intelligence, interests and intent of the traveler [learner] as it is of the contours of the route. This variability is not only inevitable, but wondrous and desirable. Therefore, no effort is made to anticipate the exact nature of the effect on the traveler, but a great effort is made to plot the route so that the journey will be as rich, as fascinating and as memorable as possible.[55]

By creating and facilitating an atmosphere of learning within the life-walk metaphor, both teacher and student take the educational journey together. When I was learning Swedish in Gothenburg, my teacher understood the need for the process as well as for the destination. My teacher saw her role as a facilitator who led us through and to our final destination, as we each individually journeyed toward learning the Swedish language.

Initially, she conducted a needs analysis so that we might explore the "why" behind learning Swedish. She placed the focus on the students' motivations and interests for learning the language. Her learning activities were designed to equip us to use the language in everyday settings. In order to ease us into fluency, she had us turn and talk to our partner before we spoke to the whole class. She facilitated our learning through monitoring – listening to our conversations. These were excellent exercises for working on fluency and accuracy, and by the end of the course local shopkeepers and neighbors could understand us.

An example of the journey metaphor was recorded in my language journal.

> Katarina taught us how to order coffee and pastry in the local café. By first modeling the situation, she engaged our five senses, which helped us to better differentiate a successful encounter from an unsuccessful one. Through a mutual exchange of laughter and understanding, everyone comprehended the situation well and felt confident enough to go to the café and order. Though I was nervous, my joy at actually receiving what I had ordered far outweighed my anxiety beforehand! Afterwards, all of us sat around a large table and discussed our experience. This is where

---

55. Herbert M. Kliebard, "Metaphorical Roots of Curriculum Design," *Teachers College Record* 74 (1972): 404.

our instruction deepened. Katarina took the next step to assist us in evaluating and strengthening our performance by further teaching us the appropriate hand gestures – correlating our speech and our actions. By operating as both facilitator and instructor, Katarina engaged us in the learning process and created an atmosphere conducive to appropriate implementation. Learning the balance of fluency and accuracy, coupled with the suitable behavior, taught me essential truths about teaching and learning that I still apply in my classrooms, today. Although learning a language is difficult, it should not be boring or frustrating for the adult learner, due to poor teaching or inappropriate methods. Katarina's journey surpassed lecture and memorization – she created an atmosphere of interaction that was exciting and memorable for us all.[56]

According to Ward, exploration and discovery are vital to the life-walk educational process.[57] Unlike the previous methods, the learning experiences and styles of all the learners are important to the educational process. Freire's version of the life-walk metaphor suggests a pedagogy that places the teacher and learner on equal plains.[58] Freire suggests two essential elements: the concept of "conscientization" and the inclusion of "praxis." These two processes are described below:

"Conscientization" refers to the personal and critical examination of one's own learning. Rather than agreeing with and repeating what is being taught, adult learners are to be continually involved in a conscious examination of the facts, as they relate to their own experiences and that of their community.[59] The process of conscientization is realized through dialogue where all participants are engaged in a common search for truth. Freire refers to this form of dialogue as "the horizontal relationship between persons."[60]

"Praxis," on the other hand, refers to the reflection between theory and practice.[61] Praxis is a necessary element for the learner who wishes to incite change in themselves and their community.[62] The correlation between conscientization and praxis "helps the learner 'to transform the world through

---

56. Pierson, "Reflection on Educational Metaphors," 57.
57. Ward, *Evaluating Metaphors of Education.*
58. Freire, *Pedagogy of the Oppressed.*
59. Ibid.
60. Paulo Freire, *Education for Critical Consciousness* (New York: Seabury, 1973), 45.
61. Freire, *Education for Critical Consciousness.*
62. Wicket, *Models of Adult Religious.*

man's reflection on himself and the world' and to take direct, considered action upon them" both.[63]

The two components of Freire's essential process of dialogue, reflection and action, are each integral to this approach. For, Freire argues, reflection without action degenerates into "verbalism," and action without reflection degenerates into "mindless activism."[64]

Groome,[65] White[66] and Wickett[67] all suggest that Freire's concepts have value in adult religious higher education – especially by recognizing the importance of learners' experiences in the educational process. Specifically, Wickett observes that adult learning is less likely to happen without this integral component of the learners' reflection on their own personal and social realities. He notes that Freire's emphasis on problem posing, in which all participants in the educational experience work together, requires reflection by teachers, as well as learners. Contextualized to an adult religious education situation, learners who have the opportunity to articulate and reflect on their own learning may have a better idea of how to respond to their personal needs and goals, as well as those of their community, through the use of critical reflection and praxis.[68]

Based on the journey metaphor, communicative methods for teaching and learning language begin with the theory of language "as communication."[69] Richards and Rogers also suggest that communicative approaches appeared at a time when the method was ready for a paradigm shift. I believe such methodology appeals to a more humanistic technique, in which interactive communication processes hold priority.

Unlike earlier methods, communicative approaches focus primarily on the role of the learners in the process of second language acquisition. Breen and Candlin explain these types of learner roles:

> The role of learner as negotiator – between the self, the learning process and the object of learning – emerges from and interacts

---

63. Freire, *Pedagogy of the Oppressed*.
64. Freire, *Education for Critical Consciousness*, 75.
65. Thomas Groome, *Christian Religious Education: Sharing Our Story and Vision* (San Francisco, CA: Jossey Bass, 1999).
66. J. White, *International Religious Education; Models, Theory, and Prescription for Interage Life and Learning in the Faith Community* (Birmingham, AL: Religious Education Press, 1988).
67. Wicket, *Models of Adult Religious*.
68. Ibid.
69. Richards and Rodgers, *Approaches and Methods*, 159.

with the role of joint negotiation within the group and within the classroom procedures and activities, which the group undertakes. The implication for the learner is that he should contribute as much as he gains and thereby learn in an interdependent way.[70]

According to Richards and Rogers, this collaborative approach may be unfamiliar to some adult learners who were trained in classical approaches.[71] In order for a collaborative form of learning to be effective, traditional teachers and learners may need special training in its techniques and procedures.[72] However, while special training is frequently beneficial, educators may simply need to assess needs, rethink some of their methods, and creatively facilitate meaningful experiences to practice the content. I describe my Swedish teacher as one who applies the life-walk metaphor in her daily teaching. Her teacher as facilitator taught the students to value and engage in the language learning experience. In fact, she modeled how they could take control of their own language learning and determine their own destinations. Making connections to real-world use is a challenge in any learning environment, but the teacher who attempts to offer students not only language but tools to continue that learning outside the walls of the formal classroom, is truly equipping students for their own language learning journey.

As stated in the introduction, language learning is not a one-size-fits-all proposition. Rather, it is a dynamic process that requires total commitment from the students and their teacher. By helping students understand their own styles of learning, and giving them strategies to capitalize on their strengths, successful communication is attainable. In my personal experience as a language learner, I not only learned the language, but also successfully executed the practice of language. In turn, when I studied at a university in Sweden, I used some of the same principles my teacher modeled. By including cognitive, linguistic and affective factors into our learning, a teacher can duly capture the journey metaphor.

---

70. Michael Breen and Christopher Candlin, "The Essentials of a Communicative Curriculum in Language Teaching," *Applied Linguistics* 1, no. 2 (1980): 110.

71. Pierson, "Reflection on Educational Metaphors," 59.

72. Ibid.

## *Scriptural Reflection*

There are many metaphors in Scripture that exemplify the journey metaphor. One of the most poignant is found in Psalm 23. The metaphor that seems prominent in the mind of David is that of the shepherd who guides and journeys with the sheep. The shepherd metaphor is used throughout the Old Testament (Ps 78:71–72; 2 Sam 5:2; Isa 44:28; Jer 3:15; 23:1–4: Mic 5:4). The Lord as the shepherd of his people Israel dominates passages as well (Pss 23:9; 79:13; 80:1; 95:7; 100:3; Gen 48:50; Isa 40:11; Jer 17:16; 31:10; 50:19). The Shepherd metaphor also appears multiple times in the New Testament in reference to Jesus as Shepherd (John 10:11–13; Heb 13:20; 1 Pet 5:4; Rev 7:17).

David may have sung Psalm 23 as he watched over his flocks. Perhaps as he meditated on his surroundings he thought about God as Shepherd who guided and cared for him. David certainly understood the responsibilities of a shepherd and in this psalm he attaches these responsibilities to his Shepherd, God himself. His Shepherd leads him to still waters just as David leads his sheep to streams that are still. The Shepherd often restores David just as David lets his sheep rest and does not drive them too hard. Because David trusts his Shepherd, he takes the journey that God directs him on without fear of evil because he knows God will protect him. The shepherd has to be flexible because of the changing needs of the sheep. For example, if they are tired from the journey, the shepherd lets them rest. If they stray on the journey, the shepherd uses his rod and staff to get them back on the path. The metaphor of a shepherd has much to say to educators who seek to provide a positive journey for his or her students.

We are physical creatures, but we are also spiritual ones. We are whole people – we smile, we laugh, we get nervous – and therefore it is very important to understand that the Shepherd embraces us, his sheep, as whole persons. We are not just a body or just a soul, we are created in his image as it says in 1 Thessalonians 5:23, "May God himself, the God of peace, sanctify you through and through. May your whole spirit, soul and body be kept blameless at the coming of our Lord Jesus Christ." When looking at the metaphor of the shepherd, the positive journey that educators provide is a holistic one.[73]

---

73. For a more complete understanding of the mind-body connection, see Anthony A. Hoekema, "The Whole Person," in *Created in God's Image* (Grand Rapids, MI: Eerdmans, 1986), 203–226.

## Post-Methods: An Array of Metaphors

According to Brown, the post-method era of language teaching was a concept that arose around the turn of the twenty-first century.[74] Kumaravadivelu called for a pedagogy of particularity where he expressed the need for "soundly conceived pedagogical approaches that attended to the particularities of contexts."[75] He suggests that the post-methods era is a transitional period and that its pedagogy is a work in progress. According to Celce-Murcia, the goal is to help prospective teachers develop their own effective pedagogies that will create meaningful collaboration among learners, teachers and teacher educators.[76] Brown poses the question, "Was the proclamation of a post-method condition merely a matter of semantic quibbling?" The answer may well be "maybe." Larsen-Freeman and Anderson among others have remained comfortable with maintaining the notion of methods.[77] Brown rightly summarizes this, saying "the profession has attained a modicum of maturity where we recognize that the diversity of language learners in multiple worldwide contexts demands an eclectic blend of tasks, each tailored for a specified group of learners studying for particular purposes in geographic social and political contexts."[78]

An eclectic approach to teaching requires understanding and critical reflection in terms of methods that are readily available to us based on the context of teaching and learning. Brown says, "Your approach to language teaching methodology is a theoretically well-informed global understanding of the process of learning and teaching. It is inspired by the interconnection of all your reading and observing and discussion and teaching and that interconnection underlies everything you do in the classroom."[79]

### *Scriptural Reflection*

The essence of one metaphor that describes the post-methods era is difficult to identify. Rather an array of metaphors may be more applicable. When we

---

74. Brown and Lee, *Teaching by Principles*, 40.

75. Ibid.

76. Marianne Celce-Murcia, "Teaching English as a Second or Foreign Language," in *An Overview of Language Teaching Methods and Approaches*, 4th ed. (Boston, MA: Heinle CENGAGE Learning, 2014), 11.

77. Diane Larsen-Freeman and Marti Anderson, *Techniques and Principles in Language Teaching*, 3rd ed. (Oxford, UK: Oxford University Press, 2011), xvi.

78. Brown and Lee, *Teaching by Principles*, 40.

79. Ibid., 42.

focus on the "I Am" statements that describe Jesus Christ in the writings of the apostle John, we discover an array of metaphors. For example, in John 6:35, Jesus compares himself to the bread of life which sustains life. In John 8:12 Jesus calls himself "the light of the world." In John 14:6 he refers to himself as "the way, the truth and the life – no one comes to the father but by me." And in John 15:5 he compares himself to a vine and his followers as branches of the vine. In Revelation 21:6 Jesus refers to himself as the Alpha and Omega, the beginning and the end.

Other metaphorical references are made about followers of Christ. For example, in Matthew 5:13 Jesus refers to his followers as "salt of the earth." In this metaphor, Christians are compared to salt which is both a preservative and a flavoring. Another example is 1 Corinthians 5:17 – "Therefore, if anyone is in Christ, he is a new creation; the old has gone, the new has come." In these examples metaphors are used to help us understand who Christians are in relationship to Christ.

Some negative metaphors were also used to portray Christ incorrectly. These metaphors were condescending and inappropriate. An example is in Matthew 11:19: "The Son of Man came eating and drinking, and they say, 'Here is a glutton and a drunkard, a friend of tax collectors and sinners.' But wisdom is proved right by her deeds." Therefore, metaphors that have a condescending tone are inappropriate for the classroom.

Another example from Scripture that may illustrate the complexity discussed above may be found in the phrase, "the body of Christ." Paul uses this body metaphor in 1 Corinthians to describe the situation in the city of Corinth. For example, in 1 Corinthians 10:16 Paul refers to the body of Christ in reference to the Lord's Supper. In using the physical image of the body, Paul illustrates the unity between Christ and his church. In another passage, 1 Corinthians 12:27 Paul refers to the church as unified in the body of Christ. In other words, there are different members but there is only one body. Events that were taking place in the church at Corinth endangered this unity so Paul offers the metaphor of the body to help the Corinthians understand that a body divided cannot flourish. The body is living and dynamic and each part is essential.

However, the body metaphor can have a negative impact as well. When the church moves away from its purpose and turns into a business enterprise, we can envision the scene when Jesus entered the temple courts in Matthew 21:12 and drove out all who were buying and selling there. He overturned the tables of the money changers and the benches of those selling doves saying,

"It is written... My house will be called a house of prayer, but you are making it 'a den of robbers'" (v. 13). When we liken language learning to a business metaphor – "learn a language in 3 easy lessons" – we move away from the dynamic process of language acquisition and sell it as just a commodity.

## Conclusion

The methods we choose or integrate are not set in stone. Much like the journey metaphor, it is a dynamic composite of well-informed beliefs that can change across time and in various contexts we can apply what is best for our students. The interaction between the methods we use and the contexts we teach in is key to effective language teaching. Both the art and science of teaching are addressed and the landscape of language learning broadens as we consider metaphors which both express and describe what we mean as teaching and learning language.

A valid alternative of the journey metaphor is worth exploration, especially when compared to the historical methods of teaching and learning we have examined in this essay. A range of well-chosen methods promoted by an informed teacher can enhance the process of language learning in any context. An interdependence between the teacher and students may provide an opportunity for learning that solidifies the foundation needed for students to become a final metaphor – that of lifelong learners.

## Bibliography

Apps, J. "Metaphors in Education." Unpublished lecture notes presented at the LEPS/ACE Department, Northern Illinois University, DeKalb, Illinois, 1995.

Benge, Janet, and Geoff Benge. *Eric Liddell: Something Greater Than Gold*. San Diego, CA: YWAM Publishing, 1998.

Breen, Michael, and Christopher Candlin. "The Essentials of a Communicative Curriculum in Language Teaching." *Applied Linguistics* 1, no. 2 (1980): 89–112.

Brown, H. Douglas. *Principles of Language Learning and Teaching*. 6th ed. White Plains, NY: Addison Wesley Longman, 2014.

Brown, H. Douglas, and Heekyeong Lee. *Teaching by Principles*. 4th ed. White Plains, NY: Pearson Education, 2015.

Celce-Murcia, Marianne. "Teaching English as a Second or Foreign Language." In *An Overview of Language Teaching Methods and Approaches*, 4th ed., 2–14. Boston, MA: Heinle CENGAGE Learning, 2014.

Chomsky, Noam. *Syntactic Structures*. The Hague, Netherlands: Mouton, 1957.

Freire, Paulo. *Education for Critical Consciousness*. New York: Seabury, 1973.
———. *Pedagogy of the Oppressed*. New York: Seabury, 1970.
Groome, Thomas. *Christian Religious Education: Sharing Our Story and Vision*. San Francisco, CA: Jossey Bass, 1999.
Habermas, Ronald T., and Klaus Issler. *Teaching for Reconciliation: Foundations and Practice of Christian Education Ministry*. Grand Rapids, MI: Baker, 1992.
Herron, Carol. "Foreign Language Learning Approaches as Metaphor." *The Modern Language Journal* 66, no. 3 (1892): 235–242.
Hoekema, Anthony A. "The Whole Person." In *Created in God's Image*, 203–226. Grand Rapids, MI: Eerdmans, 1986.
Joyce, Bruce R., and Marsha Weil. *Models of Teaching*. 4th ed. Needham Heights, MA: Allyn and Bacon, 1992.
Kliebard, Herbert M. "Metaphorical Roots of Curriculum Design." *Teachers College Record* 74 (1972): 404.
Knowles, Malcolm. "Contributions of Malcolm Knowles." In *The Christian Educator's Handbook of Adult Education*. Edited by K. Gangel and J. Wilhoit, 91–103. Wheaton, IL: Victor Books, 1993.
Lakoff, George, and Mark Johnson. *Metaphors We Live By*. Chicago, IL: University of Chicago Press, 2003.
Larsen-Freeman, Diane, and Marti Anderson. *Techniques and Principles in Language Teaching*. 3rd ed. Oxford, UK: Oxford University Press, 2011.
Nattinger, James R. "Communicative Language Teaching: A New Metaphor." *TESOL Quarterly* 18, no. 3 (1984): 391–407.
Oxford, Rebecca. *Language Learning Strategies: What Every Teacher Should Know*. New York: Newbury House, 1990.
Pierson, Cheri. "Reflection on Educational Metaphors for Teaching English as a Second Language to Adult Learners." *PAACE Journal of Lifelong Learning* 17 (2008): 51–61.
———. "TESOL Classroom Dynamics Practicum Course Notes." Wheaton College, 2016.
Richards, Jack C., and Theodore S. Rodgers. *Approaches and Methods in Language Teaching*. 2nd ed. Cambridge: Cambridge University Press, 2001.
Ricoeur, Paul. *The Rule of Metaphor: Multi-Disciplinary Studies of the Creation of Meaning in Language*. Translated by Robert Czerny, Kathleen McLaughlin, and John Costello, SJ. Toronto: University of Toronto Press, 1977.
Smith, David, and Barbara Carvill. *The Gift of the Stranger: Faith, Hospitality, and Foreign Language Learning*. Grand Rapids, MI: Eerdmans, 2000.
Smith, David L. *A Handbook of Contemporary Theology: Tracing Trends and Discerning Directions in Today's Theological Landscape*. Wheaton, IL: Bridge-Point/Victor Publisher, 1992.
Vanhoozer, Kevin J. *Is There a Meaning in This Text?: The Bible, the Reader, and the Morality of Literary Knowledge*. Grand Rapids, MI: Zondervan, 1998.

Ward, Ted W. *Evaluating Metaphors of Education*. Monrovia, CA: MARC Publications, 1996.

White, J. *International Religious Education; Models, Theory, and Prescription for Interage Life and Learning in the Faith Community*. Birmingham, AL: Religious Education Press, 1988.

Wicket, R. *Models of Adult Religious Education Practice*. Birmingham, AL: Religious Education Press, 1991.

Young, M. "Planning Theological Education in Mission Settings." In *With an Eye on the Future*. Edited by D. Elmer and L. McKinney, 69–86. Monrovia, CA: MARC Publications, 1996.

# 8

# Managing Twenty-First-Century Classes Biblically

*Marilyn Lewis*

## Preview

The question of what it means to be a Christian language teacher has been addressed in more than one forum in recent years. Snow, in *English Teaching as Christian Mission*, dealt with intercultural considerations and questions of elitism, among others.[1] A decade later the subtitle of Dormer's *Teaching English in Missions* suggests a balance to aim for: effectiveness and integrity.[2] This essay considers one specific aspect of the Christian English teacher's role: managing classes biblically.

The topic of biblically managing language classes might sound specific but the contexts it applies to are varied. Learners may be immigrants to an English-speaking country focusing on conversational language, or they may be international university students who need to read and write at an advanced level. As the field of TESOL becomes more and more specialized, we also find courses for professional groups (e.g. language for medical staff), and for students interested mainly in English language literature. The students may

---

1. Donald B. Snow, *English Teaching as Christian Mission: An Applied Theology* (Scottdale, PA: Herald Press, 2001).

2. Jan Edwards Dormer, *Teaching English in Missions: Effectiveness and Integrity* (Pasadena, CA: William Carey Library, 2011).

be based in their own country or overseas. The teacher may share a culture with the learners or be from a very different background, with all the different expectations about classroom management that this situation brings. With these diverse contexts and teacher-student combinations in mind, we approach our subject.

This essay is addressed to English language teachers who want to do more than simply "keep order" in their classrooms. It starts by examining definitions and questions, such as what exactly is covered by the term "classroom management" and whether we can refer to language teaching as a "calling." Then we consider biblical principles which can guide teachers in the day to day working out of their profession. Next the topic is narrowed down to specific classroom incidents which teachers face as well as ways of developing regular classroom routines. The conclusion suggests how teachers can continue to develop professionally in the area of classroom management.

## Definitions

### *Defining Classroom Management*

Scrivener opens his book *Classroom Management Techniques* with a concise definition: "Your classroom management is the way that you manage students' learning by organizing and controlling what happens in your classroom."[3] For some readers the words "organizing and controlling" may recall their own experiences when keeping a class subdued enough to learn summed up a first-year teacher's goal. Over the years, words like "misbehavior" or "being naughty" for children and "inattention" for older learners have been replaced in some educational systems by terms like "being off task" to describe the learners and "classroom management" for the teacher's role. By whatever label, in this essay we are reflecting on what difference it might make to the management of specific incidents, as well as to the general atmosphere of learning in a language classroom, if the teacher were following basic Christian principles.

Scrivener expands his definition of classroom management to include a teacher's conscious decision "*not* to organise and control"[4] or the "delegat[ion] or relinquish[ing of] such control to the learners."[5] Further, he suggests that

---

3. Jim Scrivener, *Classroom Management Techniques* (Cambridge: Cambridge University Press, 2012), 1.
4. Ibid.
5. Ibid.

"it is also what happens (or doesn't happen) when you avoid or remain ignorant about these choices."[6] The words "organizing" and "control" (or lack thereof) are repeated, although Scrivener does not avoid the term "discipline," with thirty-three references to it in his index.[7]

Wright, in an earlier book on the same topic, prefers the active notion of "managing" to the better-known term "management." He believes that the former "captures the dynamic and unfolding nature of classroom life."[8] The three themes developed by Wright are "human relations and the emotional dimensions," the concept of participation, and "the ever-present factors of time and space."[9] Among his many helpful points is the question of adaptability: "As social, political and economic conditions change through a teacher's career, educational practices may have to change . . ."[10] His words came back to me recently when I was asked at the end of a session on classroom management in a country in Asia, why I had not mentioned using the stick on children. Corporal punishment may be illegal in many countries, but what if you find yourself in a context where you are expected to use it?

Introducing his chapter "The Language Classroom: Roles, Relationships and Interactions," Hall speaks of "the social and pedagogic character of English language classrooms,"[11] a character that is not static from one classroom to the next, let alone from one continent to another.

The target readership for this essay is Christian classroom language teachers at whatever stage of their careers they find themselves and with whatever aged students. Therefore, let us turn from published wisdom to consider what unpublished practicing teachers understand by the term "classroom management." When I ask workshop participants to complete the sentence, "Classroom management includes managing . . ." the list typically includes comments about the teacher (behavior, voice, preparation, etc.), the learners (grouping arrangements, behavior, etc.) and the lesson (timing, resources, outcomes, etc.). In focusing on teachers, and in this case teachers for whom the Bible is a basic source of guidance, let us next consider descriptions of our role.

---

6. Ibid.

7. Ibid., 301–302.

8. Tony Wright, *Classroom Management in Language Education* (Basingstoke, Hampshire, UK: Palgrave Macmillan, 2005), 3.

9. Ibid.

10. Ibid., 284.

11. Graham Hall, *Exploring English Language Teaching: Language in Action* (London: Routledge, 2011), 3.

## *Is Language Teaching Really a "Calling"?*

People sometimes ask whether teaching, and specifically language teaching, is a Christian calling in the way that term is traditionally associated with people like Albert Schweitzer, Paul Brandt or Mother Teresa. Definitions of "Christian calling" have broadened over the decades. There was a time when young people in churches were encouraged to think about whether they were being "called to be missionaries." If not, they had a range of worthwhile professions and trades open to them. Of course, they would still be Christians, but they would not feature in gold letters on the church's list of missionaries. Snow suggests that even today, a Christian English teacher might find difficulties in "explain[ing] the value of his or her work"[12] in another country to fellow church members. World events and the requirements of governments internationally have led to a change in terminology away from the word "missionary," or is it more than just a word change?

The part played by Christians in education has been noted even by historians with no personal connection to the Christian faith. Writing one hundred years ago about the educational history of his own country, India, Mazumdar had this to say: "At this period [1859] the Christian missionaries acted as strong auxiliaries towards the spread of education, and though their primary object was to facilitate the propagation of the Christian gospel, the schools and colleges which they founded in connection with the universities became powerful adjuncts to the cause of secular education also."[13] Yancey makes the same point about education in a different part of the world. "Hospitals and schools founded by missionaries rank amongst the finest in the Arabian Gulf states."[14]

According to Stott, "if we are Christians, we must spend our lives in the service of God and man . . . the only difference between us lying in the nature of the service we are called to." Bosch had a similar interpretation. According to him, the Christian faith "is intrinsically missionary," a characteristic it shares "with several other religions, notably Islam and Buddhism, and also with a variety of ideologies, such as Marxism."[15]

---

12. Snow, *English Teaching as Christian Mission*, 17.

13. Amvika Charan Mazumdar, *The Indian National Evolution: A Brief Survey of the Origin and Progress of the Indian National Congress* (Madras: G. A. Natesan, 1915), 351–352.

14. Philip Yancey, *Vanishing Grace* (London: Hodder & Stoughton, 2014), 103.

15. David J. Bosch, *Transforming Mission: Paradigm Shifts in Theology of Mission* (Maryknoll, NY: Orbis, 1991), 8–9.

As a starting point to defining Christian mission, of which he sees the Christian educator as an important part, Stott turns to the conversation between Alice and Humpty Dumpty in *Alice in Wonderland*. According to Humpty, "some words are like a portmanteau – there are two words packed up into one word." Although Stott partly agrees with Humpty in that "some words *are* like portmanteaux" he disagrees that meanings can be imposed on them arbitrarily.[16]

Assuming that the readers of this essay are Christians and language teachers and that they sometimes have concerns about managing their classes, let us turn now to one source of advice, the Bible.

## Biblical Advice

Much of what the Bible has to say about the role of a believer in society can be applied to the Christian teacher's role in the classroom, even when the word classroom is missing from a particular verse. As just one example, in Leviticus 19:18 we are told to love our neighbor as ourselves. For part of the week at least, the students in front of us are our neighbors and, hard as it may be on particular days, they are therefore to be loved, not just silently in our hearts but visibly through our actions.

At a recent training event for new language teachers in Northeast India, the participants were asked to suggest, in a word, Bible principles which might guide us in our managing of classes. On the whiteboard they then listed their suggestions, some of which are included in this section.

How might these and other qualities recommended for God-followers transfer into specific attitudes and actions in managing the language classroom? Of the many possible suggestions, the next part of this essay concentrates on four aspects: our roles as servants, as leaders, as salt of the earth, and as people of wisdom.

### Teachers as Servants

We are told that "Those who are greatest among you should take the lowest rank, and the leader should be like a servant" (Luke 22:26 NLT), a verse paraphrased by Beers and Beers as "Good leaders lead by serving, not by

---

16. John R. W. Stott, *Christian Mission in the Modern World*, 2nd ed. (London: Falcon, 1977), 12–13.

ordering others around."[17] Elsewhere believers are asked to have a servant heart, or the humility of a slave (Phil 2:5–8). Certainly there are days when teachers feel like slaves, and not only in relation to their students. Beers and Beers have a few pointers under the heading of service. In referring to Jesus's washing of the disciples' feet in John 13:5, they remind us that a "servant gladly performs tasks that others consider beneath them."[18] Then they paraphrase Matthew 20:26–27 as "a servant minister[ing] to others regardless of their status in life."[19] In classrooms we needn't look far to find such tasks or people.

Easily said, but while the one needing help is being attended to, what happens to the rest of the class? Teachers have to consider when, for how long, and of course how they offer help to those who need it. During group work they move around the room, checking to see who needs encouragement, support, guidance or redirecting. As one example of humility, experience suggests that crouching down to the level of group members (or sitting on a chair for the less supple) seems to show a more cooperative approach than towering over students asking, "Everything fine here?"

## *Teachers as Leaders*

The concepts of servanthood and leadership might at first glance appear to have opposite meanings, yet as we noted above in Luke 22:26, the two are biblically linked. The expression "to lead by example" is well known. In the language classroom, these words are particularly relevant because using a new language is, among other things, a skill, and skills are learned partly by imitation. Taking the idea of example one step further, a teacher's efforts to learn the language of class members can be a powerful example, especially when the teacher is willing to speak of difficulties as well as demonstrate triumphs. A more relaxed atmosphere can develop when classes see their teachers leading by example, as they try to master their students' first language.

The "learning to learn" approach emphasizes the process of learning as much as the goal of performance. Recently two of us explored the tutor-learner relationship in our book that links the teaching and the learning process. Among other points, we used the metaphor of a mountain guide to illustrate a teacher's role. A guide demonstrates how to do the climbing and invites

---

17. Ronald A. Beers and V. Gilbert Beers, *The Complete Book of Life's Questions: With Answers from the Bible* (Carol Stream, IL: Tyndale House, 2007), 388.

18. Ibid., 632.

19. Ibid.

the trainee climber to copy. Similarly, language teachers can speak to a class about the learning (climbing) process by reporting on their own experiences in learning another language.[20]

There is plenty of published advice about introducing students to learning strategies. One recent overview refers to five categories, any or all of which teacher-leaders could mention in connection with their own language learning.[21] Table 8.1 suggests in the right-hand column what a teacher who leads by example might say to the class.

Table 8.1: Teachers' Self-Reported Strategies

| Type of Strategy | Examples |
| --- | --- |
| Affective strategies (feelings) | *Someone told me I should encourage myself by thinking each day of something I can do better now than I could at the start of the year.* |
| Cognitive strategies (thinking) | *I try to make comparisons and contrasts between phrases in my language and the new one.* |
| Memory strategies | *When it comes to tricky grammar points I sometimes make up a rhyme to help me remember them.* |
| Organizational strategies | *I have colored stick-it pages with new phrases from my week's reading. It might seem strange but I put them on the bathroom mirror.* |
| Social strategies | *I spend a few minutes from time to time trying to talk on the phone with another person in my language class.* |
| Metacognitive strategies (thinking about learning) | *After class my friends and I talk about who is best at what (such as grammar or pronunciation or writing), and then we arrange to go for coffee so that person helps the rest of us.* |

## *Teachers as Salt*

Then there is the invitation to be the salt of the earth (Matt 5:13). Kapolyo's comment on this verse is that "disciples who refuse to live lives that are true to their calling . . . will have no influence and will become unserviceable,

---

20. Tasha Bleistein and Marilyn Lewis, *One-on-One Language Teaching and Learning: Theory and Practice* (London: Palgrave Macmillan, 2015), 33–35.

21. Hall, *Exploring English Language Teaching*, 148–149.

worse than useless."²² We can ask ourselves, in general or specific terms, what being salt might mean in the classroom. If one purpose of salt is to liven or spice up a meal, then how might a "salty" teacher add to the atmosphere? The term suggests proactive behavior that goes far beyond simply reacting to the next incident.

In some lesson planning frameworks, it has been the practice to start with a short section labeled "motivation." While pleased to see this factor highlighted, we might wonder at the implication that motivation is something done at the start of the class and then finished. How can motivation work through all stages of a lesson?

Scrivener has suggestions for creating a classroom atmosphere where students actually want to attend to the lesson, including one series of techniques that apply to situations where the class and teacher are housed in a limited space. Any of these could improve motivation. One is that students need time to let off steam. The language classroom can be a pretty intense place as students move between meeting a new language and using it themselves. Many teachers find that after a short break everyone returns with more energy and interest.[23]

Variety is another way of adding salt to a lesson. Teachers learn to vary the speed, pitch and intonation of their voice. They vary the order of the lesson (revision sometimes first, sometimes last), they vary the teaching method (teach by telling, teach by asking), and so on.

Salt also comes through the teacher's personality. There is no such thing as the "teacher image." God-given gifts of all kinds find their natural expression in the language classroom. It is sad to see someone who is lively and interesting during the coffee break with colleagues, but who puts on a "teaching" demeanor on entering the classroom.

## *The Quality of Wisdom*

A search through several reference books for language teachers fails to find the word "wisdom" in the index. Yet the Bible is not short of advice about being wise. A dictionary often used in English language defines wisdom as

---

22. Joe Kapolyo, "Matthew," in *Africa Bible Commentary*, ed. Tokunboh Adeyemo (Nairobi: WordAlive, 2006), 1146.

23. Scrivener, *Classroom Management Techniques*, 13–25.

"the ability to use your knowledge and experience to make good decisions and judgements."[24] The Bible goes further:

> The wisdom that comes from heaven is first of all pure; then peace-loving, considerate, submissive, full of mercy and good fruit, impartial and sincere. Peacemakers who sow in peace reap a harvest of righteousness. (Jas 3:17–18)

Huge as the challenge is, it can be achieved and it is often visible, as illustrated by one teacher's report:

> I was teaching in a place where it was extremely dangerous to mention our Lord's name. Actions were all that was left to me. On one occasion a student asked, "Why are you and your friends always so kind and happy?" Before I could word a response, another person in the class said, "I know why. It's because you are Christians." I could hardly believe anyone would say that word, and in fact the class leader quickly changed the topic.

Consider discernment, which Beers and Beers call "a stepping-stone to wisdom."[25] They suggest that "Discerning people demonstrate peace, love and gentleness, mercy and goodness – characteristics that come from God."[26] In many classroom moments the Christian teacher longs for swift heaven-sent wisdom or discernment in order to decide, instantly, on a course of action. We turn now to some of these moments.

## Managing Specific Incidents

The requirements for a teacher who wants to manage a class biblically are mounting up. We want to be merciful, even to the less compliant class members, and we want our own actions and attitudes to mirror those we are imposing on the class. Not only must we have no favorites, but we must be sincere, peaceful, loving, gentle, merciful and good. A Christian teacher frequently needs wisdom. Advice, both secular and biblical, moves between the general and the specific, concerning what to do as certain situations arise.

---

24. *Cambridge Advanced Learner's Dictionary* (Cambridge: Cambridge University Press, 2003), 1465.
25. Beers and Beers, *Complete Book*, 217.
26. Ibid., 219.

Scrivener pays attention to particular times when a teacher has to consider what to do, ranging in seriousness from late arrivals to "serious discipline issues."[27] He also lists many possible responses including distraction, turning to sources of support, and even "apologizing when appropriate."[28] Stepping back from the difficult moment, he speaks about "setting the stage for positive behavior,"[29] advice we are examining biblically in this essay. With Scrivener's much longer list in mind, we look now at just four times when wisdom is needed instantly, rather than after an overnight reflection.

## *A Deliberately Defiant Act*

Deliberate defiance is often, but not always, associated with children, and frequently comes from one of those students who are difficult to appreciate. Their behavior takes different forms, but in one way or another, they seem to make learning difficult for others. Proverbs is a frequently quoted source here, including one verse which is popular in pulpits: "Train a child in the way he should go, and when he is old he will not turn from it" (Prov 22:6). Habtu agrees with those who say that "the way he should go" means "a child's unique character and gifts."[30] However, he also believes with Kidner that the main message of the verse is to respect children's individuality rather than their self-will.[31]

Fortunately for teachers of adults, not all references to discipline in Proverbs relate to children. In fact we are told that the book's "purpose is to teach people to live disciplined and successful lives, to help them do what is right, just and fair" (Prov 1:1, 3 NLT).

Teachers need to have in their head the many options available in the face of willful defiance. Returning to textbooks and talking with colleagues from time to time builds up a store of options. Then, experience suggests that in response to the arrow prayer, that almost wordless plea upwards for immediate guidance, the wisdom to choose the best option will come from a higher source than the textbook we followed during our teacher training course or even from

---

27. Scrivener, *Classroom Management Techniques*, 301.
28. Ibid.
29. Ibid.
30. Tewoldemedhin Habtu, "Proverbs," in *Africa Bible Commentary*, ed. Tokunboh Adeyemo (Nairobi: WordAlive, 2006), 803.
31. Derek Kidner, *Proverbs*, reprint, Tyndale Old Testament Commentaries (Leicester: IVP, 1988), 147.

years of accumulated professional experience: "Trust in the Lord with all your heart; do not depend on your own understanding. Seek his will in all you do and he will show you which path to take" (Prov 1:7 NLT).

## *The Repentant Student*

Occasionally a student who has been difficult seems to be sorry. The parable of the prodigal son comes to mind here. Of course, it is worth noting that this student may also be the defiant student and that the penitence, though genuine, may be having a second or third airing. What is the Christian teacher's response?

C. S. Lewis had this to say: "I remember Christian teachers telling me long ago that I must hate a bad man's actions, but not hate the bad man; or, as they would say, hate the sin but love the sinner."[32] This biblical-sounding piece of advice was actually first used by Saint Augustine, according to Serpa:

> It's from St. Augustine. His Letter 211 (c. 424) contains the phrase *Cum dilectione hominum et odio vitiorum*, which translates roughly to "With love for mankind and hatred of sins." The phrase has become more famous as "love the sinner but hate the sin" or "hate the sin and not the sinner" (the latter form appearing in Mohandas Gandhi's 1929 autobiography).[33]

The essence of the message is to separate our feelings about the behavior from our feelings about the student. As one child wrote in an end-of-year thank-you note to her Christian teacher, "Even when we are naughty and you have to sort us out you look as if you like us."

## *The "Smart" Questioner*

This behavior can come from adult students as well as from children. The student appears to be asking a trick question, in an attempt to catch the teacher out. There are many reasons for behaving in as godly a way as possible, one being that the questioner is not the only one listening. If the question has been heard by the rest of the class, they will be watching your response. Here are two options.

---

32. C. S. Lewis, *Mere Christianity* (New York: Macmillan, 1952), 102.
33. Vincent Serpa, "Who Said, 'Love the Sinner, Hate the Sin'?," *Catholic Answers*, accessed 11 August 2014, http://www.catholic.com/catholic-login-status.

Jesus's frequent response to the Pharisees' questions suggests one move: answer a question with a question. This can be done respectfully and can lead to weeding out the genuine question from the rest. At other times it is possible to act as if you think the question is sincere (which occasionally it is), even putting your decision into words, "I'm going to assume you really want to know the answer to that question." As in all these instances, your attitude will probably speak louder than your words.

## *That's Not Fair!*

We recall the impartiality urged by James (3:17, 18). All the logical thinking about the difference between treating everyone the same (being fair) and yet taking individual cases into account by making exceptions comes into play during snap second decision making. Students are quick to detect favoritism. Giving a reason for your "unfair" action can sometimes soothe hurt feelings, but it is not always a good idea to set up a contest in which you have the trump card.

One childhood memory does not relate to behavior in the classroom, but to the way one of our teachers responded to a "that's not fair" incident reported to her. The conversation between teacher and one of our classmates was overheard by all of us.

"Someone's stolen my lunch money."

"Where did you put it?"

"In my blazer pocket."

"And where was your blazer?"

"In the cloakroom."

"Do you remember what we recited this morning in assembly?"

[At that time in our country even state schools had hymns, Bible reading and prayers each morning.]

"You mean *Our Father*?"

"Yes. Start saying it and I'll stop you when you reach the relevant part."

The girl recited the prayer until she reached the words "Lead us not into temptation."

Then the teacher stopped her. "Today you led some girl into temptation. Maybe her parents didn't have enough food for her lunch or enough money for her to buy it. It was wrong to leave that money in your pocket in the cloakroom."

At the next break several of us discussed the teacher's words. Was she condoning theft? Was she fair to the injured party? During my teaching career, her words have often returned to me as an illustration, among other things, of how there is often more than one possible response to untoward incidents.

## Managing Regular Classroom Routines

We turn next to less dramatic moments. How can teachers manage regular classroom routines in ways that are biblical?

### *Organizing Group Work*

In traditional, teacher-fronted classes, the metaphors for teachers' roles could have included circus director, performer or sergeant major. In today's student-centered language classroom the teacher is not the only player in the game of creating a positive experience. Students' relationships with one another are a large part of what people look forward to (or not) as they walk into the room. Some out-of-class friendships may already exist, but there are ways of making sure that everyone is included in these.

Group work often includes tasks, that important part of the language classroom that allow students to engage with one another. What is so good about students talking to one another? When group work started to become popular in language classrooms, some feared it would lead to people picking up bad habits from one another. Research suggests otherwise, as in the work of Philp et al. into peer interaction. They found a number of benefits from having students talking to one another as part of the language lesson, some relating to social outcomes and others to language results.[34]

There is more time for each student to practice the new language and less embarrassment over mistakes. The talk can be more authentic in the sense that the players are equal. When students make mistakes, everyone works towards

---

34. Jenefer Philp, Rebecca Jane Adams, and Noriko Iwashita, *Peer Interaction and Second Language Learning* (London: Routledge, 2014).

clarification more than correction, as happens when the teacher is in charge. Finally, in terms of the classroom atmosphere, the social aspect is enhanced.

It is one thing to have carefully planned group work, but what can teachers do when the unexpected happens? They might be half an hour into a two-hour lesson where students are working in groups, when two students arrive late. Of course there are many solutions but showing love (1 Cor 13), offering encouragement (1 Thess 5:11) and exercising self-control (Gal 5:22) are three broad principles. Perhaps "assume the best till you know the worst" is a piece of folk advice that has some biblical underpinning in those verses. Any of the following solutions might demonstrate that love and self-control:

- Invite them each to join a different group.
- Spend time helping them catch up before joining in.
- Ask them to sit together and read the instructions. Tell them they can catch up during report back time.

### *Flexibility in Lesson Planning*

Lesson planning is one important element in any pre-service course for language teachers. Yet managing a class also involves flexibility or, as it has been labeled in a more professional sounding term, "interactive lesson planning," Why might a teacher change plans halfway through a session?

Two of us who were interested in this question monitored our own "mind-changing" over a period of a few weeks with an academic writing class. We categorized our reasons into pedagogical and organizational, the pedagogic including both affective and cognitive causes. In one instance, a class needed cheering up after a serious talk on the results of plagiarism, and in another, a student suggested a change in the plan. Although the study had no biblical basis, re-reading the article shows biblical injunctions of encouraging others, showing mercy and, of course, reflecting love as important elements in moment-to-moment classroom decisions.[35]

In a recent workshop for language teachers, I invited people to consider what principles might guide their decision making in departing from a lesson plan for one of the following prompts:

- You notice that some students in the back row are inattentive.
- A question shows that someone did not understand your explanation.

---

35. Martin White and Marilyn Lewis, "I Changed My Mind: Teachers' Interactive Decision Making," *Guidelines* 26, no. 1 (2004): 4–9.

- You suddenly think of a more interesting activity.
- Students take longer than you had expected to complete a task.
- Not enough students have done the homework.
- Too much time is being spent moving from one grouping to another.
- The task they have started doing seems too easy.
- You seem to be doing too much of the same thing.

A number of answers were suggested. However, we were all willing to admit that in reality our reactions to some of these situations can easily be negative: annoyance at the inattentive ones, impatience at those who were slow to understand or complete a task and so on. Blaming others is easier in the classroom than in most other areas of life, but a check on the fruits of the Spirit suggests alternative responses.

## *Asking Questions*

One part of the classroom language of teachers is asking questions. These can have many purposes. Consider, for example, the following examples.

- Who can tell me one way of asking for things politely?
- So what's the best answer to the question . . . ?
- Anyone get that answer wrong?
- Do I hear someone talking?
- Why don't you people listen when I explain something?

Students learn to distinguish between questions requiring an answer and those that are rhetorical, open-ended and closed questions, questions relating to lesson content and those asked for management reasons. Students as young as kindergarten age very quickly learn that questions like these are all normal ways that teachers speak. They will often incorporate them into their games when they play school with their dolls and animals.

Teachers' language has come under the scrutiny in the current trend in language teaching towards authenticity. This term applies to the tasks we set for learners, to the situations in which language is presented and, of course, to the language itself. As an aside, when I went to study at university in France as an adult, it turned out that I was using a tense of the verb which had disappeared, as people told me, "before World War II." (To clarify, this was before I was born.) Asking authentic questions in the language classroom creates the sense that this is a real part of life, rather than a museum. For example, questions can be used as a means of leading students to make discoveries about language. The teacher can introduce such a session with words like these.

> Today, instead of telling you the rules for talking about . . . , I'm going to ask you some questions to help you discover the rules for yourself. This will take a bit longer than just telling you, but it means you will remember the rules better."

Immediately there is a sense of cooperative learning. The teacher has announced what is going to happen and why. Of course on other days the method and reason for it will be different but the students can once again have these steps explained to them.

Teachers do not always know how they sound to their students. Doing some action research can provide answers. One teacher chose to examine her classroom questioning by recording herself as she asked students about their understanding in the course of an Indonesian language lesson. Here are some of the questions she heard herself asking:

- Ok. Do you now understand the functions of _____ and _____?
- [Reads sentence from course book.] Any problems there?
- You asked why we can't use _____, didn't you?
- Oh. Here, listen. Here is a question. Can you repeat that please?[36]

In her self-critical analysis of these and many other questions, she felt that she often discouraged a cooperative learning atmosphere in a number of ways. For example, asking a closed question ("Do you now understand . . . ?") meant that only those who did understand were likely to nod their heads. Asking for any problems, she found, was followed by a two-second pause before she moved on, again discouraging any genuine questions. More positively, she was pleased to note that she reframed one student's question to make sure she had understood it, and she called the whole class's attention to another student's question before starting to answer it, thereby implying that the question was a good one.

## Conclusion

As we have seen, the topic of classroom management is addressed in many books for teachers. Our question has been how we can develop the traits

---

36. Hong Sing Tjoo and Marilyn Lewis, "Spontaneous Grammar Explanations," *Babel* 33, no. 3 (1998): 23.

recommended both secularly and biblically. We have also touched on the idea of learning from examples, both positive and negative, which we have experienced ourselves as learners. Inevitably there will be points where the reader might have thought, "Why isn't there a clear answer of what to do in this situation?" Just as our Lord did not have a pat answer that he reiterated to all questioners, so we have suggested that there is often more than one possible reaction to a situation.

In the end, lives that are put daily into God's hands will have solutions come to them which rise above their own wisdom. Teachers, like everyone else, will also make mistakes. As long as we are still on earth, we will continue to have end-of-day moments when we ask ourselves, "Why on earth did I do or say that? It would have been so much better to do something else." Forgive yourself! He will. Learn from your mistakes.

Wright, whose discussion was referred to earlier, raised three questions about how to grow professionally: "How can teachers be assisted in learning *during* their working lives? How do they continue learning? What opportunities are available to them?"[37] This essay is one small attempt to respond to the first question by sampling biblical references to discipline and leadership. What about the continued learning? How can teachers prepare for their ongoing roles as assiduously as a new teacher prepares tomorrow's lessons? If the task were to be done in our own strength, we would have resignations at the first tricky classroom situation.

For the Christian teacher, three forms of ongoing learning come to mind: reading the Scriptures, talking to God and turning to others who have been put in our path as mentors or supporters. These people can include the many writers who have prepared thoughtful commentaries on the Bible. Being steeped in biblical teachings is a process that continues throughout life as we search the Scriptures: "Your laws please me; they give me wise advice" (Ps 119:24 NLT). In our reading we find many examples that feed into wise and God-given classroom management.

Second, this reading is supported by prayer: "[Daniel] prayed three times a day, just as he had always done" (Dan 6:10 NLT). With the psalmist we can ask in our daily devotions, "Show me the right path, O Lord; point out the road for me to follow" (Ps 25:4 NLT). These prayers will be both the ongoing prayers to be made kind, merciful and so on, and also the arrow prayers referred to above, those we send up in the heat of the moment when a decision cannot wait for

---

37. Wright, *Classroom Management*, 284 (emphasis original).

the evening prayer time. If teachers are fortunate, they also have others to turn to although, as Reheboam discovered when he was given contradictory advice from two sources (1 Kgs 12:8), heavenly wisdom must often come into play.

Finally, here is a specific suggestion for taking up the challenge of ongoing professional development: examine classroom management as personal or group Bible study. Take a recent book on the topic and check the key terms it uses throughout. For instance, Scrivener has references to the authority of the teacher, the classroom environment, discipline and learner-centered approaches, among many thought-provoking headings.[38] Wright's index points to sections on affective difficulties, social forces, learner anxiety and teachers' beliefs, to mention just a few.[39] The teacher wanting to think further could take these terms and examine each of them scripturally. How does the recent educational advice match scriptural principles?

The Bible may not include a sentence starting "When you turn round from the board and note a rugby scrum forming at the back of a room . . ." but there is no shortage of advice for relating to one another for the twenty-first-century language teacher.

## Bibliography

Beers, Ronald A., and V. Gilbert Beers. *The Complete Book of Life's Questions: With Answers from the Bible*. Carol Stream, IL: Tyndale, 2007.

Bleistein, Tasha, and Marilyn Lewis. *One-on-One Language Teaching and Learning: Theory and Practice*. London: Palgrave Macmillan, 2015.

Bosch, David J. *Transforming Mission: Paradigm Shifts in Theology of Mission*. Maryknoll, NY: Orbis, 1991.

*Cambridge Advanced Learner's Dictionary*. Cambridge: Cambridge University Press, 2003.

Dormer, Jan Edwards. *Teaching English in Missions: Effectiveness and Integrity*. Pasadena, CA: William Carey Library, 2011.

Habtu, Tewoldemedhin. "Proverbs." In *Africa Bible Commentary*. Edited by Tokunboh Adeyemo. Nairobi: WordAlive, 2006.

Hall, Graham. *Exploring English Language Teaching: Language in Action*. London: Routledge, 2011.

Kapolyo, Joe. "Matthew." In *Africa Bible Commentary*. Edited by Tokunboh Adeyemo. Nairobi: WordAlive, 2006.

---

38. Scrivener, *Classroom Management Techniques*.
39. Wright, *Classroom Management*.

Kidner, Derek. *Proverbs*. Reprint. Tyndale Old Testament Commentaries. Leicester: IVP, 1988.
Lewis, C. S. *Mere Christianity*. New York: Macmillan, 1952.
Mazumdar, Amvika Charan. *The Indian National Evolution: A Brief Survey of the Origin and Progress of the Indian National Congress*. Madras: G. A. Natesan, 1915.
Philp, Jenefer, Rebecca Jane Adams, and Noriko Iwashita. *Peer Interaction and Second Language Learning*. London: Routledge, 2014.
Scrivener, Jim. *Classroom Management Techniques*. Cambridge: Cambridge University Press, 2012.
Serpa, Vincent. "Who Said, 'Love the Sinner, Hate the Sin'?" *Catholic Answers*. Accessed 11 August 2014. http://www.catholic.com/catholic-login-status.
Snow, Donald B. *English Teaching as Christian Mission: An Applied Theology*. Scottdale, PA: Herald Press, 2001.
Stott, John R. W. *Christian Mission in the Modern World*. 2nd ed. London: Falcon, 1977.
Tjoo, Hong Sing, and Marilyn Lewis. "Spontaneous Grammar Explanations." *Babel* 33, no. 3 (1998): 22–25.
White, Martin, and Marilyn Lewis. "I Changed My Mind: Teachers' Interactive Decision Making." *Guidelines* 26, no. 1 (2004): 4–9.
Wright, Tony. *Classroom Management in Language Education*. Basingstoke, Hampshire, UK: Palgrave Macmillan, 2005.
Yancey, Philip. *Vanishing Grace*. London: Hodder & Stoughton, 2014.

# 9

# Dialogue, Divinity, and Deciphering the Self: Calling Out God's Image in the Language Classroom

*Will Bankston*

Reflecting on the death of his good friend Charles Williams and its effects on his friendship with J. R. R. Tolkien, C. S. Lewis pens one of his most profound passages. He writes, "In each of my friends there is something that only some other friend can fully bring out. By myself I am not large enough to call the whole man into activity . . . Now that Charles is dead, I shall never again see Ronald's reaction to a specifically Caroline joke. Far from having more of Ronald, having him 'to myself' now that Charles is away, I have less of Ronald."[1]

Lewis is illuminating one of the great potentials of dialogue. Every verbal exchange between two or more persons "calls out" specific parts of its participants. In the above case, there exists something inside Tolkien, referred to here as Ronald, that only Williams's sense of humor could elicit. And with

---

1. C. S. Lewis, *The Four Loves* (New York: Harcourt, 1960), 92.

Williams's passing, that part of Tolkien will lay dormant for the rest of his life. As Lewis laments, "I have less of Ronald." Even more, a kind of unveiling accompanies this calling out. As "a specifically Caroline joke" draws out its own unique response from Tolkien, Tolkien himself finds out more fully what dwells inside him. He has come to know himself better. And of course, this process is not limited to the joys of friendship. All manner of dialogue, whether the words be common, kind, or cutting, expose our hiddenness.

This phenomenon has direct bearing on the language classroom where dialogues constitute a staple of educational instruction. As teachers, we aim to produce communicative classrooms, remembering that the ultimate goal of language learning is communication. Naturally requiring mutual exchange, dialogues push us along toward this pedagogical pursuit. However, dialogues are more than mere mediums. They are also models. Regardless of their intentions, they have a prescriptive effect on how students speak in the target language and culture. So then, reflecting on Lewis's insights, we must ask ourselves whether or not we are modeling dialogues that "call out" the most important aspects of a student's self. Otherwise, the self-knowledge we elicit will likely be little more than arbitrary. For instance, the insight gained into one's self by explaining which merchandise he or she would purchase from an advertisement prompt is not meaningless knowledge, and, in fact, it relies on essential grammar, vocabulary, and functions. But, if that is the only kind of self-knowledge that our classroom produces, we have devalued not only dialogue, but also its divine source and redemptive purpose.

At this point, the relation between classrooms that call out the self and the domain of theology may not be clear. To be sure though, there is a direct connection. John Calvin's insights are of particular importance here. He begins *The Institutes of the Christian Religion* with a chapter entitled "The Knowledge of God the Creator,"[2] whose first two subsections are "Without Knowledge of Self There Is No Knowledge of God" and "Without Knowledge of God There Is No Knowledge of Self." From the outset, Calvin wants us to grasp the inseparable nature of these two forms of knowledge. As he writes, "In the first place, no one can look upon himself without immediately turning his thoughts to the contemplation of God, in whom he 'lives and moves' [Acts 17:28]."[3] By recognizing that "the mighty gifts with which we are endowed

---

2. John Calvin, *Institutes of the Christian Religion*, ed. John T. McNeill, trans. Ford Lewis Battles (Louisville, KY: Westminster John Knox, 1960), 1.1.1.

3. Ibid.

are hardly from ourselves,"[4] all the while perceiving our "ignorance, vanity, poverty, infirmity, and – what's more – depravity and corruption,"[5] we are directed toward knowledge of God. As the crown of his creation, we have the privilege of bearing the very image of God. Even more, despite our best efforts at repression, we cannot help but know this.

Paul makes this inevitable, existential awareness explicit in Romans 1:20, declaring, "For his invisible attributes, namely, his eternal power and divine nature, have been clearly perceived, ever since the creation of the world, in the things that have been made."[6] When we look into ourselves, examining our "mighty gifts," we confront the evidence of his handiwork and even the image of himself that he has imprinted upon us. However, at the same time, we also find the results of the fall, the sin that has infected every bit of our being. This, too, directs us to God. Calvin knows "we cannot seriously aspire to him before we begin to become displeased with ourselves."[7] And so within ourselves we find the consequences of a good creation, created by a good creator, which, through rebellion, willfully subjected itself to sin. We find potentials that reach beyond the most naïve optimism juxtaposed with corruptions that delve deeper than the most cynical pessimism. We are complicated, incomprehensible even to ourselves. But just as the length and angle of a shadow have much to tell us about their solar source, so, too, will true self-knowledge always point us to the knowledge of God. Calvin assures us, "Accordingly, the knowledge of ourselves not only arouses us to seek God, but also, as it were, leads us by the hand to find him."[8] And herein lies the connection between dialogues and theology.

As well-designed dialogues elicit essential and accurate self-knowledge, they likewise elicit knowledge of God. And so, we must never underestimate the truly transformative power of dialogue. Granted, classroom activities will rarely if ever attain the authenticity occasioned by Tolkien and Williams, but the difference is one of degree, not direction. In what follows we will investigate dialogue and its effect on the self through a thoroughly theological lens. This will take us through a range of interdisciplinary enclaves and pains will be

---

4. Ibid.
5. Ibid.
6. All of the Scripture quotations in the essay are from the ESV.
7. John Calvin, *Institutes*, 1.1.1.
8. Ibid.

taken to directly apply our gleanings to the language classroom. Toward this end, we will strive to answer three important questions:

- Why is dialogue possible?
- Why is dialogue purposeful?
- Why is dialogue powerful?

To be fair, the possibility, purpose, and power of dialogue, just like the knowledge of the self and the knowledge of God, cannot be so neatly pried apart as our method might suggest. In fact, since what follows is based on the inherent interconnectedness of these two forms of knowledge, our three attributes of dialogue will be likewise intertwined. A dialogue's possibility will presuppose its purpose and power, and so will its purpose and power presuppose the other two. However, we must start somewhere and the first piece of our triad, possibility, ushers us immediately to him who makes all things possible, namely our Triune God.

## Why Is Dialogue Possible?

The short answer to why dialogue is possible might be summed up in the assertion that God is who God is and he has made us in his image. Regarding dialogue, he is the God who dialogues and has made us to do the same. Of course, lurking in this statement are questions such as: what does it mean for God to dialogue, how is God's dialogue different from ours, and does God dialogue with us? And perhaps, from the outset, some may feel uncomfortable with the thought of God dialoguing. This is certainly warranted if one understands our use of dialogue as a kind of negotiation in which two sides strive for a common agreement, both sides changing their minds in the process. I believe that kind of dialogue, vital as it is, only happens between humans.[9] However, if readers disagree with this theological position, it will not affect their reception of this essay's more general use of dialogue. For our purposes, we are speaking of dialogue in its most basic form, which accords with its common use in the language classroom. That is, any verbal exchange between persons. But this is not without purpose, and, as we will see, there is a deep change enacted in humans who properly pursue dialogue, a change that, like all possibilities, rests in God. Therefore, to begin formulating answers

---

9. For a supporting theological analysis of biblical accounts that would seem to suggest that God does change his mind, see Kevin J. Vanhoozer, *Remythologizing Theology: Divine Action, Passion, and Authorship* (Cambridge: Cambridge University Press, 2010), ch. 1.

to the questions raised in this section, we must turn our attention to our dialogical God.

## *Divinity and Dialogue*

The Russian literary critic, Mikhail Bakhtin, in describing the back and forth, dialogical nature of all language, makes a definite distinction between God and humanity. From birth we are immersed and socialized in a web of verbal exchanges to which we must inevitably interact. Contrasting man's linguistic entanglement with God's position outside this dialogical web, Bakhtin writes of mankind, "He is not, after all, the first speaker, the one who disturbs the eternal silence of the universe."[10] Bakhtin is right to understand human dialogue as a finite act. We can never fully transcend the particularities of our time and place, contexts that must always frame our communication. However, in a properly theological sense, God is not a being that exists in "eternal silence." Rather, God is triune.

Existing as three persons, God exists in an eternal, Trinitarian relationship of love and, within that rapturous delight, he is eternally able to commune with himself. Love therefore is eternal and prior to creation. That is, love presupposes multiple persons in relationship, and if God existed as only one person, then love would be contingent on his creation of other persons. Dialogue, like love, also requires multiple persons. And so creation made neither love nor communicative exchanges possible, but they exist as an outpouring of the love and communion that transpires eternally in our Triune God.

New Testament scholar Vern Poythress directs our attention to a glimpse of what we might call the Trinitarian dialogue in John 16:13–15.[11] In this

---

10. Sue Vice, *Introducing Bakhtin* (Manchester: Manchester University Press, 1997), 52.

11. Vern Poythress, *In the Beginning Was the Word: Language – A God-Centered Approach* (Wheaton, IL: Crossway, 2009), 18. However, when we speak of God dialoguing with words, we do well to stay within the confines of the economic Trinity, rather than to project this particular kind of verbal exchange onto the immanent Trinity. That is, God in his outward "economic" actions towards us for the sake of redemption has revealed verbal dialogical interactions between the three divine persons. We must be cautious though in ascribing "dialogue" (as we understand it) to God in his inward "immanent" actions, that is, as he is in himself. However, as Vanhoozer points out, "[t]he way the Father and Son interact in time (i.e. the economy) corresponds to the relationship of Father and Son in eternity" (Kevin J. Vanhoozer, *Faith Speaking Understanding: Performing the Drama of Doctrine* [Louisville, KY: Westminster John Knox, 2014], 75). Accordingly, while we must not speculate on the specifics of God's inward interactions, we are sure that there are communicative exchanges amid the communion of the divine persons in the immanent Trinity. Accordingly, when speaking of God dialoguing with himself, we do well to keep this communicative caveat in mind.

passage Jesus tells his disciples of the Spirit's role in testifying about him. Amid this description, Jesus tells us of the Spirit that "whatever he hears he will speak." Poythress points out that the Spirit hears the words of the Father about the Son, and may even hear the words of the Son as well. Accordingly, Poythress asserts, "the persons of the Trinity function as members of a language community among themselves."[12] And certainly we cannot forget the glimpses we are shown of the dialogue of creation. As God creates man in his own image, he says, "Let us make man in our image, after our likeness" (Gen 1:26). This image, just like him, is dialogical.

We might also consider the prayers that Jesus offers to the Father, from the high priestly prayer of John 17 to the agony of Gethsemane. Even more, as Jesus emerges from the waters of baptism, the heavens open as the Father tells him, "You are my Son; with you I am well pleased" (Luke 3:22). However, in stark contrast, as Jesus suffers on the cross, enduring the rejection that we deserve from the Father, the darkened sky is silent, even to his cries of "My God, my God, why have you forsaken me?" (Matt 27:46). It appears as if for a moment, the divine dialogue has been hushed, and this silence is the sign of ultimate suffering.[13]

### *An Analogical Understanding of the Divine Dialogue*

Of course, we must exercise caution in our understanding of dialogue if we apply it to an activity exercised in the Trinity. Recognizing the Godhead as beyond human conceptualization, we should proceed carefully and ensure that our efforts are grounded in the framework of the Cappadocian fathers. These three early-church theologians fitted together the much-debated ontological categories of "nature" and "person" into the formulation Christendom has ever since affirmed as orthodoxy. That is, the Trinity exists as three persons in one nature. Gregory of Nazianzus, one of these fathers, writes that the three persons of the Godhead are "not unequal, in substances or natures, neither

---

12. Vern Poythress, *In the Beginning*, 18.

13. I say "appears" in light of what is referred to as the *extra Calvinisticum*. That is, the eternal Son was not contained within the finitude of humanity and so, to cite one such implication, the communion between the divine persons was never ruptured or breached throughout Christ's earthly life, even amid the suffering of his human nature.

increased nor diminished by superiorities or inferiorities; in every respect equal, in every respect the same."[14]

The primary notion of person here is one grounded in Trinitarian relations and it should be kept distinct from modern, psychological concepts of human personhood. Nonetheless, when we consider human dialogue, we presuppose both a sameness and an otherness that makes such interaction both possible and purposeful. We dialogue with fellow humans, but with humans other than ourselves. The Trinity, too, exhibits qualities of otherness and sameness amid its differing persons of the same unindividuated nature. Surely any communication carried out in the Trinity, however, cannot be adequately framed within the parameters of a human referent. In fact, we commit the mistake of making God in our own image if we posit human dialogue as the rubric for understanding Trinitarian dialogue. Rather we must always cede conceptual priority to God as he has revealed himself in Scripture; for he is the one in whose image we have been made. As such, we must carry out a sensitive balancing act. As theologian Michael Horton writes, "created in God's image, humankind can be described as an analogy of God: similar but never the same."[15] Likewise, in comparing our communication with that of God, Kevin Vanhoozer, pulling from the language of the Fourth Lateran Council, writes, "For the Creator/creature distinction . . . implies a 'still greater dissimilarity than similarity' between God and human beings."[16] We are finite and so is our dialogue, as Bakhtin observed. In contrast, God is infinite and so must be his dialogue. However, we cannot forget Calvin's insight into the inseparable connection between the knowledge of ourselves and the knowledge of God. We bear his image and, marred though it is by sin, that image still points us back to him.

## *Joining the Eternal Dialogue to Ours*

Accordingly we are left with two kinds of dialogue, that which takes place within the Trinity and its finite analogue that is carried out among humanity. However, without the intrusive self-communication of God, never the twain

---

14. "On Holy Baptism," Oration 40.41, in NPNF 2, 7: 375, quoted in Gregg R. Allison, *Historical Theology: An Introduction to Christian Doctrine* (Grand Rapids, MI: Zondervan, 2011), 240.

15. Michael Horton, *Introducing Covenant Theology* (Grand Rapids, MI: Baker Academic, 2006), 22.

16. Vanhoozer, *Remythologizing Theology*, 25.

shall meet. With this qualification in mind, there is a sense in which we can affirm Bakhtin's remark on God's disturbance of eternal silence. As Karl Barth writes, "God did not need to speak to us. What He says by Himself and to Himself from eternity to eternity would really be said just as well and even better without our being there, as speech which for us would be eternal silence."[17] That is, we would have no access to the eternal communication of the Godhead by way of our own efforts. It rests fully on his initiative, and we receive it solely as a grace. So high above our finitude, and present sinfulness, does such speech rise that, left to our own devices, it would be as "eternal silence." In effect, if God speaks to us, he must accommodate himself to our creaturely capacities, an action which Calvin likens to a nurse who must "lisp" with an infant.[18]

But thankfully, since our creation, humanity has received this communicative grace of God, through which he brings us into dialogue with himself. Cornelius Van Til points out that humanity has always required such "supernatural, positive thought-communication on the part of God to man."[19] It has proved a natural necessity of the human condition from Eden onward. That is, "God spoke to Adam even in paradise."[20] Even before the fall, we needed the words of God, and, in his love, he supplied them. And of course, he continues to supply them in and through Scripture. As such, when we doubt not just the content of these words but also their very existence as God's speech, we fall victim to the lie of the serpent. This is why Karl Barth identifies "the presumption to ask, 'Did God say?' (Gen 3:1)" as a "primal error" that ruins theology.[21] Doubting God's speech to us will necessarily shipwreck any and all attempts to know God, and by extension, ourselves. Instead, as Vanhoozer declares, "The proper starting point for Christian theology is God in communicative action."[22]

---

17. Karl Barth, *Church Dogmatics, Vol 1.1, Sections 1–7: The Doctrine of the Word of God*, trans. G. W. Bromiley, G. T. Thomson, and Harold Knight, Study Edition (London; New York: Bloomsbury T&T Clark, 2010), 136.

18. John Calvin, *Institutes*, 1.13.1.

19. Gregg L. Bahnsen, *Van Til's Apologetic: Readings and Analysis* (Philipsburg, NJ: P & R, 1998), 712.

20. Ibid.

21. Karl Barth, *Evangelical Theology: An Introduction*, trans. Grover Foley (New York: Holt, Rinehart & Winston, 1963), 125.

22. Kevin J. Vanhoozer, *The Drama of Doctrine: A Canonical-Linguistic Approach to Christian Theology* (Louisville, KY: Westminster John Knox, 2005), 63.

Investigating creation, what is often called God's general revelation, will occasion much knowledge. To that end, the insights gained from dialogues with those around us certainly fall into this category, as we ourselves are his creation. But does God's speech as our "proper starting point" undercut the importance of our human-to-human dialogues, especially those with no explicit reference to God's speech with us? Calvin makes an important distinction here, distinguishing between the knowledge of God as creator and the knowledge of God as redeemer. As Paul makes clear in Romans 1, we all have knowledge of the former, and as dialogues call out ever deeper parts of ourselves, this knowledge will necessarily deepen, even despite our unrighteous efforts at the opposite. However, the knowledge of God as redeemer requires God's communicative action in and through Scripture. And, as we will see, it alone can bring God as creator into its proper focus, showing us where the fault lies for creation's evident corruption and in whom our hope rests for its certain redemption. But towards that end, the more we learn of ourselves, the more we know that we need a redeemer not only for salvation, but also to understand the complicated cosmos we find ourselves within.

## *Eliciting His Image in the Classroom*

As language instructors, we cannot forget the divine image present in each of our students. Not only does it remind us of the serious stewardship that teaching entails, but it also demands curriculum that calls out this image. However, materials for the language classroom are often chosen according to only one category of appropriateness. That is, they must be the appropriate difficulty for the language proficiency of the learners. Certainly if the materials and the activities they spark prove too easy or difficult for the students, this disconnect will impede learning. And of course, any appropriately graded material must also be implemented with sound teaching principles. But, theologically speaking, this is not enough. We need materials that foster dialogues of deep self-knowledge. Again, our God is the God who dialogues, and he dialogues of nothing arbitrary. As much as feasibly possible, we should dialogue accordingly.

To gain practical perspective of what such anti-arbitrariness might look like in the classroom, we do well to look firsthand into a language learning textbook. Specifically, we will frame the discussion around the speaking classroom, but the same principles of verbal exchange apply to listening, reading, and writing. At the Southeast Asian university at which I recently taught, the most popular textbook series for speaking instruction was *Interchange*. This set of textbooks is well designed and takes students through a range of topics by way of an effective and engaging pedagogy. However, in light of the image we bear, we need to ask whether or not the topics engaged penetrate sufficiently deep into the self. As an example, the thirty-two model dialogues, labeled as *Conversations*, in the fourth edition of *Interchange: Intro*,[23] which is the first book in the series, certainly address a range of topics. Examining this diversity, we might group them into the following twenty categories of self-knowledge:

- Your name
- Your classes
- The items you use, give, and receive
- Where you are from and where you grew up
- Your first language
- The people in your family
- Your age
- Your clothes and appearance
- Your response to bad weather conditions
- The time zone you live in
- The foods you like
- Your job
- Your schedule
- The kind of house or apartment you live in
- The sports you play or like to watch
- Your talents
- How you celebrate your birthday
- Your health
- Directions to places you want to go
- What you do for fun and how you spend your vacations

Surely this is not a bad list, and, in many ways, it is quite comprehensive. However, these topics can tend toward mere surface knowledge of the self. The deeper parts of the person will likely lay dormant. To be fair though, this is not the fault of the textbook. Given the international circulation of such texts, they need to be cross-culturally safe. In a sense, anything more than superficial might enter a minefield of cultural mores as appropriate conduct and questions vary from one people group to another. Composing

---

23. Jack C. Richards, *Interchange: Intro Student's Book*, 4th ed. (Cambridge: Cambridge University Press, 2012).

and implementing a curriculum that calls out the self therefore falls upon the shoulders of culturally competent teachers. With an understanding of what dialogue topics will prove searching but not scandalous, they should seek to impart much more than mere linguistic knowledge. They should strive to make the classroom a site of sincere self-discovery, and, thereby, a place in which students are directed to the God who makes all dialogue possible.

## Why Is Dialogue Purposeful?

Recognizing that dialogue is possible because we have been made in the image of our dialogical God, we need to inquire into its purpose. We need to know what dialogue is for. We might summarize our answer, quoting the first response from the Westminster Shorter Catechism (a document inherently dialogical in structure) as "To glorify God, and to enjoy him forever." This is the chief end of man and, presumably, all human activities. But, as humans, this purpose will always be fulfilled in degrees, as we find ourselves ever more fit for this end as we progress through the sharpening of present sanctification and on into the never-ending ages of the eschaton. In turn, let us examine dialogue as a vehicle that pushes us along this process of ever increasing fitness for fellowship with God.

### *Knowing the Self through the Other*

The process of being "called out" by dialogue is an integral part of the inevitable human process of *becoming*. For the entirety of our existence, and not just in the present age, we will undergo this transformation, each becoming either more or less like what God intends for humanity. As C. S. Lewis says of this fateful fork in the road, we will either be "a creature which, if you saw it now, you would be strongly tempted to worship, or else a horror and a corruption such as you now meet, if at all, only in a nightmare."[24] Lewis later lays out this existential dichotomy as the difference between growing into "immortal horrors or everlasting splendors."[25] The ultimate purpose of dialogue is to be a tool by which God guides us toward fruition and away from decay. This purpose requires dialogues that elicit deep self-knowledge, the kind that will

---

24. C. S. Lewis, "The Weight of Glory," in *The Weight of Glory and Other Addresses*, 1st Touchstone edition (New York: Simon & Schuster, 1996), 39.

25. Ibid.

most fully bring both our mighty gifts and our corruption into the light of life. Levity, no matter how loquacious, is never enough. We, as language teachers, must never forget this responsibility. Lewis compels us onward, reminding us, "All day long we are, in some degree, helping each other to one or other of these destinations."[26]

Of course, none of us is "large enough to call the whole man into activity."[27] But there is one who is and he gives us the privilege of being used by him to bring out others through the conduit of community. Again, we are always becoming, but he is not. As the great Dutch theologian Herman Bavinck explains, "The contrast between being and becoming marks the difference between the Creator and the creature. Every creature is continually becoming."[28] Similarly, Vanhoozer, when articulating a scripturally sanctioned understanding of perfection, as opposed to our autonomous human conceptualizing of it, writes, "The Bible depicts the perfection of God in terms of the eternal relations and communications between Father, Son, and Spirit and their free and gracious overflow into the realm of created being. There is no higher standard of perfection than God himself in his fully realized being-in-communicative-activity."[29] This "overflow" of God's own Trinitarian dialogue splashes onto us, revitalizing petrified possibilities for the proper kind of human "becoming," the kind that will form us into "everlasting splendors."

To rightly recognize these possibilities for what they are though, we must understand the corruption from which we must be cleansed. In contrast to Vanhoozer's description of "the perfection of God," Martin Luther describes a sinner as "the person curved in on himself,"[30] a posture at utter odds with the eternally other-orientation of each person in the Trinity. And, of course, God knows himself completely. But, ironically, the inward-focused frame that Luther warns against, despite its concentration on the self, blinds the self to the self. Nowhere is more self-focused than hell and, accordingly, no other place has less self-knowledge.

---

26. Ibid.

27. Lewis, *Four Loves*, 92.

28. Herman Bavinck, *The Doctrine of God*, trans. William Hendriksen (Edinburgh: Banner of Truth, 1977 [1951]), 49, quoted in D. A. Carson, *The Difficult Doctrine of the Love of God* (Wheaton, IL: Crossway, 2000), 54–55.

29. Vanhoozer, *Remythologizing Theology*, 483.

30. Michael Reeves, *Delighting in the Trinity: An Introduction to the Christian Faith* (Downers Grove, IL: InterVarsity, 2012), 94.

## *An Apprehensive Apprehension of the Self*

At this point, we do well to think more clearly about what is meant by knowledge in this respect. In his editing of Calvin's *Institutes*, John T. McNeil provides a footnote explaining that by "knowledge," Calvin did not intend only "objective knowledge." This was part of it, but not nearly all of it. McNeil proposes "existential apprehension" as a corresponding, modern-day equivalent.[31] That is, such knowledge awards awareness and understanding of the human condition. And, in a sense, the first step towards this knowledge is the realization of how little we know of ourselves. Even more, that of which we are knowingly ignorant should give us pause. This is what separates true self-knowledge from self-esteemism. Augustine illustrates well this recognition, which we might call *existential apprehensiveness*. Experiencing an alarming coming to terms with himself, he is provoked to profess, "For there is in me a lamentable darkness in which my latent possibilities are hidden from myself, so that my mind, questioning itself upon its own powers, feels that it cannot rightly trust its own report."[32]

What, however, separates this kind of realization from suppositions such as Freud's unconscious? We might compare Augustine's realization with the following bit of deeply delving dialogue from Chaim Potok's novel *The Chosen*, in which two young, devout Jewish boys discuss the principles of psychoanalysis:

> "Our unconscious is not a nice place . . . It's full of repressed fears and hatreds, things we're afraid to bring out in the open."
>
> "And these things rule our lives?"
>
> "According to some psychologists they do."
>
> "You mean these things go on and we don't know anything about them?"
>
> "That's right . . . What's inside of us is the greatest mystery of all."
>
> "That's a pretty sad thing to think about. To be doing things without really knowing why you're doing them."

---

31. Footnote 1 in John Calvin, *Institutes*, 1.1.1.

32. Conf. X, xxxii, quoted in Peter Brown, *Augustine of Hippo: A Biography*, 2nd ed. (Berkeley, CA: University of California Press, 2000), 172.

Danny nodded. "You can find out about it, though. About your unconscious, I mean. That's what psychoanalysis is all about."[33]

In a sense, there is great similarity here between Augustine and Freud. But ultimately this is because both have simply opened their eyes to the world around them and inside them. They both know that something is wrong with the world and that this something lurks even deep within themselves. As Tim Keller explains, no one can navigate life with any degree of coherence without answers, however provisional or misdirected, to certain essential questions, one of which might be paraphrased as: what is wrong with the world?[34] Regarding Freud and Augustine, they both know that something is wrong, that things are not the way they should be. And this is the presupposition of the above question. That is, before we ask what is wrong, we must know that something is indeed wrong. But Freud's answer to this question, his diagnosis of the unconscious, veers from reality, and so his treatment, psychoanalysis, is equally askew.

## *Simplistic Structures for Complex Selves*

However, as we interact with others through sincere dialogue, we gather more and more data points related to this question. We uncover clues as to what is wrong with the world and, in effect, ourselves. Speaking from personal experience, I never thought I struggled with anger and frustration till I was married and I did not begin to realize the immensity of this struggle until I had children. Years of family interactions have called out parts of myself that need to be understood and confronted. And these sobering bits of self-knowledge are not obstructions or obstacles. They are mercies. As Augustine prays, "I beseech You, God, to show my full self to myself."[35] One of the most effective ways that God shows us ourselves is through such dialogue with others.

But, again, along with corruptions, dialogues also call our mighty gifts into light. If all that was ever elicited from us was corruption, we might be inclined to believe the psychoanalytic assessment. Literary theorist Terry Eagleton writes of Freud's prognosis, "His estimate of human capacities is on the whole conservative and pessimistic: we are dominated by a desire for

---

33. Chaim Potok, *The Chosen* (New York: Ballantine, 1967), 156.

34. Timothy Keller, *Every Good Endeavor: Connecting Your Work to God's Work* (New York, NY: Dutton, 2012), 157.

35. Conf. X, xxxvii, quoted in Brown, *Augustine of Hippo,* 172.

gratification and an aversion to anything which might frustrate it."[36] And this is the inevitable simplicity to which human philosophies ultimately succumb. They will always expound human nature monotonously, with either dreary pessimism or bland optimism. In Freud's case, he certainly errs on the former. However, and here rests one of the core truths about Christianity, the pessimism of human philosophies does not dive low enough nor does their naivety reach high enough.[37] That is, Freud, in his pessimism, is not pessimistic enough. The trouble is not that we want "gratification." That would be a much too minor thing to account for the wickedness in the world. Rather the problem is that we want to be God. And herein lies the crux of our corruption.

Philosopher Albert Wolters casts considerable light upon this dark depravity, warning us, "The great danger is always to single out some aspect or phenomenon of God's good creation and identify it, rather than the alien intrusion of human apostasy, as the villain in the drama of human life."[38] He goes on to give some examples of what form this singling out has historically taken. To cite a few examples: Plato blamed the body, Rousseau human culture, and Heidegger technology.[39] However, only our own rebellion against God's godship, what D. A. Carson has called the "de-godding of God,"[40] can adequately answer the question of what is wrong with the world. It is the "alien intrusion" of human revolt against God that brought sin into God's good creation. It has left us, as well as the rest of creation that we steward, with a complex mix of God-reflecting goodness and sin-infected infirmity. Without this understanding, as Wolter explains, we will condemn some good part of creation as the culprit, something that God made and declared good. In so doing, we not only try to fit a complex reality into an overly simplistic structure, we also implicate God rather than ourselves as the cause of our corruption. And this, too, is just another way in which we attempt to throw God from his throne.

---

36. Terry Eagleton, *Literary Theory: An Introduction* (Minneapolis, MN: University of Minnesota Press, 1996), 139.

37. This notion is taken from Timothy Keller, *Rejecting the Real Jesus,* Podcast audio. Redeemer Sermon Store, MP3, 22 September 1996, http://sermons2.redeemer.com/sermons/rejecting-real-jesus.

38. Albert Wolters, *Creation Regained: Biblical Basics for a Reformational Worldview,* 2nd ed. (Grand Rapids, MI: Eerdmans, 2005), 61.

39. Ibid.

40. D. A. Carson, "Three More Books on the Bible: A Critical Review" in *Collected Writings on Scripture* (Wheaton, IL: Crossway, 2010), 297.

## *The Enmity and Ignorance of Interpretative Rebellion*

It might seem that we have veered far from the topic of dialogue, but this context of "de-godding" is essential in rightly arranging the self-knowledge that dialogues elicit. As dialogues reveal more and more our own selves to us, we must interpret these pieces of information. Diverse fields of study have shown that there are no such things as "brute facts," data devoid of interpretation. That is, facts do not speak for themselves. They are only understood inside of an interpretative framework. The theologian and apologist Cornelius Van Til,[41] the literary theorist Terry Eagleton,[42] and even the philosopher of science Thomas Kuhn are all in agreement on this.[43]

And so when dialogues bring our gifts and corruption into the light, how will we arrange this data? Will we attribute the goodness we find to a masked "desire for gratification?" Will we blame the badness on something outside ourselves, on something like a Marxist notion of class struggle? Will we interpret it according to the prevailing norms of our respective societies? In the case of my own national culture, such norms would likely attribute the good wholly to my own nature and blame the bad on some external and repressive interference. My culture assures me that, deep down in myself, there is only goodness. However, not only can this not account for the complexity of reality, it also contradicts the interpretative framework supplied by Scripture.

In turn, the question of interpretative frameworks leaves us, in a sense, at the same crossroad as Adam and Eve, as they decided whether to trust God or the serpent as to the workings of the world.[44] As dialogues produce self-knowledge, we are prodded to one of two paths. We may try to rebelliously stuff this information into a framework that is much too simple and of our own making. Or we may let God's word arrange these data points according to the true shape of the complex world that he has created and we have corrupted.

Furthermore, in our fallen state, we stand not only ignorant of God, but also in enmity with him. John Webster makes a similar point explaining that we can never forget the role that sin plays in understanding and embracing the truth of God and ourselves. When genuinely grasped, it necessarily brings repentance before and reconciliation with the one, true God. As Webster writes,

---

41. Bahnsen, *Van Til's Apologetic*, 38.

42. Eagleton, *Literary Theory*, 75.

43. Thomas Kuhn, *The Structure of Scientific Revolutions*, 3rd ed. (Chicago: University of Chicago Press, 1996), 111.

44. Bahnsen, *Van Til's Apologetic*, 152.

"Calvin's account of Scripture in Book I of the *Institutes* is part of a broader and soteriologically oriented presentation of the knowledge of God through which alone we are restored to truthful self-knowledge."[45] All of our faculties, including those involved with knowing, have been polluted by the alien infection of sin. And so, "For Calvin, the cognitive activities of humankind are caught up in the drama of sin and redemption: far from being a reliable faculty or set of skills unaffected by our depravity, human knowing is a field of vicious and willful rejection of God."[46]

We naturally want to usurp God and, therefore, we strive to interpret all knowledge, including that of the self, according to frameworks of our own choosing. As teachers in the language classroom, calling out knowledge of the self will always fight against this ignorance, showing the inadequacy of any merely human framework. However, only the Holy Spirit can turn this enmity into embrace, opening students' hearts to seek the God who, alone, can tell them who they are. Towards this end, every bit of self-knowledge is a means by which the Holy Spirit can incite such love.

So then, modifying a notion from literary theorist Stanley Fish, the question becomes, to which interpretative community does each person belong? Which authorities decide what is good and proper interpretation for our particular group? As Fish says of members of each such community, "a way of thinking, a form of life, shares us, and implicates us in a world of already-in-place objects, purposes, goals, procedures, values, and so on."[47] In this sense, we may take the path of pride, sharing a form of life cut off from God, immersed in mere manmade mirages and interpreting the world through illusions rather than illumination. Or, by God's grace, we may be taken up into the eternal interpretative community, the only one that precedes the actual "world of already-in-place objects," namely the Trinity. And to be sure, joining the interpretative community of the Godhead is salvation, enjoying the eternal fellowship with the Father, Son, and Holy Spirit, and interpreting everything accordingly. This, again, is our chief end. However, even amid this community, we do not cast out all mystery from ourselves. But, thankfully, just as God knows himself fully, he knows us to our deepest depths and the Spirit draws

---

45. John Webster, *Holy Scripture: A Dogmatic Sketch* (Cambridge, UK: Cambridge University Press, 2003), 70–71.

46. Ibid.

47. Stanley Fish, *The Stanley Fish Reader*, ed. H. A. Veeser (Malden, MA: Wiley-Blackwell, 1999), 41.

us into a dialogue of prayerful petition with a fullness of self-knowledge that we ourselves could never muster. As Romans assures us,

> Likewise the Spirit helps us in our weakness. For we do not know what to pray for as we ought, but the Spirit himself intercedes for us with groanings too deep for words. And he who searches hearts knows what is the mind of the Spirit, because the Spirit intercedes for the saints according to the will of God. (Rom 8:26–27)

And such dialogue, too deep for human words, propels us along toward the ultimate purpose of all dialogue, which is the unending process of becoming an "eternal splendor." So while the cause of our corruption takes us lower than any human philosopher dares to go, God likewise lifts us higher than even the most optimistic manmade meanderings. These are the heights and depths of Christianity, which alone can account for the complexity of the self. As Lewis observes, "I believe in Christianity as I believe that the Sun has risen, not only because I see it, but because by it I see everything else."[48]

### *Interpreting the Unexpected in the Classroom*

Unexpected situations, those that attack our assumptions, tend to be particularly adept at drawing out our mix of mighty gifts and corruption, a complexity for which only Christianity can properly account. Again, the forms these take in the classroom will rarely attain the authenticity of encounters outside the classroom, but the difference, as stated before, is one of degree, not direction. In turn, dialogues that present students with surprising situations of real consequence can call out parts of the self often unknown or unnoticed. *Interchange: Intro*, the text examined in the previous section, supplies the skeleton of one such exchange. This dialogue takes place as Kate and Joe are leaving a restaurant:

| | |
|---|---|
| Kate: | Oh, no! Where are my car keys? |
| Joe: | I don't know. Are they in your purse? |
| Kate: | No, they're not. |
| Joe: | Maybe they're on the table in the restaurant. |
| Server: | Excuse me. Are these your keys? |

---

48. C. S. Lewis, "Is Theology Poetry?" in *The Weight of Glory and Other Addresses*, 1st Touchstone ed. (New York: Simon & Schuster, 1996), 106.

| | |
|---|---|
| Kate: | Yes, they are. Thank you! |
| Server: | You're welcome. And is this your wallet? |
| Kate: | Hmm. No, it's not. Where's your wallet, Joe? |
| Joe: | It's in my pocket . . . Wait a minute! That *is* my wallet![49] |

This is only a skeleton though because, with the text's understandable aim of being culturally safe, it operates from an interpretative framework of assumed optimism in the actions of others. That is, the server's noble actions do not seem to surprise Kate and Joe in the least. The only violations of Joe's expectations concern the placement of his wallet and not the makeup of a person. What is subtly presented is a philosophy that we are good deep down, an inoffensive framework for the global community. The server only did what anyone would do in such a situation.

In turn, engaging the dialogue theologically, teachers should supplement this dialogue with activities that make students step back and analyze other ways of interpreting this data. For example, teachers could add to the dialogue, making the interaction more nuanced. Perhaps, for example, Kate is the server's professor and what she left at the table was the answer key to an upcoming exam. What *would* the server do? What *should* the server do? Similarly, students could wrestle with the question of whether or not the scripted exchange agrees with their own views and experience. Even more, the students might be given the opportunity to apply their own interpretative frameworks of the self, preferably articulating what exactly those frameworks are. For example, they might learn much about themselves by re-enacting this dialogue with additions and changes that accord with the contours of their own personal views of humanity. Again, any human framework will fail to account for the complexity of the self, so teachers should not be surprised if the modified dialogues oscillate between the commonly assumed optimism and the dreary pessimism described above. In fact, through such activities, the hope is that students will perceive that the self requires a much more complex interpretation, one that only our creator can provide.

## Why Is Dialogue Powerful?

After investigating God's image in us, which makes dialogue possible, and God's intention for us, which makes dialogue purposeful, we do well to examine

---

49. Richards, *Interchange: Intro Student's Book,* 11 (emphasis original).

the power of dialogue. In particular, we need to take a closer look at human language and culture, making certain that they are capable of mediating the transformational dialogues to which we aspire. If our words lack the power to reveal reality, then they likewise forfeit any hope of showing us ourselves. Language constitutes a kind of lens through which we view the world, and we must be confident that it does, in fact, have the power to sharpen our vision.

### *Words and the World*

With that said, one of the most rewarding experiences that comes with studying a foreign language is the opportunity to view reality through a different set of categories. Language classrooms must never lose sight of this. For example, we see this phenomenon in C. S. Lewis's affection for the existential acuteness of the German word *sehnsucht*.[50] It is a term with no direct English equivalent and it describes a kind of insatiable or uncontrollable searching or longing, a concept that framed much of Lewis's most persuasive apologetic writings. That is, this term accurately articulated the desire that all people inherently feel toward God, which, in ignorance of him and in enmity toward him, they vainly seek to satisfy through much too meager means. In a similar fashion, the Vietnamese language has articulated certain concepts in ways that have powerfully changed my own understanding of them. For instance, one way to express the verb "learn" is to combine the verbs "study" and "ask." I appreciate this twofold dynamic that pairs studying with the humbling posture of asking questions, implying a relationship of dialogue with a learned mentor. In that sense, proper learning requires community. One may perhaps study in the isolation of a library carrel, but this is less than learning in the proper sense.

Language connects us to reality and I believe that the two terms above bring two particular aspects of reality into clearer focus. In so doing, they also grant their speakers essential insights into the self. Language then functions as a kind of mediator between humanity and reality. There is no such thing as a thought free of language. And this has proved a troubling truth for philosophy in its quest to understand human knowledge. If language mediates our life in the world, then any endeavor to understand knowledge, including knowledge of the self, must address language in some form.

---

50. C. S. Lewis, *Surprised by Joy: The Shape of My Early Life* (Orlando, FL: Harcourt, 1955), 7.

Philosophy has certainly taken up this challenge. Vanhoozer assures us, "Indeed, it would be no exaggeration to say that language has become the preeminent problem of twentieth-century philosophy."[51] However, the consensus of strong postmodernism regarding this issue is disconcerting. Language has been condemned as an arbitrary (and generally repressive) system that enforces a futile structure on a chaotic world. Language can never hope to be true, only useful.[52] The examples from German and Vietnamese mentioned above might be interesting, but not insightful. Even more, given the disconnect between the order of every linguistic system and the undecipherable disorder of reality, language never really touches reality. Instead, words create an artificial world of false structures in which we live and move and have our being. Dialogue then would have no power to reveal the self, but only to further obscure it. And to be sure, there would be no self, only the arbitrary accumulation of the language systems that each person has inherited.[53]

## *The Word and the World*

So we arrive at an important question, one that probes the foundational relationship between the world we inhabit and the words we use. Namely, do words construct our world? And, perhaps surprisingly, the answer is yes, although not in the way that postmodern philosophies claim. God spoke the world into being. Every inch of creation owes its existence to his words, or, more appropriately, his Word. The apostle John tells us, "In the beginning was the Word, and the Word was with God, and the Word was God. He was in the beginning with God. All things were made through him, and without him was not any thing made that was made" (John 1:1–3).

Even more, John goes on to write, "And the Word became flesh and dwelt among us, and we have seen his glory, glory as of the only Son from the Father, full of grace and truth" (John 1:14). The Word through which God creates

---

51. Kevin J. Vanhoozer, *Is There a Meaning in This Text?: The Bible, the Reader, and the Morality of Literary Knowledge* (Grand Rapids, MI: Zondervan, 1998), 17.

52. For the purposes of this essay, the nuances of post-structuralistic theories, like those of Jacques Derrida and the later work of Roland Barthes, and those of socio-pragmatic theories, like those of Richard Rorty and Stanley Fish, have been lumped together under the larger label of postmodernism. For excellent discussions on the finer points of these positions see Anthony C. Thiselton, *New Horizons in Hermeneutics: The Theory and Practice of Transforming Biblical Reading*, 20th ann. ed. (Grand Rapids, MI: Zondervan, 1992).

53. For an insightful summary of the strong postmodern consensus on language see Vanhoozer, *Is There a Meaning in This Text?*, chs. 2, 3, and 4.

and sustains the entire coherent, and not chaotic, cosmos became a man and dialogued with other humans. The Word in which all of reality holds together (Col 1:16–17), has entered into a specific linguistic system. The Word took on the body and culture of a first-century Palestinian Jew. And yet, the author of Hebrews can confidently assert, "He is the radiance of the glory of God and the exact imprint of his nature, and he upholds the universe by the word of his power" (Heb 1:3). What else can we say, but, "O Deconstruction, where is your sting?"

That is, the finite particulars of human culture and language were no barrier to Jesus's revelation of the Father. They constituted the very vessels of this revelation. The incarnation placed Jesus in the midst of a specific time, place, and people and he ministered accordingly. And given his human audience, he could not have done otherwise. As D. A. Carson writes, "Finite human beings have no culture-free access to truth, nor can they express it in culture-free ways."[54] And truly Jesus, God's Word, is God's ultimate act of dialogue with humanity.

One particularly stirring example of Jesus's revelatory dialogue is that of John 4, when Jesus speaks to the Samaritan women at the well. After a back and forth of verbal exchanges that press into the woman's past marriages and her current case of cohabitation, we are met with a moment of confessional clarity that would render the most uncomfortable of conversations well worth the cost. His knowledge, his authority, his care and concern, have called out a hope in her, perhaps one long forgotten. She says to Jesus, "I know that Messiah is coming (he who is called Christ). When he comes, he will tell us all things" (4:25). We can only imagine what she must have felt when he replied, "I who speak to you am he" (4:26). And of course, we can never separate the language of the exchange from the cultural context that gives it life.

There is a scandal that runs throughout this scene, but we often unknowingly minimize it, attributing it merely to Jesus's interaction with a Samaritan woman, a conversation partner that astounded the disciples. "For Jews have no dealings with Samaritans" (4:9). However, if we understand this scene in accordance with Hebrew cultural conventions, the full scandal of the scene comes into view. A well is the least likely location where Jesus would have been thought to meet this adulterous Samaritan woman. The real scandal is the

---

54. D. A. Carson, "Recent Developments in the Doctrine of Scripture," in *Collected Writings on Scripture* (Wheaton, IL: Crossway, 2010), 102.

setting-infused suggestion of betrothal between the Messiah and a woman of no appeal and complete aversion to Jesus's Jewish contemporaries.

Hebrew literature scholar Robert Alter has pointed out a number of type-scenes employed in the Old Testament. Explaining this literary convention, he says that it is "dependent on the manipulation of a fixed constellation of predetermined motifs."[55] "Essentially, it constitutes the particular *people*, *places*, and *procedures* in a scene that awaken certain expectations in the audience as to what will happen next."[56] He offers the betrothal type-scene as an example, laying out its prescribed procedures. In simplified summary, it involves a man from a foreign country interacting with a woman or women at a well, the drawing of water, the running home of the female party to announce the man's arrival, and the betrothal of the two parties.[57] As he points out, we see this play out between Isaac and Rebekah, Jacob and Rachel, and Moses and Zipporah. In turn, the convention imposed an expectation of betrothal between a man and woman who made each other's first acquaintance at this setting of well-worn significance.

Alter's literary analysis gives no attention to the New Testament. However, Jesus, working as God's ultimate act of dialogue, is coordinating the contexts of creation and convention to communicate something about himself with incomparable rhetorical power. He is the Samaritan's true bridegroom. "To the same degree that his living water trumps the stagnant water of the well, so Christ's devotion to her trumps that of the six men she has previously known."[58] Such is his love for the church, his beloved bride. This realization provides us the most important self-knowledge of all. That is, we are his bride. We are his. We are the ones for whom he gave up everything in order to cleanse us from our spiritual adultery, our idolatrous infidelity. And the love he has for us supplies us a worth that would make even the loftiest human philosophy seem degrading by comparison.

## *What Words Can Do*

Christ shows us that human words and the cultures they function within are capable of performing a truly amazing feat. They can reveal our Triune

---

55. Robert Alter, *The Art of Biblical Narrative*, 2nd ed. (New York: Basic Books, 2011), 60.
56. Cheri Pierson, Will Bankston, and Marilyn Lewis, *Exploring Parables in Luke* (Carlisle, UK: Langham Global Library, 2014), 130 (emphasis original).
57. Alter, *Art of Biblical Narrative*, 61–69.
58. Pierson, Bankston, and Lewis, *Exploring Parables in Luke*, 137.

God. The God who dialogues has given us language to dialogue truly about him. At the same time, it is clear that language does not always clarify the knowledge of God or of the self. At times, language can distort certain aspects of reality, thereby working at cross-purposes with Christ. For instance, the word "boredom" can tempt us with a dangerous entitlement to be entertained. Of course, reality in no way assures or even encourages such expectations. In fact, operating with "boredom" as a navigating notion, we will find reality more thoroughly blurred. Even more, languages can work not just to blur reality, but also to block it. Consider Lesslie Newbigin's experience in learning the Tamil language. At a certain point in his studies he realized that he had not yet come across a word for "hope." He recalls, "When I questioned my Hindu teacher about this, he asked me in turn what I meant by hope. Does hope mean anything? Things will be what they will be."[59] This, of course, does not suggest that the Tamil language does or could not express the concept of hope, but rather the way in which worldview and language can work to reinforce each other for good or ill. And of course, certainly any language can also be used for ill ends through speech-acts such as lying or intimidating.

The insight of Albert Wolters, examined in the previous section, supplies us a map for untangling the blessings and curses of language. Postmodern philosophy, it might be argued, has condemned language as the cause of what is wrong with the world. Language is seen as a kind of prison that bars us from reality and as a kind of power that represses any thoughts hostile to its arbitrary order. In this way, an inherently good part of creation, language, is "singled out" as the culprit of the world's woes. Again, this is too simplistic, as all human philosophies ultimately are. Instead, language, like each part of creation, has felt the infection of human sin and exhibits a mingling of mighty gifts and corruptions. We were created good and so was language.

However, we often lapse into the assumption that "to err is human." As D. A. Carson contests though, it is not error that is inherent to humanness but rather finitude.[60] The same holds true for our language. In turn, speaking of Scripture, Carson asserts, "human words, when so superintended by God himself, can convey divine truth – not exhaustively, of course, but truly."[61] Surely our words never claim the inspiration of Scripture, but, nevertheless, human words can finitely reveal the infinite. And so we should never doubt

---

59. Lesslie Newbigin, *The Gospel in a Pluralistic Society* (Grand Rapids, MI: Eerdmans, 1989), 101.

60. Carson, "Recent Developments," 96.

61. Ibid.

their ability to reveal the finite, namely ourselves, as we dialogue with one another. Ultimately, we are not the product of our words, but the product of the Word. He is the one who created us and he needs "no one to bear witness about man, for he himself knew what was in man" (John 2:25). Knowing himself and us perfectly, he assures us that the words that connect us to reality and to other persons are a powerful medium of truth.

Even more, as dialogue brings the revelation of God from one combined context of culture and language to another, the church's knowledge of God grows. Missiologist Andrew Walls puts this point perfectly, writing, "It is a delightful paradox that the more Christ is translated into the various thought forms and life systems with our various national identities, the richer all of us will be in our common Christian identity."[62] Towards that end, Vanhoozer offers the example of the Council of Nicaea, as the church translated Paul's assertion of Jesus's "equality with God" in Philippians 2:6–11 into the affirmation that Jesus and God are *homoousios* with each other. He explains, "*Homoousios* – literally, 'of the same substance' – is doubly a translation: from Hebrew to Greek; from poetry (or hymn) to metaphysics."[63] And so as the language and culture of early church verse encountered that of Greek philosophy, a cross-cultural dialogue ensued that increased humanity's knowledge of God. Just as the German and Vietnamese examples more fully open our eyes to reality, so does Nicaea's appropriation of *homoousios*. And of course, a fuller knowledge of God will always supply us a fuller knowledge of self, a particularly powerful point for the inherently cross-cultural nature of the language classroom. As Lewis goes on to comment after reflecting on the death of his good friend Charles Williams, "In this, Friendship exhibits a glorious 'nearness by resemblance' to heaven itself where the very multitude of the blessed (which no man can number) increases the fruition which each of us has of God . . . The more we thus share the Heavenly Bread between us, the more we shall have."[64]

## *Language and the Culture of the Classroom*

In full affirmation of human finitude, Jesus revealed the Father through a coordinated combination of language and culture. We as language teachers should likewise look for ways that dialogue can be made more powerful

---

62. Andrew Walls, *The Missionary Movement in Christian History: Studies in the Transmission of Faith* (Maryknoll, NY: Orbis, 1996), 54.
63. Vanhoozer, *Drama of Doctrine*, 342.
64. Lewis, *Four Loves*, 92–93.

through the combination of these finite, yet wholly capable mediums. We cannot forget that every dialogue takes place within a situational and cultural context. Even more, these factors infuse every utterance with deeper meaning. Remembering Jesus's manipulation of Hebrew literary conventions and his confrontation of contemporary prejudices as he spoke with the woman at the well, let us return to the dialogue between Kate, Joe, and the server. In the textbook, the dialogue is paired with Figure 9.1:[65]

**Figure 9.1**

All three persons involved in the conversation appear to be of the same ethnicity. There is, of course, nothing wrong with this. However, approaching the classroom theologically, we can learn from Jesus's example. In that sense, teachers might bring the dialogue into the students' own culture, recasting the speakers as the cultural equivalents of Jews and Samaritans or that of fishermen and Pharisees. Similarly, the new cast of characters could be framed by settings that carry strong cultural implications, utilizing locations as Jesus did the well. Certainly this needs to be done with cultural sensitivity and competent care. But, properly implemented, students may have the chance to confront bits of their self not normally elicited, amid the safety of the communicative classroom. At the very least, students will benefit by having the

---

65. This graphic is taken from Richards, *Interchange: Intro Student's Book*, 11.

dialogues transposed onto settings more immediate to their own experience. Many students are worlds away from the fine dining restaurant pictured above, but would be quite familiar with settings like coffee shops or bus stations, making the dialogue more authentic, meaningful, and relevant to their own experiences. By taking these tactics together, the teacher will have provided students a great service, properly stewarding the divine image that they bear.

## Concluding Considerations

Novelist and essayist Francine Prose writes of the words spoken by fictional characters, "what is dialogue after all, but the speech that could only come from the mouth of one character in all of fiction, and from the mind of one writer?"[66] We have striven to talk of reality, not fiction, but still, our reality is a story. And we, too, owe our existence to the words, or, more appropriately, the Word of God, our author. We bear his image and he has given us the privilege of uniqueness. Just as only a joke from the mouth of Charles William's could evoke a particular part of Tolkien, so the many different dialogues in which we participate call out specific aspects of our mysterious selves. The deeper a dialogue penetrates, the greater the self-knowledge brought into the light.

To be sure, this is a vital process, one that will shape us for all of time. Through it all, God alone makes it possible, purposeful, and powerful. And this is how it should be since the end of any self-knowledge is richer knowledge of him. In any context, and no less in the language classroom, such twofold knowledge is our goal. Like God, we aim to communicate, to dialogue. Our God is anything but arbitrary, and we should dialogue accordingly.

## Bibliography

Allison, Gregg R. *Historical Theology: An Introduction to Christian Doctrine*. Grand Rapids, MI: Zondervan, 2011.
Alter, Robert. *The Art of Biblical Narrative*. 2nd ed. New York: Basic Books, 2011.
Bahnsen, Gregg L. *Van Til's Apologetic: Readings and Analysis*. Philipsburg, NJ: P&R, 1998.
Barth, Karl. *Church Dogmatics, Vol 1.1, Sections 1-7: The Doctrine of the Word of God*. Translated by G. W. Bromiley, G. T. Thomson, and Harold Knight, Study Edition. London; New York: Bloomsbury T&T Clark, 2010.

---

66. Francine Prose, *Reading Like a Writer: A Guide for People Who Love Books and for Those Who Want to Write Them* (New York, NY: HarperCollins, 2006), 192.

———. *Evangelical Theology: An Introduction*. Translated by Grover Foley. New York: Holt, Rinehart & Winston, 1963.

Brown, Peter. *Augustine of Hippo: A Biography*. 2nd ed. Berkeley: University of California Press, 2000.

Calvin, John. *Institutes of the Christian Religion*. Edited by John T. McNeill. Translated by Ford Lewis Battles. Louisville, KY: Westminster John Knox, 1960.

Carson, D. A. *The Difficult Doctrine of the Love of God*. Wheaton, IL: Crossway, 2000.

———. "Recent Developments in the Doctrine of Scripture." In *Collected Writings on Scripture*. Wheaton, IL: Crossway, 2010.

Eagleton, Terry. *Literary Theory: An Introduction*. Minneapolis, MN: University of Minnesota Press, 1996.

Fish, Stanley. *The Stanley Fish Reader*. Edited by H. A. Veeser. Malden, MA: Wiley-Blackwell, 1999.

Horton, Michael. *Introducing Covenant Theology*. Grand Rapids, MI: Baker Academic, 2006.

Keller, Timothy. *Every Good Endeavor: Connecting Your Work to God's Work*. New York: Dutton, 2012.

———. *Rejecting the Real Jesus*, podcast audio. Redeemer Sermon Store, MP3, 22 September 1996. http://sermons2.redeemer.com/sermons/rejecting-real-jesus.

Kuhn, Thomas S. *The Structure of Scientific Revolutions*. 3rd ed. Chicago: University of Chicago Press, 1996.

Lewis, C. S. *The Four Loves*. New York: Harcourt, 1960.

———. *Surprised by Joy: The Shape of My Early Life*. Orlando, FL: Harcourt, 1955.

———. "Is Theology Poetry?" in *The Weight of Glory and Other Addresses*. 1st Touchstone edition. New York: Simon & Schuster, 1996.

———. "The Weight of Glory." In *The Weight of Glory and Other Addresses*. 1st Touchstone edition. New York: Simon & Schuster, 1996.

Newbigin, Lesslie. *The Gospel in a Pluralistic Society*. Grand Rapids, MI: Eerdmans, 1989.

Pierson, Cheri, Will Bankston, and Marilyn Lewis. *Exploring Parables in Luke: Integrated Skills for ESL/EFL Students of Theology*. Carlisle, UK: Langham Global Library, 2014.

Poythress, Vern S. *In the Beginning was the Word: Language—A God-Centered Approach*. Wheaton, IL: Crossway, 2009.

Potok, Chaim. *The Chosen*. New York: Ballantine, 1967.

Prose, Francine. *Reading Like a Writer: A Guide for People Who Love Books and for Those Who Want to Write Them*. New York: HarperCollins, 2006.

Reeves, Michael. *Delighting in the Trinity: An Introduction to the Christian Faith*. Downers Grove, IL: InterVarsity, 2012.

Richards, Jack C. *Interchange: Intro Student's Book*. 4th ed. Cambridge: Cambridge University Press, 2012.

Thiselton, Anthony C. *New Horizons in Hermeneutics: The Theory and Practice of Transforming Biblical Reading*, 20th ann. ed. Grand Rapids, MI: Zondervan, 1992.

Vanhoozer, Kevin J. *The Drama of Doctrine: A Canonical-Linguistic Approach to Christian Theology*. Louisville, KY: Westminster John Knox, 2005.

———. *Faith Speaking Understanding: Performing the Drama of Doctrine*. Louisville, KY: Westminster John Knox, 2014.

———. *Is There a Meaning in This Text?: The Bible, the Reader, and the Morality of Literary Knowledge*. Grand Rapids, MI: Zondervan, 1998.

———. *Remythologizing Theology: Divine Action, Passion, and Authorship*. Cambridge: Cambridge University Press, 2010.

Vice, Sue. *Introducing Bakhtin*. Manchester: Manchester University Press, 1997.

Webster, John. *Holy Scripture: A Dogmatic Sketch*. Cambridge: Cambridge University Press, 2003.

Walls, Andrew F. *The Missionary Movement in Christian History: Studies in the Transmission of Faith*. Maryknoll, NY: Orbis, 1996.

Wolters, Albert M. *Creation Regained: Biblical Basics for a Reformational Worldview*. 2nd ed. Grand Rapids, MI: Eerdmans, 2005.

# 10

# Yahweh's Taxonomy of the Deeper Dimensions

*Melissa Smith*

In spiritual realms, the deeper dimensions have long been revered. Go farther and push deeper, the message seems to be, and we reach the heart of God. Sometimes these deeper dimensions are seen as an interior versus exterior battle. This, in part at least, is what Saint Teresa of Avila was getting at in her analogy of prayer.[1] She describes the people in the outer rooms of their soul's castle as consumed with the world and its insidious reptiles:

> In the same way, there are souls so infirm and so accustomed to busying themselves with outside affairs that nothing can be done for them, and it seems as though they are incapable of entering within themselves at all. So accustomed have they grown to living all the time with the reptiles and other creatures to be found in the outer court of the castle that they have almost become like them; and although by nature they are so richly endowed as to have the power of holding converse with none other than God himself, there is nothing that can be done for them. Unless they strive to realize their miserable condition and to remedy it, they will be

---

1. Saint Teresa of Avila, *Interior Castle*, trans. E. Allison Peers (New York: Start Publishing, 2012).

turned into pillars of salt for not looking within themselves, just as Lot's wife was because she looked back.[2]

However, as the intercessor travels through the interior castle of the soul, she presses onward toward the throne room and inward toward deep intimacy with His Majesty the King of Kings. Thus, the battle against the exterior is won.

A. W. Tozer also juxtaposes the deeper dimensions against the surface, a place for followers of Jesus to eschew. The surface shares the problems of the external and the deep the blessings of the internal. Though written more than half a century ago, we have only to substitute "technological age" for "machine age," and Tozer's explanation of the surface is strikingly applicable in today's world:

> The idea of cultivation and exercise, so dear to the saints of old, has now no place in our total religious picture. It is too slow, too common. We now demand glamour and fast flowing dramatic action. A generation of Christians reared among push buttons and automatic machines is impatient of slower and less direct methods of reaching their goals. We have been trying to apply machine-age methods to our relations with God. We read our chapter, have our short devotions and rush away, hoping to make up for our deep inward bankruptcy by attending another gospel meeting or listening to another thrilling story told by a religious adventurer lately returned from afar.
>
> The tragic results of this spirit are all about us. Shallow lives, hollow religious philosophies, the preponderance of the element of fun in gospel meetings, the glorification of men, trust in religious externalities, quasi-religious fellowships, salesmanship methods, the mistaking of dynamic personality for the power of the Spirit: these and such as these are the symptoms of an evil disease, a deep and serious malady of the soul.[3]

Tozer employed different words and analogies, but the message echoes Saint Teresa's. When preoccupied with the reptiles of the world, our relationship with Jesus, if we have one, is meaningless. Our lives are filled with empty outward pleasures while inwardly we are bankrupt. Saint Teresa describes such souls as

---

2. Ibid., 18–19.
3. A. W. Tozer, *Pursuit of God* (Harrisburg, PA: Christian Publications, 2011), 63–64.

"infirm," almost incurable. Tozer describes their condition as "an evil disease, a deep and serious malady of the soul."

Interestingly, this objection to the surface is also seen in the field of language teaching. A simple perusal of one chapter in a well-known and oft-used textbook for students of TESOL, for example, reveals complaints similar to Saint Teresa and Tozer's. In *Teaching by Principles*,[4] Brown and Lee assess various methods of language teaching over the last one hundred years. The most negative of their assessments is reserved for the Grammar Translation Method.[5]

> It is ironic that this method has until very recently been so stalwart among many competing models. It does virtually nothing to enhance a student's communicative ability in the language. It is "remembered with distaste by thousands of school learners, for whom foreign language learning meant a tedious experience of memorizing endless lists of unusable grammar rules and vocabulary and attempting to produce perfect translations of stilted or literary prose."[6]

As they continue their assessment, other methods fare better, but many still share at least one or two drawbacks with Grammar Translation, primary of which is their failure to go below the surface and put language into practice. The Audiolingual Method is cited for "its ultimate failure to teach long-term communicative proficiency."[7] They call the Silent Way "too harsh a method and the teacher too distant, to encourage a communicative atmosphere."[8] Throughout their discussion, they warn against overemphasizing surface-level memorization, rote learning, and form-focused instruction. In addition, from their description of Communicative Language Teaching, we learn that this current, and seemingly better, approach "*extends beyond* the merely grammatical elements of communication into... 'real-life' communication... fluency," and even further into the ability to create new utterances.[9]

---

4. H. Douglas Brown and Heekyeong Lee, *Teaching by Principles: An Interactive Approach to Language Pedagogy*, 4th ed. (White Plains, NY: Pearson Education ESL, 2015).

5. Ibid., 18.

6. Jack C. Richards and Theodore S. Rodgers, *Approaches and Methods in Language Teaching* (Cambridge: Cambridge University Press, 2001), 6; quoted in Brown and Lee, *Teaching by Principles*, 18.

7. Brown and Lee, *Teaching by Principles*, 22.

8. Ibid., 26.

9. Ibid., 31 (emphasis added).

This essay explores this push to go deeper in both the spiritual and educational realms. Its premise is that language teachers can and should plumb the deeper dimensions with their students as the Master Teacher does with his. The exploration begins by digging further into his deeper dimensions. While examining his goals for his students, we will use one of the world's tools to measure his depths and vice versa. Then, we will follow Yahweh one step deeper into the moral dimension. After comparing and contrasting his ideas with the world's, we will explore how we might take our students into the deeper realms of the moral dimension. Finally, we will look at the meaning that can be found in teaching in the moral dimension.

## The Deeper Dimensions

### Yahweh and the Deeper Dimensions

Saint Teresa of Avila and Tozer did not base their ideas about the deeper dimensions on human wisdom. Nor was Saint Teresa the first to use analogies to explore the depths of the spiritual realms. As revealed in his book, Yahweh loves the deeper dimensions and has used analogies to express their depths. In Psalm 1, he compares true followers who delight in his law to trees planted beside a stream, and so we picture them rooted in the soil of his Word and drinking deeply of his living water. The wicked, in contrast, are like worthless fluff blown away by the wind. In the parable of the sower, the shallow are eaten by birds, choked out by weeds, or wilt in the sun while the rooted flourish (Matt 13:1–9).

Long before Saint Teresa of Avila, Jesus used a building analogy as he encouraged people to dig deep and lay their foundation on rock instead of sand (Matt 7:24–27; Luke 6:47–49). Later his followers refer to him as the one and only foundation (1 Cor 3:10–11). Then, Paul ties it all together by encouraging us to dig deep and avoid the fluff of "empty philosophies and high-sounding nonsense that come from human thinking and from the spiritual powers of this world, rather than from Christ" (Col 2:6–10 NLT).

Since ancient times, Yahweh has objected to the surface and urged his followers to strive against it. Accusations of lacking depth weave in and out of Old Testament prophesy where Yahweh chastised his people for refusing to put faith into practice (Ezek 33:31–33) and for giving him lip service with human rules "learned by rote" while in their hearts building altars to another (Isa 29:13 NLT). Centuries later, the situation clearly had not changed when Jesus used the words of Isaiah to accuse religious leaders of the same lack of depth as their ancestors (Matt 15:1–10). He referred to an interior versus exterior battle when he reproached them for cleaning the outside of the cup while inwardly rotting away (Matt 23:25–28). Subsequently, his authors repeated similar warnings throughout the New Testament.

> But don't just listen to God's word. You must do what it says. Otherwise, you are only fooling yourselves. For if you listen to the word and don't obey, it is like glancing at your face in a mirror. You see yourself, walk away, and forget what you look like. But if you look carefully into the perfect law that sets you free, and if you do what it says and don't forget what you heard, then God will bless you for doing it. If you claim to be religious but don't control your tongue, you are fooling yourself, and your religion is worthless. Pure and genuine religion in the sight of God the Father means caring for orphans and widows in their distress and refusing to let the world corrupt you . . . If you are wise and understand God's ways, prove it by living an honorable life, doing good works with the humility that comes from wisdom . . . But the wisdom from above is first of all pure. It is also peace loving, gentle at all times, and willing to yield to others. It is full of mercy and the fruit of good deeds. It shows no favoritism and is always sincere. And those who are peacemakers will plant seeds of peace and reap a harvest of righteousness. (Jas 1:22–27; 3:13–18 NLT)

> We have much to say about this, but it is hard to make it clear to you because you no longer try to understand. In fact, though by this time you ought to be teachers, you need someone to teach you the elementary truths of God's word all over again. You need milk, not solid food! Anyone who lives on milk, being still an infant, is not acquainted with the teaching about righteousness. But solid food is for the mature, who by constant use have trained themselves to distinguish good from evil. (Heb 5:11–14)

These passages bring the exterior versus interior battle into our world today. As followers of Jesus, we are to listen and remember so that we can move beyond spiritual dullness and into understanding. We, then, are ready to progress to solid food. These deeper realms of relationship require us to put basic teaching into practice, in obedience, and involve an ability to judge good from evil. All this solid food leads toward the ultimate goal of a life lived out in holiness and righteousness, set apart by humility, wisdom and peace.

## *Bloom's Taxonomy*

An educational tool that has been used for more than half a century is what is known as Bloom's Taxonomy. Published in 1956, it was originally designed as a means of classifying and measuring objectives but has been used in an array of ways and for various purposes.[10] It has often been seen as a tool for deepening learning from knowledge retention and comprehension into a "fuller range of cognitive processes."[11] Based on revisions made in the 1990s, the taxonomy expands from *remembering* and *understanding* to a fuller range that includes: *applying, analyzing, evaluating,* and *creating*.

As an illustration of how the levels work, some potential goals for readers of this essay are listed in Table 10.1. Notice that they follow a typical sentence pattern used in Western education circles to express learning outcomes.

The first two learning outcomes indicate knowledge *about*. As they go deeper, readers put knowledge into practice. In other words, hopefully you, the reader, will do more than simply skim the surface of this essay but will make your own decisions about how, why, and even if to take your students into the deeper dimensions and then end up with a plan for change.

Viewed through the lens of Brown and Lee's[12] assessment of teaching methods, Bloom's Taxonomy could provide guidance for developing learners' communicative ability. Teaching would need to result in more than simply memorizing disconnected words and rules. Instead, language should be *remembered* and *understood* (in context). Outcomes also need to lead toward *applying* (contextualized) language by putting it into practice. They might include *analyzing* the language in focus or using it to *analyze* something else within the context. Then, learning outcomes for that unit could culminate in a project where students share opinions and *evaluate* ideas while *synthesizing* (the original term used for the creating level) everything learned into something new, all while using language to *create* spontaneous utterances.

Viewed through a different lens, Yahweh's in particular, Bloom's Taxonomy might not simply be human understanding of learning processes but rather human discovery of Yahweh's wisdom. The next few paragraphs will explore

---

10. David R. Krathwohl, "A Revision of Bloom's Taxonomy: An Overview," *Theory into Practice* 41, no. 4 (2002): 212.

11. Richard E. Mayer, "Rote versus Meaningful Learning," *Theory into Practice* 41, no. 4 (2002): 226.

12. Brown and Lee, *Teaching by Principles*.

this idea by applying this principle to Yahweh's practices in order to see what wisdom might emerge.

**Table 10.1: Bloom's Goals for This Essay**

| Level | Purpose | By the end of this essay, readers will be able to: |
|---|---|---|
| remembering | recalling or recognizing information | list two scriptural analogies that show the deeper dimensions of relationship with Yahweh. |
| understanding | grasping the meaning of information | explain how Yahweh takes his students beyond basic teachings. |
| applying | using information | illustrate how Bloom's Taxonomy might apply to Yahweh's goals for his students (including themselves). |
| analyzing | seeing patterns or breaking information into parts | compare Yahweh's means of taking students into the deeper dimensions with the world's means. |
| evaluating | judging the value of information | investigate the importance of the deeper dimensions for language learning and life. |
| creating | putting information together in order to make something new | plan for teaching that takes students into the deeper dimensions. |

## *Yahweh's Learning Outcomes*

Although sometimes obscure to his students, Yahweh's teaching, like this essay and our teaching, has intentions. As was illustrated earlier, he expects us to be weaned from milk and move on to meat; he leads us toward change and desires to see truth lived out in holy lives. He may not have a written curriculum or lesson plans, but he certainly seems to have "outcomes" in mind and to set "benchmarks" for his students.

## Sentence Pattern

If the Master Teacher wrote out his goals according to the accepted pattern used in Western education today, he might have at least one adaptation. The responsibility to reach certain results, under his guidance, does not rest solely on the shoulders of his students. They are not left alone to produce certain outcomes but are, mercifully, enabled by his Spirit. Thus, his sentence pattern for his learning outcomes might read like this:

> By the end of _____, students will be able *and enabled* to _____.

## Long-term Outcomes

One time limit for Jesus's overall goals for his students might be the end of life on this earth. Drawing from his prayer in John 14, some of his learning outcomes within this period might focus on union with him through holiness. This union was certainly a result of reaching the innermost room of the castle of which Saint Teresa of Avila spoke. A. W. Tozer describes such oneness this way:

> Has it ever occurred to you that one hundred pianos all tuned to the same fork are automatically tuned to each other? They are of one accord by being tuned, not to each other, but to another standard to which each one must individually bow. So one hundred worshippers met together, each one looking away to Christ, are in heart nearer to each other than they could possibly be were they to become "unity" conscious and turn their eyes away from God to strive for closer fellowship. Social religion is perfected when private religion is purified. The body becomes stronger as its members become healthier. The whole Church of God gains when the members that compose it begin to seek a better and a higher life.[13]

In human terms, we might express the Master Teacher's unity goals this way:

- By the end of life on this earth, students will be able and enabled to be one with me as I am with my Father.
- By the end of life on this earth, students will be able and enabled to be holy as I am holy.

---

13. Tozer, *Pursuit of God*, 88.

### Lesson Objectives

In his classroom and the one-on-one tutoring he does, Jesus leads his students through "lessons" and "learning activities," all aiming toward his overall outcomes. In human terms, we could express some of his lesson and activity objectives this way:

- By the end of this morning's devotions, this student will be able and enabled to quote Ephesians 4:22–24.
- By the end of this week's devotions, this student will be able and enabled to explain how to be holy according to Ephesians 4:17–32.
- By the end of this sermon, students will be able and enabled to compare the world's standards with my holiness and illustrate areas of divergence.

If the Master Teacher were to stop there, his students might end up with a thorough understanding of the concept of holiness. Knowledge *about*, in his classrooms, however, is not enough; his students also need the wherewithal (enabled by his Spirit) to take action. Thus, he seeks to turn his students' hearts of stone into flesh, resulting in obedience (Ezek 36:24–32). He desires to go beyond basic or head knowledge and so offers his students meat and not simply milk such that they can judge good from evil and act rightly (Heb 5:11–14). His objectives for his students, then, extend to include ones that take them out of the classroom and into life. In human terms, they could be expressed this way:

- By the end of this period of study, this student will be able and enabled to monitor her or his personal holiness.
- By the end of this experience, this student will be able and enabled to make a plan with specific steps toward being holy as I am holy.

Table 10.2 below illustrates where each of these objectives might fall on Bloom's Taxonomy.

Although Yahweh's goals for his students may not be as linear as this analysis using Bloom's Taxonomy might suggest, what seems clear is that his teaching has a point and is intended to lead toward specific outcomes. What also seems clear is that the results are meant to move students into a "fuller range of cognitive processes,"[14] from the outer rooms to the inner, from surface to deep, from knowledge *about* to union with him lived out in the world.

---

14. Mayer, "Rote versus Meaningful Learning," 226.

Table 10.2: Yahweh's Goals

| Learning Objectives | Level |
|---|---|
| By the end of this morning's devotions, this student will be able and enabled to quote Ephesians 4:22–24. | remembering |
| By the end of this week's devotions, this student will be able and enabled to explain how to be holy according to Ephesians 4:17–32. | understanding |
| By the end of this sermon, students will be able and enabled to compare the world's standards with my holiness. | analyzing[15] |
| By the end of this sermon, students will be able and enabled to illustrate areas of divergence between the world's standards and my holiness. | applying |
| By the end of this period of study, this student will be able and enabled to monitor her or his personal holiness. | evaluating |
| By the end of this experience, this student will be able and enabled to make a plan with specific steps toward being holy as I am holy. | creating |

Analyzing Yahweh's goals in this way may, first of all, make us better students as we see the depths to which he desires us to go. As teachers, it may add meaning to our teaching to realize a reason beyond education principles for taking students into the deeper dimensions. However, before we can explore this meaning, we need to go one step farther, for Jesus's desired outcomes for his students do not stop at planning for change but require actual change that is both outward and inward.

## The Moral Dimension

### Yahweh's Moral Dimension

Yahweh's point in replacing a heart of stone with "a tender, responsive heart" was to lead to willing and active obedience (Ezek 26:25–27 NLT). His intent in feeding his students meat was that they would not only "know how to do what

---

15. As Krathwohl explains, the revision of Bloom's Taxonomy allows for some overlap between levels and some flexibility in the hierarchy. Thus, the analyzing and applying levels are switched here to fit with a natural progression of the proposed outcomes.

is right" but turn head knowledge into actions and also attitudes, producing a "good crop for the farmer" rather than "thorns and thistles," and then, whether by example or instruction, begin to teach others (Heb 5:11–6:12 NLT). In human terms, these objectives might be expressed in the following way:

- By the end of this period of testing, this student will be able and enabled to take steps toward outward and inward change.
- By the end of this unit (including the study, experiences and period of testing) this student will be able and enabled to lead others toward outward and inward change.

In other words, the Master Teacher's goals for his students intend to take them even further and deeper than Bloom's Taxonomy might suggest. Bloom's Taxonomy seems to get students to the point of planning for action, possibly beyond (the intent of the creating level). Jesus wants them not only to take action but also for the right reasons. Thus, if rather than using Bloom's Taxonomy to analyze Yahweh's goals, we use Yahweh's goals to analyze Bloom's Taxonomy, we may discover that it needs to "go deeper into a moral dimension, a potential seventh level, where learners combine information with experiences in order to make and act on moral decisions,"[16] with right motives and attitudes. Table 10.3 on the following page illustrates how Yahweh's taxonomy might work.

Yahweh's Taxonomy of the Deeper Dimensions, if we can refer to it as such, includes a moral dimension, a place where his students not only learn but are also transformed and then act. Moreover, their actions are not simply outward obedience. They are right motives, attitudes, beliefs, and ideas that inspire righteous words, actions, and even thoughts. Or, traversing Yahweh's moral dimension may begin with righteous behavior and end with inner holiness as he plumbs the depths of our soul and brings about transformation. Ultimately, this union – between outward self, inward soul, Yahweh, and his holiness – harmonizes into a symphony of praise to the King (Rom 12:1–2).

---

16. Melissa K. Smith, "Bloom's Taxonomy Plus the Moral Dimension," *Master Teaching* (blog), 4 June 2014 (8:05am), http://masterteaching.leapasia.org/2014/06/04/blooms-taxonomy-plus-the-moral-dimension/.

Table 10.3: Yahweh's Goals Plus the Moral Dimension

| Learning Objectives | Level |
|---|---|
| By the end of this morning's devotions, this student will be able and enabled to quote Ephesians 4:22–24. | remembering |
| By the end of this week's devotions, this student will be able and enabled to explain how to be holy according to Ephesians 4:17–32. | understanding |
| By the end of this sermon, students will be able and enabled to compare the world's standards with my holiness. | analyzing |
| By the end of this sermon, students will be able and enabled to illustrate areas of divergence between the world's standards and my holiness. | applying |
| By the end of this period of study, this student will be able and enabled to monitor her or his personal holiness. | evaluating |
| By the end of this experience, this student will be able and enabled to make a plan with specific steps toward being holy as I am holy. | creating |
| By the end of this period of testing, this student will be able and enabled to take steps toward outward and inward change. | moralizing |
| By the end of this unit (including the study, experiences, and period of testing) this student will be able and enabled to lead others toward outward and inward change. | moralizing |

## *The World's Perspective*

This idea of a moral dimension is not without precedent in the world's approaches to education. In the Colonial Era in the United States, for example, the primary purpose of education was "to train children to act morally," which is exactly what the McGuffey Readers seemed to be doing by the mid-1800s.[17] Chinese history takes this practice of moral education back even farther to philosophers like Confucius to whom are attributed ideas like "教书育人"

---

17. Hunter Brimi, "Academic Instructors or Moral Guides? Moral Education in America and the Teacher's Dilemma," *The Clearinghouse: A Journal of Educational Strategies, Issues, and Ideas* 82, no. 3 (2009): 126.

"Teach books; educate human beings." Historically in China, the purpose and end of education is to cultivate virtuous human beings.

## *A Difference in Depth*

Although precedent for the moral dimension may be found in various cultures around the world, human ideas diverge from Yahweh's. In particular, there is often a difference in depth. My Chinese colleagues, for example, will as yet identify virtue as the primary purpose and end of education, but the modern interpretation of this seems to be "turning every citizen into a man or woman of character and cultivating more constructive members of society."[18] This approach seems to engender a focus on cleaning the outside of the cup with little attention to the inside. A similar assessment might be made of American education practices: "Simply put, when it comes to moral values, American policymakers primarily want students to act appropriately, whether they have internalized a real sense of moral virtue or not."[19]

This difference in depth is an issue not only in today's secular world but also in the religious where virtue seems defined by Christian society rather than transcendent biblical principles and morality is often equated with political platforms. This in part is what Philip Yancey is getting at as he reminisces about the church experiences of his childhood up to the present day. Then, the focus was on outward "lifestyle issues such as hair- and skirt-lengths, movies, dancing, smoking, and drinking."[20] Though the behavior in the crosshairs is somewhat different today, the outward focus is not, and according to Yancey, "too often . . . matches line for line that of conservative – or liberal – politics and not the priorities of the Bible."[21]

Though followers of Jesus may go further, hopefully, into Yahweh's Taxonomy of the Deeper Dimensions than our secular counterparts, we often fail to go deep enough. In part, we suffer from the age-old problem of the Pharisees and their litany of rules governing outward behavior rather than inward virtue. Today, the issue seems rooted in a tendency to skip from Scripture to application without first looking for deeper, underlying principles that confront the heart issues that shape behavior.

---

18. Li Lanqing, *Education for 1.3 Billion* (Beijing: Foreign Language Teaching and Research Press and Pearson Education, 2004), 301.
19. Brimi, "Academic Instructors," 126.
20. Philip Yancey, *Vanishing Grace* (Grand Rapids, MI: Zondervan, 2014), 229.
21. Ibid., 253.

## *Issues of Practice*

Not only is there a problem with depth but also with practice. Currently, there seems to be some disagreement about whether or not morality belongs in education. Glenn Sanders, a Christian college educator, places himself on one side where he and others hold the belief that classrooms should foster students' moral development.[22] To represent the opposing view, he quotes from William Chace, former president of both Wesleyan and Emory Universities. Part of that quote is included here:

> Some critics will complain that the university is not fulfilling its role as moral academy devoted to the inculcation of specific values. Given its lamentable record in only fitfully honoring that responsibility, I conclude, with mixed regret and relief, that it should no longer try to do so.[23]

Accompanying this disagreement is a strong belief that for one person to impose her or his morals on another is wrong. This issue has been raised in the field of TESOL. In their exploration of evangelicals in language teaching, Varghese and Johnston interpret TESOL organization's mission statement as "a responsibility not to try to persuade students to adopt their beliefs and values but to accept students' views on a basis of equality," and they contend that "part of respecting someone else's culture involves letting them continue to hold their own spiritual values."[24]

Varghese and Johnston make some important points. They acknowledge that all teachers, no matter their beliefs and whether they are aware or not, hold values that they offer up to students. Furthermore, their point that we should respect our students' values and not impose our own has validity. In *English Teaching as Christian Mission*, Don Snow makes this point and warns Christian teachers of the dangers of unknowingly pressuring students toward their values by force of their position over them.[25]

---

22. Glenn E. Sanders, "How Christian Practices Help to Engage Students Morally and Spiritually: Testimony from a Western Civilization Course," in *Teaching and Christian Practices*, eds. David I. Smith and James K. A. Smith (Grand Rapids, MI: Eerdmans, 2011), 157.

23. William M. Chace, *100 Semesters: My Adventures as a Student, Professor, and University President, and What I Learned Along the Way* (Princeton: Princeton University Press, 2006), 330; quoted in Sanders, "How Christian Practices Help," 158.

24. Manka M. Varghese and Bill Johnston, "Evangelical Christians and English Language Teaching" *TESOL Quarterly* 41, no. 1 (2007), 26–27.

25. Donald B. Snow, *English Teaching as Christian Mission* (Scottdale, PA: Herald, 2001), 76–77.

However, the attitude that respect means acceptance and anything otherwise becomes imposition is problematic. It may, first of all, cause teachers to think they cannot raise moral issues in the classroom, and that if they do, they are breaking the rules. Christians, who admittedly may be judged more harshly,[26] may fear that they will be seen as attempting to proselytize and coerce. Furthermore, if teachers do dip into the moral dimension, they may avoid their own ideas and opinions, going so far as not even to present them in an objective manner as one possibility among many. Consequently, students are left with half the story, and teachers, who already deal with dehumanizing pedestals and power distance, come across, perhaps, as amoral individuals.

"Automaton" might be too strong a word to describe what students become in this setting, since most teachers would, presumably, acknowledge that their students are at least mental and emotional beings. However, these views about the moral dimension might feed into a practice of treating students as something less than human when, on the contrary, students face moral dilemmas not only in life but also in the classroom, as any teacher who has dealt with cheating or bullying, to list just two, would attest.

What this leads to in language classrooms, as Smith and Carvill suggest, is teaching that portrays people as paper doll-like figures without heart or soul.[27] Students are taught to buy and sell but not to talk about using money wisely or donating it to a cause. They learn how to visit other countries, go to stores, stay in hotels, and go to school, but rarely do they learn about going to church, wrestling with dilemmas, or pondering the deeper questions of life. They practice language to greet, thank, complain, borrow, and request but not to delight, mourn, feel guilty, repent, hope, fear, and believe.

## The Lens of Yahweh's Wisdom

Yahweh's Taxonomy of the Deeper Dimensions indicates that we may need to take learners deeper than the world might suggest. Like both Bloom's and current TESOL practices, it tells us to take our students beyond memorizing and understanding language to being able to use it to analyze, evaluate, and create something new. Yahweh's taxonomy, then, might dig even deeper so that they are also using language to choose between right and wrong behavior while regulating inward motivations. Although we cannot necessarily expect

---

26. Varghese and Johnston, "Evangelical Christians," 26.

27. David I. Smith and Barbara Carvill, *The Gift of the Stranger: Faith, Hospitality, and Foreign Language Learning* (Grand Rapids, MI: Eerdmans, 2000).

students to enact change, we can challenge them to examine their behavior and attitudes and plan for change. The question, of course, is how to do so in appropriate ways given the limitations within which we work. The next few paragraphs will examine appropriate ways and means.

### *Yahweh's Place in Moralizing*

Whether our students believe in him or not, Yahweh is the source of wisdom that helps them "understand what is right, just, and fair" and "find the right way to go" (Prov 2:1–15 NLT). Whether we overtly acknowledge him or not, in Jesus, teachers and students "live and move and exist" (Acts 17:28 NLT), evaluate, create, and moralize. The issue is not his sovereignty or even his presence in our classrooms. Rather, it concerns whether we should explicitly bring him in when taking students into the moral dimension.

On the one hand, fear of breaking the rules or appearing to proselytize is not good motivation for leaving Yahweh out of the picture. Fear is never good justification. Neither is it helpful to overcompensate in such a way that we appear to agree with ideas that are contrary to Jesus's values. Moreover, teachers do their students a disservice if they only give them part of the picture: Islam and Buddhism but not Christianity; Hanukkah and Santa Claus but not Jesus; their emotional, mental, and physical selves but not their spiritual.

On the other hand, a desire to be respectful and appropriate is good reason for caution. The classroom, where we have a captive audience who in some cultures is obligated to listen, is usually not the setting for the details of our faith. In another place, I expressed the caution this way:

> *Moralizing is not free rein to talk about God or the Bible or share our faith in the classroom.* Rather it's giving learners tools to make wise decisions about right and wrong, regulate their behavior, and take action. We may broaden their view with a personal experience, proverb, or quote. What we don't do is pressure or dictate, aware of the influence we wield as teachers.[28]

The personal experiences we share may reflect our faith. The proverb or quote may come from the Bible and be identified as such. Or we may take an underlying biblical principle and apply it to real life without overtly identifying its source.

---

28. Smith, "Bloom's Taxonomy Plus," (emphasis original).

However, caution is in order. Talking about Jesus, even under the guise of moralizing, does not drive our teaching. The point is not to start with the moral principle and build our lesson around it. Moralizing, rather, supports language goals and takes them deeper. Moralizing is also not an occasion for teacher (or students) to get on a soapbox and pontificate, especially about personal opinions or the rules of religion. Moreover, it is not a platform for setting students straight. In fact, often instead of "telling," we should be helping students "come to their own conclusions."[29]

Sometimes, in our moral level teaching, conclusions are never reached. Instead, we simply raise the questions, evoke reflection, and encourage learners to seek trusted counsel. Then, we get on our knees and ask the Spirit of Jesus to take them further and deeper. It is there, on our knees, where we encounter Yahweh in one of his most fruitful places. It is there where the Advocate groans for our students while convicting them of sin, righteousness and judgment (Rom 8:26–28; John 16:5–11).

## The Love Your Neighbor Framework

### *The Primary Purpose of Moralizing*

If Jesus is not necessarily an explicit part of the moralizing that takes place in our classrooms, what, then, is its purpose? Drawing on some ideas laid out by Smith and Carvill in *The Gift of the Stranger*,[30] I would like to propose that the purpose of moralizing in the classroom is to help students love themselves and others, a Love your Neighbor Framework.

David Smith summarizes the premise of *The Gift of the Stranger* this way: "The Christian learner of other languages and cultures stands under a twofold calling: to be a blessing as a stranger and to exercise hospitality to strangers."[31] Doing so, he and Carvill reflect in their book, "fulfills the command to love God and to love one's neighbor as oneself."[32] While their suggestions may be largely directed at Christians learning another language, their ideas are also applicable in classrooms filled with students of other beliefs or lack of them. Whether or not students love God, taking them into the moral dimension can

---

29. Ibid.
30. Smith and Carvill, *Gift of the Stranger*.
31. "The Gift of the Stranger Revisited," *Journal of Christianity and Foreign Languages* 7 (2006).
32. Smith and Carvill, *Gift of the Stranger*, 84.

teach them to love their neighbor as they love themselves, and in so doing, we may make them better citizens of the world and more compassionate members of our classroom team, all while reflecting light.

## *One Moral Principle*

The problem is reaching this purpose given the textbooks and content we have to work with. In certain settings, teachers may have the freedom to design their own materials that reflect some of the themes Smith and Carvill describe in their book. However, many teachers of English around the world are assigned curriculum that seems far removed from anything resembling a Love your Neighbor Framework. Consider these typical unit topics in English textbooks:[33]

- environment
- health, exercise
- food, restaurants
- workplace, jobs, careers
- entertainment, movies, music, free-time activities, sports
- clothing, shopping, money
- housing
- travel, transportation, directions
- technology
- family, friendship, describing people
- emotions

At times, I have challenged my Chinese colleagues to identify one moral principle to focus on with each unit in their textbooks. In a place like China where virtue is considered both the purpose and end of education, unit topics often support this. However, even with the seemingly surface-level topics listed above, we may find ways of taking learners deeper by identifying moral principles that fall under the heading "love your neighbor as yourself."

## *Personal Responsibility*

If our intent is to engender better world citizens and compassionate members of our classroom team, then an important aspect of the Love your Neighbor

---

33. Two textbook series were examined in order to generate this list: *World Englishes* (Boston, MA: Heinle, CENGAGE Learning, 2010) and *Interchange,* 4th ed. (Cambridge: Cambridge University Press, 2012). Topics are grouped together into categories.

Framework is personal responsibility. Some textbook units raise meaningful issues, but they do not always go far enough. For example, in units on the *environment*,[34] a topic that comes up frequently in English language textbooks around the world, the problems are often presented well. Activities may ask students to discuss what societies or governments should do, but much less frequently are students asked to make decisions about what actions they personally could take. Rarely, if ever, does a unit end with a class project out on campus or another location picking up trash.

In China, where topics are much more conducive to moralizing, my colleagues have taught units,[35] for example, on the treatment of people with disabilities or certain jobs like garbage collectors, but still the units do not always ask students to take personal responsibility. Again, the unit may present the problem well – in what are rather inspiring readings – but the students are only asked to consider what societies or people in general should do. Rarely are they asked to consider their own behavior and attitudes. Personal experience as well as my friend with a disability would attest that in many cases both outward actions and inward beliefs are in need of transformation, transformation that could affect both their world citizenship and membership on the classroom team.

## *Loving Self and Others*

While students are taking personal responsibility, teachers can look for ways to encourage them to love themselves. Students may not be temples of the Holy Spirit, but they still might enjoy making decisions about *food*, *exercise*, and *work* vs. *rest* in ways that take care of their bodies, minds, and spirits. They may have no concept of modern-day idol worship, but they might benefit from a discussion about their potential addictions to *technology* or how to avoid worshiping their *children* and why.

At the same time, we can look for ways to encourage students to respect and love others. They may not be concerned about reflecting Jesus, but they may, for example, need to judge how they should respectfully interact with a *restaurant* server (or garbage collector) and why. They may not be interested in justice for the same reasons we are, but we can still ask them to consider

---

34. In the next few paragraphs, I have highlighted words that connect into the unit topics listed earlier.

35. *New Horizon College English 1*, ed. Zheng Shu Tang (Beijing: Foreign Language Teaching and Research Press, 2007).

how to spend *money* based on the ways *food* or *clothing* companies treat their laborers. They may not be commissioned to clean the inside of the cup, but they can still not only practice appropriate ways of *describing people* but also regulate the inward attitudes that may engender inappropriate descriptions.

## *Learners' Moral Needs*

The moral principles we choose to focus on in each unit of our textbook are based on learners' needs. My examples above come primarily from my experiences working with Chinese learners. Obviously, your students may need something different. In the same way that we identify other learner needs, we should keep the following in mind:

- **The target context**. This includes how learners may need both to use language in order to make future moral decisions and also to maneuver through life's moral dilemmas.
- **Their current level**. This includes what they already know and do and what attitudes and sources of guidance/inspiration they already have in the moral dimension. People have goodness ingrained in them culturally, and individual students may already follow a well-defined set of moral principles and for good reasons. Our students have ideas to contribute which may teach and inspire their classmates (and us). Their current level may be the best starting point for our moral dimension teaching.
- **Bridging the gap between current level and target context**. This involves both identifying moral principles and appropriate techniques.

Working cross-culturally complicates the process of identifying principles to bridge this gap. A bridge can turn out to be a gap, and an apparent gap may actually be a bridge. In other words, good that is ingrained in us culturally is not necessarily ingrained in our students. And what is ingrained in us is not always transcendent truth but could have a legitimate alternate interpretation in another society or culture. We also have to consider what approaches or techniques would best move them toward the target. Meeting their moral needs may be better accomplished with encouragement rather than criticism, questions rather than dictates, and challenges rather than concluding statements. Recently, I have also discovered the possibilities inherent in using learners' own culture, their ancient wisdom (a Chinese proverb, for example), to stir up reflection.

## *The Role of the Teacher*

Perhaps the single most important way we can plumb the deeper dimensions is as a model. We may never once find an appropriate moment, inside class or out, to speak of Jesus with our students. However, we have no reason to hide our moral selves from them. On the contrary, they need to see us wrestling with moral dilemmas. (*Should I give money to beggars or not? Why?*) They need to know that we struggle with wrong attitudes. (*My behavior toward people is sometimes influenced by their skin color. How can I change my way of thinking?*) They also need to hear what we have learned from their moral principles and the good ingrained in them culturally. (*Chinese people are often very forgiving. I've been trying to learn to look at the whole picture of someone's life rather than judging based on one wrong idea or mistake.*)

Being a model for students, however, not only involves allowing them to see our moral selves but also, whether they see it or not, humbly growing into the deeper realms ourselves. In his attempts to take his students deeper, Glenn Sanders described his goal this way: "I want to be a moral and spiritual person teaching moral and spiritual beings in moral and spiritual ways."[36] Taking our students into the moral dimension starts with us surrendering to our Teacher's efforts to move us beyond head knowledge into practice and beyond behavior into issues of the heart. This modeling is not a precursor or a first step. It is not a level we have to reach before we are qualified to plumb the depths with our students. Rather, it is a constant. As we help our students grow morally, we humbly and steadily root deeper into Jesus.

## Meaning in the Deeper Dimensions

How often do teachers go through the motions in their classrooms, caring about students and their learning, but not thinking about a greater purpose? Even teachers who believe that they are commissioned to evangelize their students may feel that the classroom is for learning; outside is for deeper matters. Yet, this attitude steals meaning from our teaching. I have written elsewhere:

> A frequent complaint from my university colleagues is that their teaching has no point because their students are unlikely to use English in the future. Moralizing with each unit in their textbooks resonates with these teachers and in fact with most teachers I've

---

36. Sanders, "How Christian Practices Help," 157.

encountered no matter their background or beliefs. Why? Because it gives them license to teach the human beings, not simply the students, in their classrooms. It allows them to help learners acquire subject matter they *may* use while preparing them for life they *will* live.[37]

Moralizing in the classroom gives purpose to our teaching. Furthermore, when we ask learners to use what they have learned to make moral decisions, it also gives them a reason, a real-life reason, to communicate.

Moralizing also has meaning beyond our classroom and students and us. It pleases Jesus. If one of us went to Jesus and said, "Teacher, we saw someone teaching her students to cast off their evil selves, but we told her to stop because they don't believe in you,"[38] is this how he would respond? "Don't stop her or her students. No one who performs the miracle of turning from darkness toward light will long be able to speak evil of the light. Anyone who is not against me is for me. Even if they're only doing it to give a cup of water to their teacher, they will surely be rewarded."

More than pleasing him, moralizing brings glory to Jesus. One day every knee will bow to him and every tongue confess his sovereignty (Phil 2:9–11). One day people from every tribe and language will gather around his throne giving honor to his name (Rev 7:9–10). No mandate stops us from starting the process now, in our classrooms, as we point learners from around the world toward what is right and just and fair.

## Conclusion

This push to go deeper and find purpose is not merely a human concept. Rather, when we take learners into the deeper dimensions, we are imitating Yahweh who wants more from his students than head knowledge or blind obedience. When we focus in on moral principles in our teaching, we follow in his footsteps, he who lights one clear path toward him. When we lay the groundwork and then send students off to grapple and uncover, we teach like our Master. Created in his image, eternity planted in our hearts, we are given sixty-six books of guidance by which we figure out how to rightly traverse the often-rugged ground of life and teaching. Along the way, the amazing views of glory inspire our hearts to dig deep and press in.

---

37. Smith, "Bloom's Taxonomy Plus" (emphasis original).
38. This and the response below are adapted from Mark 9:38–41 NLT.

## Bibliography

Brimi, Hunter. "Academic Instructors or Moral Guides? Moral Education in America and the Teacher's Dilemma." *The Clearinghouse: A Journal of Educational Strategies, Issues, and Ideas* 82, no. 3 (2009): 125–130.

Brown, H. Douglas, and Heekyeong Lee. *Teaching by Principles: An Interactive Approach to Language Pedagogy*. 4th ed. White Plains, NY: Pearson Education ESL, 2015.

Krathwohl, David R. "A Revision of Bloom's Taxonomy: An Overview." *Theory into Practice* 41, no. 4 (2002): 212–218.

Lanqing, Li. *Education for 1.3 Billion*. Beijing: Foreign Language Teaching and Research Press and Pearson Education, 2004.

Mayer, Richard E. "Rote versus Meaningful Learning." *Theory into Practice* 41, no. 4 (2002): 226–232.

Sanders, Glenn E. "How Christian Practices Help to Engage Students Morally and Spiritually: Testimony from a Western Civilization Course." In *Teaching and Christian Practices*, edited by David I. Smith and James K. A. Smith, 157–176. Grand Rapids, MI: Eerdmans, 2011.

Smith, David I. "The Gift of the Stranger' Revisited." *Journal of Christianity and Foreign Languages* 7 (2006).

Smith, David I., and Barbara Carvill. *The Gift of the Stranger: Faith, Hospitality, and Foreign Language Learning*. Grand Rapids, MI: Eerdmans, 2000.

Snow, Donald B. *English Teaching as Christian Mission*. Scottdale, PA: Herald Press, 2001.

Teresa of Avila. *Interior Castle*. Translated by E. Allison Peers. New York: Start Publishing, 2012.

Tozer, A. W. *The Pursuit of God*. Harrisburg, PA: Christian Publications, 2011.

Varghese, Manka M., and Bill Johnston. "Evangelical Christians and English Language Teaching." *TESOL Quarterly* 41, no. 1 (2007), 5–31.

Yancey, Philip. *Vanishing Grace*. Grand Rapids, MI: Zondervan, 2014.

Zheng Shu Tang, ed. *New Horizon College English 1*. Beijing: Foreign Language Teaching and Research Press, 2007.

# Contributors

**Will Bankston** (MA TESOL & Intercultural Studies, Wheaton College Graduate School) is currently completing a Master of Divinity and an MA in Systematic Theology at Trinity Evangelical Divinity School. He serves with an educational NGO, having taught at universities in Southeast Asia and the Middle East. He is a co-author of *Exploring Parables in Luke: Integrated Skills for ESL/EFL Students of Theology* (Langham Global Library 2014) and has written numerous articles investigating the relationship between theology, language, culture, and education. His work has appeared in popular forums such as *The Gospel Coalition* and in academic journals such as *Teaching Theology and Religion*.

**Bradley Baurain** (PhD, University of Nebraska) has taught for twenty-five years in the United States, Canada, China, and Vietnam. He is currently leading the graduate-level TESOL program at Moody Theological Seminary and Graduate School in Chicago. He is the author of *Religious Faith and Teacher Knowledge in English Language Teaching* (Cambridge Scholars Publishing 2015), as well as co-editor of *Multilevel and Diverse Classrooms* (a volume in TESOL's Classroom Practice series 2010) and *Voices, Identities, Negotiations, and Conflicts: Writing Academic English Across Cultures* (Emerald 2011). He has published articles in journals including *TESOL Journal,* the *Journal of Language, Identity, and Education, ELT Journal,* and the *Journal of Aesthetic Education,* and serves on the Editorial Review Board of the *International Journal of Christianity and English Language Teaching*. His interests include teacher development, narrative inquiry, and literature in language education.

**Robert L. Gallagher** (PhD, Fuller Theological Seminary) is the department chair and director of the Master of Arts program in intercultural studies, and associate professor of intercultural studies at Wheaton College Graduate School in Chicago where he has taught since 1998. He previously served as the president of the American Society of Missiology (2010–2011), and as an executive pastor in Australia (1979–1990), as well as being involved in theological education in Papua New Guinea and the South Pacific since 1984. His publications include co-editing *Footprints of God: A Narrative Theology of Mission* (MARC 1999), *Mission in Acts: Ancient Narratives in Contemporary Contexts* (Orbis Books 2004), *Landmark Essays in Mission and World Christianity* (Orbis Books 2009), and *Contemporary Mission Theology: Engaging the Nations* (Orbis Books 2017), together with co-authoring *Encountering the History of Missions: From the Early Church to Today* (Baker Academic 2017).

**Michael Lessard-Clouston** (PhD, OISE/University of Toronto) is a professor of applied linguistics and TESOL in the Cook School of Intercultural Studies at Biola University in La Mirada, California, where he directs the MA in Applied Linguistics and teaches in its on campus and online MA TESOL programs. He has taught ESL/EFL and done teacher training in Canada, China, Indonesia, and Japan, and his research has appeared in publications such as the *Canadian Modern Language Review, Journal of English for Academic Purposes, Language, Culture and Curriculum, NECTFL Review, TESL Canada Journal*, and *TESL Reporter*. He is also author of *Teaching Vocabulary* (TESOL 2013) and founding editor of the *International Journal of Christianity and English Language Teaching*. His research interests include corpus linguistics, intercultural communication, second-language acquisition, and vocabulary learning and teaching. His current writing project is a short book on second-language acquisition applied to English language teaching.

**Marilyn Lewis** (Honorary Research Fellow, The University of Auckland) has taught English and other languages in New Zealand, India and Cambodia, and she also worked as a teacher trainer in Southeast Asia. Upon her retirement, she enjoys volunteering for teaching-related projects in Asia. She is a prolific writer and is co-author of *Studying in English: Strategies for Success in Higher Education* (Palgrave 2017), *New Ways in Teaching Adults* (TESOL Press 2015), and *Exploring Parables in Luke: Integrated Skills for ESL/EFL Students of Theology* (Langham Global Library 2014).

**Cheri Pierson** (EdD, Northern Illinois University) is an associate professor of TESOL at Wheaton College Graduate School. She specializes in teacher education, methodology, curriculum development and English for specific purposes. She is the author of *Dictionary of Theological Terms in Simplified English Student Workbook* (EMIS 2003), *Women Crossing Borders* (EMIS/Billy Graham Center 2006), co-author of *Exploring Theological English* (Piquant 2010), *Exploring Parables in Luke: Integrated Skills for ESL/EFL Students of Theology* (Langham Global Library 2014) and numerous articles in journals such as *Teaching Theology and Religion*. She lived in Sweden where she taught academic English and teacher preparation courses to students from all over Europe.

**Kaylene Powell** (MA TESOL and Intercultural Studies, Wheaton College Graduate School) resides in eastern Nebraska where she works as a writing consultant, adult ESL instructor, editor, author, and tutor. She served with an educational NGO for twelve years, just over eight of those years as an EFL teacher and teacher trainer-mentor in three different regions of mainland China. She has also instructed students from a wide variety of other countries in American ESL settings. In addition to writing academically and developing curriculum, she is also an author of both poetry and fiction.

**Melissa K. Smith** (PhD, University of Illinois) has lived in China for eighteen years. In addition to teaching part-time at Ningxia University, she runs LEAPAsia, a non-profit educational organization that supports teachers, encourages students and school children, and donates books to schools. She enjoys learning from other teachers and their mentors as she supports the professional development of both. As a teacher educator, she created and contributes to the blog, *Master Teaching*, which focuses on the integration of profession and faith.

**Karin Spiecker Stetina** (PhD, Marquette University) is an associate professor of biblical and theological studies at Talbot School of Theology, Biola University. She is passionate about teaching theology that is aimed at loving the Lord our God with all our heart, soul, mind, and strength and loving our neighbors as ourself (Mark 12:30–31). She seeks to relate theology to following Christ in daily life. She taught theology and church history for nearly twenty years at Wheaton College and at various churches. She has been a consultant and an associate editor for *Luther Digest*. Her research interests include Reformation Theology and the theology of John Calvin, Martin Luther, and Jonathan Edwards, as well as the theology of education and reading theology with discernment. She has published numerous books and articles.

Langham Literature and its imprints are a ministry of Langham Partnership.

Langham Partnership is a global fellowship working in pursuit of the vision God entrusted to its founder John Stott –

> *to facilitate the growth of the church in maturity and Christ-likeness through raising the standards of biblical preaching and teaching.*

**Our vision** is to see churches in the majority world equipped for mission and growing to maturity in Christ through the ministry of pastors and leaders who believe, teach and live by the Word of God.

**Our mission** is to strengthen the ministry of the Word of God through:
- nurturing national movements for biblical preaching
- fostering the creation and distribution of evangelical literature
- enhancing evangelical theological education

especially in countries where churches are under-resourced.

**Our ministry**

*Langham Preaching* partners with national leaders to nurture indigenous biblical preaching movements for pastors and lay preachers all around the world. With the support of a team of trainers from many countries, a multi-level programme of seminars provides practical training, and is followed by a programme for training local facilitators. Local preachers' groups and national and regional networks ensure continuity and ongoing development, seeking to build vigorous movements committed to Bible exposition.

*Langham Literature* provides majority world preachers, scholars and seminary libraries with evangelical books and electronic resources through publishing and distribution, grants and discounts. The programme also fosters the creation of indigenous evangelical books in many languages, through writer's grants, strengthening local evangelical publishing houses, and investment in major regional literature projects, such as one volume Bible commentaries like *The Africa Bible Commentary* and *The South Asia Bible Commentary*.

*Langham Scholars* provides financial support for evangelical doctoral students from the majority world so that, when they return home, they may train pastors and other Christian leaders with sound, biblical and theological teaching. This programme equips those who equip others. Langham Scholars also works in partnership with majority world seminaries in strengthening evangelical theological education. A growing number of Langham Scholars study in high quality doctoral programmes in the majority world itself. As well as teaching the next generation of pastors, graduated Langham Scholars exercise significant influence through their writing and leadership.

To learn more about Langham Partnership and the work we do visit **langham.org**

www.ingramcontent.com/pod-product-compliance
Lightning Source LLC
Chambersburg PA
CBHW071226170426
43191CB00032B/1047